family fun in Florida

Jan Godown
with Anna Annino

FALCON®

A FALCON GUIDE ®

Falcon® is continually expanding its list of recreational guidebooks. All books include detailed descriptions, accurate maps, and all the information necessary for enjoyable trips. You can order extra copies of this book and get information and prices for other Falcon guidebooks by writing Falcon, P.O. Box 1718, Helena, MT 59624 or calling toll-free 1-800-582-2665. Please ask for a free copy of our current catalog. Visit our website at www.falcon.com or contact us by e-mail at falcon@falcon.com.

Printed in the United States of America.

1 2 3 4 5 6 7 8 9 0 MG 05 04 03 02 01 00

Falcon and FalconGuide are registered trademarks of Falcon® Publishing, Inc.

Cover photos of Castillo de San Marcos and canoeing Manatee Springs State Park by Maxine Cass.
Cover photos of boys wading in the surf and astronaut at Kennedy Space Center by Timothy O'Keefe.

Cataloging-in-Publication Data
Godown, Jan, 1952-
    Family Fun in Florida / Jan Godown with Anna Annino
        p. cm. -- (A Falcon guide)
    Includes index.
    ISBN 1-56044-764-8 (sc : alk. paper)
    1. Florida--Guidebooks. 2. Family recreation--Florida--Guidebooks. I. Annino, Anna, 1991- II. Title. III. Series.

    F309.3 .G62 2000
    917.5904'64--dc21

                                                              00-64640

CAUTION

All participants in the recreational activities suggested by this book must assume responsibility for their own actions and safety. The information contained in this guidebook cannot replace sound judgment and good decision-making skills, which help reduce risk exposure; nor does the scope of this book allow for disclosure of all the potential hazards and risks involved in such activities.

Learn as much as possible about the recreational activities in which you participate, prepare for the unexpected, and be cautious. The reward will be a safer and more enjoyable experience.

♻ Text pages printed on recycled paper.

For my beloved family, Paolo Annino and Anna Annino,
who are always game to try a new site.
This book is also dedicated to the memory of two dear Bills:
Bill Mansfield and Bill Cowles,
each of whom enjoyed so much fun in Florida.

"A child's world is fresh and new and beautiful,
full of wonder and excitement. . . ."

Rachel Carson
A Sense of Wonder

ACKNOWLEDGMENTS

. . . .

Almost everyone who has walked barefoot in Florida knows a great place to take kids. So this guide is plump with suggestions shared by a beach full of helpers. They deserve a lifetime supply of coconut milkshakes for providing me with site tips, reference material, traveling companions, tour-guide services, driving and lodging, and much other help.

I thank Jim, Lindsey, and Lisanne Bailey; Bill Baker; Sandra Barrett and Claire Barrett; Russ and Robin Beck; Jody Bisz; Denise Butler; Phyllis Bosco; Mary Louise Bachman; James Call; Madeleine Carr; Susan Cerulean; Susan Cowles; Sandee and Chris Coulter; Betsy and Bernie Daley; Frank Davies; Joyce Ducas; Terry DeFoor; Susan DeFord and Ken Klein; Jennifer Dunn; Peggy Durham; Wendy, Mike, and Sarah Durant; Sara Eisler; Rusty Ennemoser; Mary Fears; Julie Ferolito; Pam Forrester; Velma Frye and Zoe Sharron; Mike Fuery; Debra Galloway; Karen and Chuck Haithcock; Bob Harris; Richard Hassler; Nancy Hamilton; Holli Hausfeld; Sylvia Herrwerth; Teresa Hollingsworth; Nikki Abels James; Jerry Johansen; Anna Johnson; Catherine, Dan, Laura, and Savannah Kelly; Joe and Linda Knetsch; Trish Higgins Kurowski; Beth LaCivita, Stan Chapman, and Abigail Chapman; Gerald Grow; Lorrie Guttman; Hope Lange; Larry Lee; Mary Ann Lindley; Cindy and Tom Lord; Jennifer Lusk; Elizabeth Masters; Marge Mansfield; Linda Maynard; Heather Mendelson; Jack McCarthy; Mary Elizabeth McIlvane; Heather McVoy; Laurie, Tom, Lacey, Andrew, Aaron, and Hollie Marie Meehan; Heather Mendelson; and Mary Moon.

I also owe thanks to Rayanne, Scott, Georgia, and Gracie Mitchell; Susan Murowski; Joan Morris; Ann, Don, Carson, and Anna Morrow; Catherine, Lee, Julia, and Suzanne Munroe; Hope Nelson; Gil Nelson; John Newton; David Nolan; David Osier; Alexandra Owen; Daniel Parker; Katie Pennie; Mollie Palmer; Audrey Parente; Jane Parrish; Angel Passailaigue; Diane Pickett; Phil Pollock; Kim Prozzi; June Wiaz and Barry, Emily, and Lily Moline; Mary Jo Tierney and Michael Wentz; Bonnie Wilpon; Judyanne Webb; Lee Rose; Emily Rosen; Bob Ruth; Roberta Sandler; Kati Schardl; Frank Stephenson; Susan, Charlie, Sarah, and Eric Stratton; Deb Swim; Allen Thompson; Brent Tozzer; Zilpha Underwood; Ellie Whitney; Ed Wilks; James Valentine; and Janet, Mike, Paul, and Christina Vitale.

Some members of Shirley Ann Dunbar's class at Holy Comforter Episcopal School filled out site forms. They are Casey Gray, Georgia Mitchell, Patrick McGrail, Jake B. Wilkins, and Anna Annino. Ideas or site forms also came from Apalachee Bend Girl Scout Troop 599, guided by Jackie Bist and Nancy Showalter. Helpers were Catie Joe Ale, Anna Annino, Annie Bist, Lacey Booth, Sonnie Mayewski, Caroline Showalter, Lindsey Showalter, and Katie Tuovila. I'm also thankful for site ideas from Apalachee Bend Girl Scout Troop 99 leaders Diane Getty and Teresa Sarbeck and troop members.

Many groups and organizations also helped me with this book, including Nick Wynn, Florida Historical Society; Patricia Wickman, Betty Mae Jumper, and Virginia Mitchell, the Seminole tribe of Florida; Barbara Shew and the Lake Helen Book Fair staff; and Doug Luciani, Kelly Grass, Brandy Henley, Kim Howes, and other VISIT Florida staff.

Other organizations that helped include Bunnie Bloom and All Florida Adventure Tours; the *Florida Hotel and Motel* magazine staff; Russell Daws and Marian Hester, Tallahassee Museum of History and Natural Sciences; Madeleine Carr and Pat Durham, Wakulla Springs State Park; and staff members of the Florida Office of Recreation and Parks, Florida Fish and Wildlife Conservation Commission, Florida Division of Forestry, the Museum of Florida History, State of Florida Library and Archives, and Leon County Public Library.

The University of Florida College of Journalism and Communications and *The Alligator* are fondly remembered for lessons taught.

I hope readers who also assisted but aren't listed here will forgive my lapse.

I especially want to thank Marian Bailey Godown, my mother, for invaluable Florida materials; my sister Joanna Godown, for keeping me company; two special Florida visitors, Nicole and Andrea Rasimas; Salvatore and Nellie Annino; and Angela Annino, for those Florida postcards.

Innumerable Florida sunrises and sunsets are reserved for my family, Paolo Annino and Anna Annino. They visited sites with or for me and went crabbing, fishing, bird and butterfly watching, and shell collecting. Anna's curiosity led the way, and Paolo's support of the project was steadfast.

Finally, I look westward to the offices of Falcon Publishing and thank Leeann Drabenstott, Chris Cauble, Megan Hiller, Erin Turner, Laura Ottoson, former Floridian Glenn Law, and especially my steady-eyed editor for *Family Fun in Florida,* Gayle Shirley.

CONTENTS

· ·

REGIONS OF FLORIDA

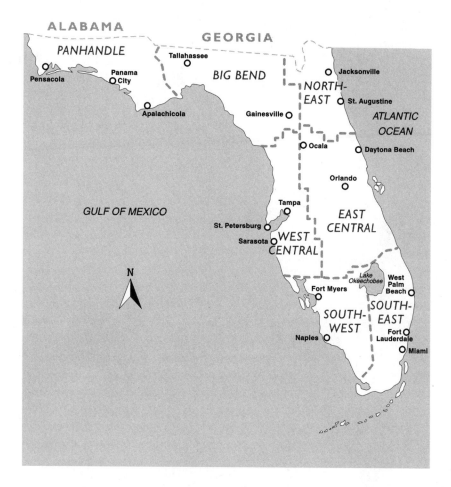

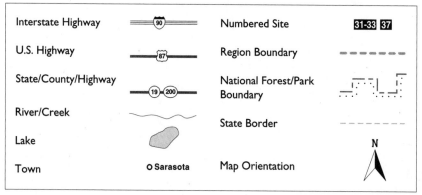

Interstate Highway	Numbered Site
U.S. Highway	Region Boundary
State/County/Highway	National Forest/Park Boundary
River/Creek	State Border
Lake	
Town	Map Orientation

Introduction

I have a mother's secret to share about how to visit Florida: Travel with someone little who finds delight in the sounds tucked inside a seashell.

Lie down on clean wet sand so your sandlot bunch can bury you, giving you a skin treatment that rivals a spa mudpack. Climb an ancient coastal Indian mound and have your young "natives" scan the horizon for a Spanish galleon's tall wooden mast. Sip chilled orange juice served in a coconut cup. Bunk overnight on a houseboat. Watch a space shuttle hurtle to the heavens. Watch a weaver create a round bowl from perfectly flat palm fronds. Listen for the sharp call of eagles floating on thermals over a historic Florida prairie. Stay dry underwater while going nose to nose with wild manatees. Lick guava ice cream in the shade of a coconut palm tree. Wear a pink flower in your hair. Float way down upon the Suwannee River. Wade into one of the natural wonders of the world—the Everglades. Watch Seminole Indians defend their land in an 1830s war re-enactment. Pet a soft ray at a saltwater touch tank. Visit a 1920s bayfront palace and its attic game room.

This family-friendly guide offers almost 500 diversions like these, with an emphasis on nature, history, science, and cultural activities. Many are inexpensive or free.

Brenda Ueland, an adventurous Midwestern mother and author of the 1930s, once recommended two parenting ploys: At mealtime, she delighted in telling her young daughter something intriguing, such as, "Do you know the papa seahorse carries the babies and gives birth to them?" Parents who tell their children arresting details about the world can soon expect their children to entertain *them* with extraordinary ideas of their own. On trips, these children are not shy about asking park rangers, for example, if birds ever hitch a ride on the backs of gopher turtles. (They do.)

Secondly, vacation bedtimes are no problem for a family that values vigorous, rambunctious frolicking across a park or beach. Such families, Ueland wrote, are likely to have children "worn down by laughter and intellectual excitement," tuckered out from tomfoolery and somersaults, and ready for dreams. So with that in mind, the free picnic, park, and beach sites described in this guide become more than quick places to visit the restroom or eat a sandwich.

Finally, let children guide you. In a museum, they may ignore the collection of paper money but return to gawk again and again at the stuffed alligator—even though you may have seen several already in the course of your trip. So what? A man who visited the 400-year-old Castillo at St. Augustine as a child once told a writer, "The first thing I did was touch the stones. I guess I did that just to have contact with the people who had put those stones there before." That child grew up to be an architect, and years later he remembered that transformative moment. Treasure those moments.

INSIDE THIS GUIDE

. . . .

Family Fun in Florida introduces a family-friendly state so big that it crosses two time zones. The peninsula stretches at least 790 driving miles, from red clay hills on the northwestern border in the Panhandle to the coral islands of the Keys. Even if you rush along via the interstates—which I do not recommend—it takes four hours to drive from Daytona Beach to Miami Beach.

Because of Florida's size, I suggest you explore no more than one or two regions per trip. Rushing to see it all means you'll deprive your children of entertaining and educational experiences. Rushing leads to speeding tickets and car wrecks. Not only should you avoid crushing your own bones, but you don't want to hit the threatened Florida black bear, the almost-extinct Florida panther, or the river otters, deer, bobcats, and other animals that cross Florida's roads. (Yes, I've seen otters cross roads.)

For purposes of this book, I've divided Florida into seven regions: the Panhandle, Big Bend, Northeast, East-Central, West-Central, Southeast, and Southwest. Each section of the book emphasizes sites with natural, historical, educational, and cultural resources. Expect a sand-bucketful of the best parks, campgrounds, children's science centers, aquariums, museums, marine science centers, art galleries, festivals, citrus-grove tours, beaches, preserves, wildlife outings, boat trips, fishing spots, underwater sanctuaries, forts, historic buildings, fossil sites, zoos, historic re-enactments, nature attractions, and gardens, as well as rainy-day and post-sunburn diversions.

Although a few sites are remote or may require an hour's mosey beyond a major highway, I've selected more that are close to major highways and interstates, to break up those long drives. For urban visitors, I've included great places to take kids in the vicinity of four beautiful city/metro regions: Jacksonville/Duval County, Tampa/Clearwater/St. Petersburg, Orlando, and Fort Lauderdale/Miami Beach. These cities are often overlooked as family vacation destinations. Yet, they are bursting with activities; consider them for your Florida trip.

This guide notes free places to visit, such as the Polk Museum of Art east of Tampa and the National Museum of Naval Aviation in the Panhandle, in addition to many free beaches and local parks. You'll read of seasonal discounts and other money-saving tips. For example, some museums offer free admission one day of the week. Many resorts offer discount coupons to area sites; ask at the check-in desk.

When it's important, I mention whether a place is best suited to older or younger children. In descriptions of sites that kids might normally consider a bore, I tell you whether the site is enlivened on a particular day because of a fun festival or the arrival of costumed re-enactors. Or I try to steer you to the one or two things in a general museum that are most likely to interest your children. I delight in finding lesser-known gems, such as the small Graves Museum, an archaeological collection in Hollywood near Fort Lauderdale that rivets my daughter's attention. Her approval means something; she is a fan of the American Museum of Natural History in New York and of the Smithsonian museums.

I also tip you off to a few special and kid-pleasing places to stay the night, such as a family-focused cottage colony under the palms at Fort Myers Beach. I tell you how to camp at Walt Disney World, and how to sleep in a lighthouse, at the base of a real NASA rocket, and in a bank.

When you aren't based at a campsite, my advice is to book a room with some kitchen amenities, even if they include only a small fridge and a microwave. It's true that a good dining-out experience in a family-friendly restaurant can turn a trip into a vacation. But fruit, bagels, pastry, juice, cereal, milk, and cheese are easy to buy and serve as your sleepy tribe awakens one by one. You may want to stop at a Florida grocery for still-warm Cuban bread, fresh mangoes or guavas, a fresh-baked key lime pie, or a tropical soda. Or you may want to find a family-friendly lodge that offers free breakfast, as do several mentioned here.

I have recommended some dining establishments that are just too much fun to pass up, such as a family restaurant on the riverfront in Fort Lauderdale that offers free boat rides after the kids chow down. Another popular place is a state park near DeLand/Daytona Beach that features a restaurant where you griddle your own pancakes. Don't leave Florida without sampling some of the regional temptations, including Cuban sandwiches, cheese grits, coconut milkshakes, alligator nuggets, key lime pie, fresh winter strawberries, black bean soup, grouper sandwiches, fried shrimp, Seminole Indian pumpkin fry bread, smoked mullet dip, crab soup, sweet Zellwood corn on the cob, tangerines straight from the tree, and tropical-flavored ice creams.

All of the site descriptions in this book include highlights, directions, fees, hours, and up-to-date contact information, such as websites and toll-free telephone numbers. Check the appendix for resources such as the state fishing agency, canoe outfitter association, nature groups, and an additional reading list. The handy index can speed you to a specific locale or topic.

This guide doesn't list every family-oriented place under our sun. Nor can this book mention every state park, beach campground, fishing hole, museum, or picnic spot. If your family's absolute favorite destination is missing, contact me care of Falcon Publishing, P.O. Box 1718, Helena, MT 59624. Thanks, and please buckle up.

TRAVEL TIPS

Automobile routes. The fastest way to travel across Florida is via our free interstate routes. They are:

- I-10, which runs east-west between Jacksonville and the Alabama border;
- I-75, which runs north-south between Georgia and Tampa and southeast to Miami;
- I-95, which runs north-south between Georgia and Miami; and
- I-4, which runs east-west between Tampa and the Orlando/Daytona Beach area.

The main toll-access highways are the Bee Line Expressway, which runs between Orlando and the Space Coast, and Florida's Turnpike, which goes from just south of Ocala to just short of Everglades National Park. This is a highly recommended route to the park.

Emergency numbers. The emergency number in all of Florida is 911. Of course, if you have quick access to emergency numbers for local law enforcement agencies and firehouses, you can use those, too. The Florida Highway Patrol is our state police on major highways. The Florida Marine Patrol covers the state waters. Beach lifeguards are a local government service. Not all seashore or lakeshore beaches employ lifeguards, so check upon arrival. A special emergency assistance number just for visitors is 800-656-8777. See the contact information on page 298 for more emergency numbers.

Sunburn, heat exhaustion. It's so easy to burn your skin in Florida. Here's what you should have on hand to help ensure an ouchless trip:

- Broad-brimmed tie-on hats, visors.
- Long-sleeved white shirts, loose white T-shirts.
- Polarized sunglasses.
- Sunscreen with an SPF of at least 15 and zinc oxide cream, along with aloe vera gel and calamine lotion for aftercare. Sunscreen now comes in a handy gel stick that is easy to apply and that sticks to kids in the water.
- Plenty of cold water and/or sports drinks. These refreshers are as essential as sand buckets and towels if you're headed to any beach or fishing spot or expect to be out boating. Another refreshing treat: Get grapes at the store and freeze them before heading to the beach.

Health supplies. Check with your doctor or pharmacist about the newest take-along aids, especially skin patches for seasickness if you intend to book an ocean fishing trip.

In addition to a traditional first-aid kit, I like to take:

- Medicated adhesive bandages.
- Calamine lotion and aloe vera gels.

- Aspergum.
- Vitamin C cough drops.
- Analgesic salve for muscle aches. Don't apply on sunburned skin!
- Sports drinks for a quick electrolyte boost.
- Juices fortified with vitamin A and calcium.
- Energy bars.
- Papaya enzyme, for seashore stings.
- Baking soda and colloidal oatmeal for soothing skin soaks.

Water safety. Life jackets are required by law if you're in a boat or personal watercraft. At the beach, read information boards posted in the sand. Never touch a jellyfish, even if it's beached. Lifeguards often treat jellyfish stings with a papaya enzyme. Carry that or a meat tenderizer with papaya as its active ingredient in your travel kit. Study posted alerts about rip tides and runouts, which are excessively strong currents that can prove life threatening.

I can tell you from experience that it's not wise to swim in marina waters or canals. They aren't designed for swimmers and can harbor dangerous, submerged obstructions, such as concrete chunks, metal trash, and sharp oyster bars.

Fort Lauderdale and Daytona Beach are famous for their excellent professional lifeguards, but not every beach in Florida employs lifeguards.

Other water tips. In the summer, shuffle along as you wade in sedate waters just offshore. This will send stingrays scurrying into deeper water. They don't attack people, but they have a long, barbed tail that carries a painful poison if you step on it or it touches your ankle.

Shark bites are rare and are more likely to plague surfers, night swimmers, or the victims of boating accidents. This is most likely to happen at inlets, which are like underwater highways for marine creatures between the ocean, gulf, and bays. Bleeding can attract sharks. If you feel something touch you in the water, as has happened to my family and friends many times, it's most likely a harmless fish, which our clear waters still hold in large numbers. Or it could be seaweed. Don't panic, but move closer to the beach just in case.

Don't wear watches or ankle or wrist bracelets in the water, especially metal ones. These can reflect light, and that can attract fish, including barracuda, which are found in the warm subtropical waters of the state, primarily near coral reefs.

To avoid cutting your toes, always wear sneakers or "surf shoes" when getting out of a boat onto a water bottom, where sharp oyster bars may lie submerged.

Boating-manatee collisions. Manatees are an endangered species, in large part because they are so easily and often hit by boat propellers or personal watercraft. When you're on the water, wear polarized sunglasses so you can see through the surface glare and watch for these gentle underwater animals. Also look for round swirls on the water surface that indicate manatees are below. Never violate a no-wake or slow-speed restriction. Stay away from shallow areas and from beds of sea grass. If you run aground, immediately pull up your prop and walk your boat through; never drag the propeller.

Storms. Lightning strikes Florida more often than any other state in the country. While I was writing this book, a storm in my hometown of Tallahassee yielded 10,000 recorded lightning strikes in one hour; yet, no one was hit.

Still, it's always a good idea to take a few precautions when lightning threatens. If a storm approaches, go inside. Expect lifeguards to eject you from the beach, even if the area is still sunny. A bolt of lightning can travel many miles.

Hurricanes and tropical storms bring local flooding, high winds, and torrents of rain. The hurricane season generally lasts from June through October, with most hurricanes occurring in September and October. Since 1967, I have weathered several. I think a wise person follows the preparation tips abundantly offered by officials and the media in advance of a hurricane's arrival, including evacuation if it's advised in your area.

The summer rainy season brings heavy, monsoonlike downpours in the afternoons, mainly in central and southern Florida. Take shelter to watch them; don't drive in them. They end abruptly, with sunshine and often a rainbow. Enjoy.

Extreme temperatures and humidity. On summer days, expect the temperature inside your parked car to climb as high as 120 degrees F if it's not parked in the shade. Allow time for the hot air to disperse before driving away. I recommend visiting Florida in the winter, when the weather is cooler. If, like many families, you must travel during summer vacations, consider dividing the day into three parts. Plan outside activities for morning and late afternoon/early evening. Reserve 11 A.M. to 4 or 5 P.M.—the time when the heat and sun's rays are most intense—for inside and air-conditioned diversions, such as museums, science centers, movies, reading, and take-along hobbies.

Snakes. Snakes are common in most Florida parks, preserves, and wilderness areas, where they put a bite on the rodent population. Few of Florida's snakes are poisonous. It's not likely you'll see them, but if you do, please appreciate them. The harmless brown snake is a common sight from a boardwalk at Manatee Springs State Park; you may see one coiled in the water-submerged base of a cypress tree. Other common and harmless snakes are the beautiful indigo, which is federally protected, and the corn snake.

Unless you are hiking in remote areas, you are unlikely to see poisonous water moccasins, rattlesnakes, or coral snakes. A rare bite from any of these snakes requires immediate attention.

Alligators. These prehistoric reptiles are easy to avoid; it just takes willpower. Too many visitors want a close-up picture. Resist the urge. Buy a postcard instead. Don't splash or swim where alligators do. That means freshwater rivers and some lakes. Warning signs are often posted along public lakes or rivers that alligators are known to patrol; heed them. If you're unsure, ask people nearby. If you see an alligator anywhere, especially on a park foot-path, don't approach it. And by all means don't attempt to feed one; it's against the law. The same goes for crocodiles, which live in salt water in extreme South Florida.

Dolphins. These creatures are benevolent but wild, nonetheless. Some male porpoises have tried to "mate" with people who try to swim with them. These large mammals can push heavily against you.

Dolphins can also fall victim to human diseases. Marine biologists urge that you appreciate wild porpoises and dolphins from a distance. Don't feed them or support a business that allows visitors to feed them for entertainment. Dolphin encounter programs that involve captive mammals and are supervised by specialists are worth checking into.

Bears. Florida's bears, which roam parts of remote southwestern Florida, the forests of Central Florida, and the two national forests in northern Florida, are generally reclusive creatures that like to avoid human contact. Few vacationers ever see them. Campgrounds in bear territory do a good job of explaining how to secure food; heed the instructions. Occasionally, a wandering bear that finds its way to civilization is removed to a more remote Florida location. If you see a bear in an urban setting, such as a back yard, call the wildlife alert hotline listed in the contact information at the back of this book.

The Florida panther, which is nearly extinct, is rarely a threat.

THE VACATION PLACE

· ·

The travel tips and insider ideas in *Family Fun in Florida* spring from the 30-plus years I have spent traveling and working in Florida—the last 9 years as a mother and family trip organizer.

I hope these ideas encourage you to explore the best of Florida with children, have fun, and save a little money at the same time. This guide is not only ideal for parents and grandparents. It also offers helpful tips for teachers, recreation group leaders, home schoolers, boys and girls club sponsors, student mentors, school trip chaperons, scout leaders, and church or synagogue youth-group leaders. May your vacation include an extra splash of fun in Florida—the vacation place.

PANHANDLE REGION

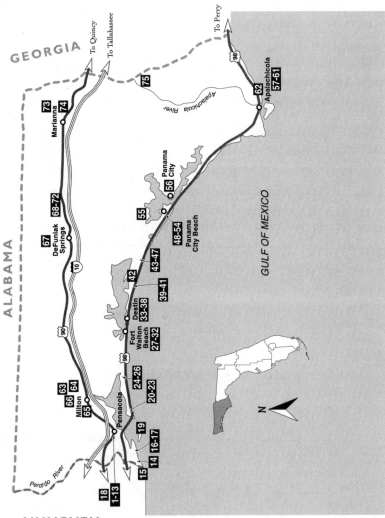

Panhandle
Region

It's no wonder this tucked-away corner of the Sunshine State, with its beaches and pinewoods, is the part of Florida that tourists are least likely to visit. You would have to drive 700 miles from the Everglades to reach the Panhandle. It sits in an entirely different time zone—Central Standard—from the rest of the peninsula. The main city, Pensacola, is as far west as Chicago.

The climate is different, too. The clear waters of the Gulf of Mexico are too chilly for winter swimming, but dolphins fish here year-round. To the delight of children, some Januarys bring a dusting of snowflakes, and on rare nights the mercury dips into the 20s and even the teens. So pack warm clothes if you settle on a winter visit to the Panhandle.

But the summer sizzles! Frisbees fly when the Panhandle becomes a crowded and splashy vacation spot from Memorial Day through Labor Day. The sunny region lures vacationers from Georgia, Alabama, Mississippi, and North Florida; they come to catch fish, drift lazily in giant inner tubes down the rivers, and search for starfish in the tide pools on the gulf shore. Canoeing on the quiet rivers and expansive bays is popular here, as is fishing the lakes for largemouth bass and poking about the fishing ports.

Though it is out of the way, the Panhandle still has a few urbanlike beaches in some locales. *Family Fun in Florida* will help you avoid densely packed condominium towers and the occasional seedy area. Instead, this guide salutes the smaller coastal villages, a national seashore park, and a string of award-winning state parks that preserve dune habitat on the barrier islands and coastal wetlands, lush watersheds, and forests.

A big part of any Panhandle visit is the chance to sample fresh seafood at casual coastal shacks. The fresh shrimp, bay scallops, red snapper, and flounder are local favorites. Panhandle oysters from Apalachicola are known around the world.

Some visitors detour to the Panhandle to soak up the history. The region's story dates back at least 5,000 years, to when natives harvested oysters, scallops, and other seafood here. Then, in the summer of 1559—six years before the Spanish founded St. Augustine—about 500 Spanish soldiers and 1,000 workers arrived from Mexico in 13 wooden ships. They settled near the site of present-day Pensacola but abandoned their colony two years later after enduring a horrendous hurricane. Later, Pensacola developed into a thriving colony.

Inland, the Panhandle looks like parts of Alabama. You'll be able to stroll up 200-foot-high hills of vivid red clay and along trails made by the Native Americans through oak and pine forests. Black bears roam here, ever wary of campers. Bogs full of insect-eating plants fascinate children. Cool, steep river ravines shelter out-of-place plants such as the rhododendron, which is more commonly associated with the Appalachian Mountains. The state's only walk-through underground cavern is preserved in an inland Panhandle state park. A clear, shallow river with a white-sand bottom attracts canoeists. A state museum honors the Panhandle doctor who invented air conditioning in the early 1800s to help comfort his patients suffering from yellow fever. You'll pass roadside pecan groves and peanut farms in this region where the climate can't support tropical oranges. But short palmettos and an occasional palm—especially the sabal, or cabbage, palm—will reassure you that you are, indeed, in Florida.

Once a timber-harvesting region, the Panhandle is experiencing a decline in this industry. Former timberlands are being developed into villagelike enclaves that de-emphasize car travel and minimize harm to fragile wetlands and shoreline. Foot and bike paths link homes and marketplaces, and houses with wraparound porches and second-story balconies are built on stilts to help protect them from hurricane floodwaters. One newer development, Seaside, was designed by architects to be a model coastal community and is so famous that it's a tourist destination.

When it's time to park the vacation backpack for the night, families will find several shady public campgrounds in the Panhandle, including some on the gulf shore. Inland, where fishing and hunting are popular, snug cabins in the forest are also available. Family-friendly destinations with kitchenettes or cottages include Purple Parrot Island Resort and Sandpiper Inn Motel and Cottages, both in Pensacola; Clarion Inn and Hampton Inn in Pensacola Beach; Heron Haven Beach Getaway in Navarre Beach; Henderson Park Inn in Destin; Frangista Beach Inn, Miramar Beach; all of Seaside; Baywoods, Choctawhatchee Bay, Porter's Court, and Portside Resort, all at Panama City Beach; the Rainbow Inn and the Gibson Inn in Apalachicola; Adventures Unlimited in Milton; and Sunbright Manor and Hotel DeFuniak in DeFuniak Springs.

To introduce your children to the region's history, consider staying at the New World Landing in Pensacola, a former 19th-century warehouse that now features charming rooms decorated on historical themes. Or try the modern, 15-story Pensacola Grand Hotel, where an authentic 1912 train depot serves as the entrance and lobby. You have to see it to believe the unique melding of old and new.

For more information contact:

• Apalachicola Chamber of Commerce
  850-653-9419
  <www.homtown.com/apalachicola>

- Emerald Coast Convention and Visitors Bureau
  800-322-3319
  <www.destin-fwb.com>
- Gulf Breeze Area Chamber of Commerce
  850-932-7888
- Navarre Beach Area Chamber of Commerce
  800-480-SAND (7263), 850-939-3267
- Northwest Florida Water Management District
  850-539-5999
- Panama City Beach
  800-PC-BEACH (722-3224), 800-553-1330
  <www.800pcbeach.com>
- Pensacola Beach Chamber of Commerce
  800-635-6803
- Pensacola Convention and Visitor Information Center
  800-343-4321 (in Florida), 800-874-1234 (outside Florida)
  <www.visitpensacola.com>
- Perdido Key Chamber of Commerce
  800-328-0107, 850-492-4660
  <www.perdidochamber.com>
- South Santa Rosa Island Welcome Center
  850-939-2691, 800-480-7263
  <www.navarrefl.com>
- South Walton Tourist Center
  800-322-3319, 800-822-6877
  <www.beachesofsouthwalton.com>

Pensacola Area

• •

Downtown Pensacola boasts multiple historic districts that can transport you back to the time of the hardy Spanish colonists, treasure-seeking conquistadors, and the square-rigged Spanish galleons in which they arrived. Narrow brick streets and buildings with balconies, inviting garden plazas, and landscaped fountains reflect a time when the European territory of Florida stretched west to the Mississippi River. You can even still visit the original 16th-century Spanish plaza.

1. Historic Pensacola Village

• •

This is Florida's equivalent of Colonial Williamsburg, a collection of stunning, restored buildings that celebrate a dramatic part of Pensacola's history.

The village features a landscaped Spanish plaza that has served as a park since the 1600s. Museums showcase period furnishings and intriguing displays, such as glass bottle traps that were baited with sugar water in the 1700s and used to catch bugs and rats. A toy store and pharmacy line a re-created Victorian street. Another feature of the historical village is the T. T. Wentworth Jr. Florida State Museum, a quirky collection housed in the former city hall, an Italian Renaissance Revival showplace. There you can see a shrunken head and a stuffed Kodiak bear and enjoy some hands-on fun at the third-floor kids' discovery center. The Pensacola Colonial Archaeological Trail is headquartered in Historic Pensacola Village, too.

In an area with more historical highlights than you can absorb in a week, this village next to Pensacola Bay may well be your best non-beach destination. Two features are especially stunning: On display here are artifacts from a British fort, built in 1778, that lay hidden under the streets of downtown Pensacola until they were excavated. Another fascinating find is a Spanish galleon, wrecked off Pensacola in 1559 and discovered centuries later. Among the items retrieved from the ship were jars of Spanish olives.

Costumed re-enactors bring to life this must-see historical complex. Plan a day around it, as there are cafés and restaurants on the shady streets and in some of the historical buildings.

Location: In downtown Pensacola, in the Seville Historic District at 205 East Zaragoza Street.

Important information: Open from 10 A.M. to 4 P.M. Mondays through Saturdays and from 1 to 4:30 P.M. Sundays. Tickets are good for two days and can be used to enter all of the museums and historical sites within the district. Children under age 4 are admitted free. For more information, call 850-595-5985 or visit <www.historicpensacola.org>. Fees are $4.50 for seniors and children 4 to 16, $5.50 for all others.

2. Pensacola Historical Museum/Old Christ Church

• •

This is part of the Historic Pensacola Village (see above), but it deserves a special mention. It is the oldest church in Florida still standing on its original spot. Old Christ Church, built in 1832 of bricks made of red clay from the nearby bluffs, was pressed into duty as a Union hospital and barracks during the Civil War. Many local residents fondly recall its days as the public library in the 1950s. Although billed as a local museum, Pensacola's history reaches far beyond the city limits. Budding historians in your family might want to soak up the atmosphere here.

Location: In downtown Pensacola at 405 South Adams Street (the intersection of Zaragoza and Adams Streets).

Important information: For more information, call 850-433-1559 or visit <www.historicpensacola.com>. Admission is included in the fee paid to enter the Historic Pensacola District (see above).

3. The Wall South and Veterans Memorial Park

This meditative place opened in 1992 with a replica of the Vietnam Veterans Memorial in Washington, D.C. Plans are to expand it, eventually memorializing those who served in every war from World War I to the present. The park affords the opportunity for an important teachable moment.

Location: In downtown Pensacola on Bayfront Parkway.

Important information: Always open. For more information, call 850-433-8200.

4. Pensacola Museum of Art/Old Jail

Take your kids to jail and let them stay a bit. This art museum, built in 1906 to serve as the city jail, features some barred cell blocks that look just as they once did—except for the art displayed quite cleverly within. The nonprofit gallery features Old Dutch masters, Chinese porcelain, and other changing exhibits.

Location: In downtown Pensacola at 407 South Jefferson Street.

Important information: Donations accepted. There's a fine gift shop with great toys. For more information, call 850-432-6247 or visit <www. artsnwfl.org/pma.

5. Quayside Art Gallery

If you have a budding artist in tow, check out the colors at this rainy-day diversion set up in an 1873 firehouse just north of the old wharves, or quays. A 2.5-ton horse-drawn steam fire engine gleamed here when the building was the Germania Steam Fire Engine and Hose Company. Today, the three floors comprise an artists' cooperative, said to be the largest in the southeastern United States. The gallery reflects Pensacola's growing appeal as an artists' community.

Location: In downtown Pensacola across from Plaza Ferdinand and the Pensacola Cultural Center.

Important information: Free. Open from 10 A.M. to 5 P.M. Mondays through Saturdays and from 1 to 5 P.M. Sundays. For more information, call 850-438-2363.

6. City of Five Flags Trolley

● ●

Rest little feet, orient yourself, and learn about city lore aboard one of the trolleys that travel through the historic district. There are two different lines, and you can board or debark at any of the stops.

Location: There are stops throughout Pensacola's historic district, including at the Historic Pensacola Village, 200 East Zaragoza Street.

Important information: For more information, call 850-595-3228.

7. Science and Space Theater

● ●

Join volunteers with the Escambia Amateur Astronomer's Association for the changing planetarium shows. This is a good alternative for children older than age 5, when it's too wet to sit around a campfire.

Location: At Pensacola Junior College, 6235 Omie Circle.

Important information: Planetarium shows are Thursday through Saturday nights. Fees are $2 for students and $3 for adults; children younger than 5 are not admitted. For more information, including show times, call 850-484-1150.

8. The Coffee Cup

● ●

This is a noisy, affordable hamburger place in an authentic 1940s diner. The grits, eggs, pancakes, and other fresh-cooked food are well known to appreciative locals. Now you know the secret, too.

Location: In downtown Pensacola at 520 East Cervantes Street.

Important information: Open for breakfast and lunch. For more information, call 850-432-7060.

9. The Yacht

Given Florida's 1,800 navigable miles of shoreline, I'm surprised that entrepreneurs don't lower the gangplank more often to shipboard eateries. This upscale restaurant is on board a 153-foot motorized yacht from the 1930s that was once owned by Carl Fisher, who developed Miami Beach from a mangrove swamp into swank winter real estate. Treat well-mannered children to Sunday brunch or the early menu, which is offered beginning at 4:30 P.M.

Location: In Pensacola, the Yacht restaurant is permanently docked in Harbor Village at Pitt Slip.

Important information: Closed Mondays. For more detailed directions and information, contact the restaurant at 850-432-3707.

10. Hopkins Boarding House

This is a plain but popular dining option in the North Hill Preservation District. Food is served on mismatched dinner plates in a house with a wide, wraparound porch, and you are seated with strangers around the dining table. Simple country fare, including mashed sweet potatoes, fried okra, baked ham, and cornbread, is passed around the table. Introduce yourself to your neighbor and participate in a unique dining experience. Explain to your children what a 1949 boarding house was like. When you're finished, take your plate to the kitchen. Pass the peas, please.

Location: In Pensacola at 900 North Spring Street.

Important information: Prepare your children to accept the lack of menu selection, as well as table mates—mostly adults—whom they've never met. Hopkins is closed Saturdays through Mondays. It's open Tuesdays through Fridays at breakfast time, lunchtime, and dinnertime. Lines are the longest on Friday nights, when lip-smackin' fried chicken is served. Call for specific times or more information, 850-438-3979.

11. Pensacola Wildlife Rescue and Sanctuary

The animal lover in your flock is sure to have questions for the volunteers at this nonprofit refuge for injured birds and wildlife. Some of the patients are permanent guests but others, fortunately, will be able to be released back into the wild.

Location: In Pensacola at 105 North S Street.

Important information: Call first for detailed directions and hours, 850-433-9453. Donations are accepted.

12. University of West Florida

• •

A college campus isn't always a vacation stop, but this riverfront university sits within a 1,000-acre nature preserve. A boardwalk runs through a wetlands, making it easy to spot alligators and turtles. This is a fine place to picnic and stretch your legs, especially if you have children who are curious about college life.

Location: Take University Parkway to the campus in Pensacola.

Important information: The preserve is easily accessible from Blue Parking Lot 20, behind Building 13. For more information, call 850-474-3000.

13. J. W. Renfroe Pecan Company

• •

Pecans are a traditional fall treat in North Florida, although they aren't often associated with the "coconut state." My family believes that Florida pecans are tastier than those from neighboring Georgia. This longtime, family-run company offers the nuts freshly shelled—salted or unsalted—and also in the shell. They make a good take-along vacation snack and an easy-to-pack gift for the pet-sitter back home.

Location: In Pensacola at 2400 Fairfield Drive.

Important information: Open from 8 A.M. to 5 P.M. Mondays through Saturdays. For more information, call 800-874-1929.

14. Big Lagoon State Recreation Area

• •

This idyllic, 700-acre campground/park sits in sandpine scrub on Big Lagoon, part of the famed Intracoastal Waterway. Enjoy sandy beaches and swimming in the calm, shallow water. There are also three nature trails (including one to an unusual pitcher-plant bog), ranger-guided walks, marsh boardwalks from which to view herons and other feeding birds, an interpretive visitor center, picnic areas, and an observation tower. Early risers and dusk walkers might spot the wary, resident gray foxes.

Location: On County Road 292A about 10 miles southwest of Pensacola.

Important information: Open daily from 8 A.M. to sunset. For more information, call 850-492-1595 or visit <www.dep.state.fl.us/parks>.

15. Perdido Key State Recreation Area

About 15 miles southwest of Pensacola at the Alabama border, this state park preserves 2.5 miles of rolling sand dunes on a barrier island otherwise crowded with condominiums. Enjoy the boardwalks, notice the wind- and wave-sculpted scrub oaks and other trees, and learn about coastal habitat at the visitor center. The island also features an isolated unit of the Gulf Islands National Seashore, accessible only by foot. A survey by the University of Maryland named this stretch of beach one of the best in the nation. There are showers to wash off sand and salt water. Johnson Beach is a fine swimming spot, and it offers primitive campsites accessible only by foot or boat.

Location: About 15 miles southwest of Pensacola off State Road 292, at the eastern end of Perdido Key.

Creek, Español, and Français spoken here

We don't know what **language** was spoken by the families who hunted mastodons in the Panhandle some 10,000 years ago, but Creek was the language of Florida's more recent Native Americans, who migrated to North Florida from Alabama and other regions beginning in the 1700s. A Creek Council in Pensacola keeps this heritage alive, and the E-CHOTA Cherokee Reservation holds an American Indian Festival in April at Mossy Head, 20 miles west of DeFuniak Springs.

Spanish was the first European language used throughout Florida. In Pensacola, this is apparent in the melodic names of plazas, streets, and neighborhoods. While the name Pensacola sounds Spanish, it is said to come from the way the Spanish interpreted a Native American word, *Panzacola,* which meant "long-haired people."

The region's occasional and always brief French rule, which ended for good in 1722, is evident in words like *bayou* and in Pensacola's vibrant Mardi Gras festivals.

For more information, contact the Creek Council at 850-444-8410, E-CHOTA Cherokee Reservation at 850-892-2562 or 850-892-2875, and Mardi Gras at 850-932-2259 or 850-934-0337.

Important information: For more information, contact 850-492-1595 or visit <www.dep.state.fl.us/parks>. For information about Gulf Islands National Seashore, contact 850-934-2600 or visit <www.nps.gov/guis>.

16. Fort Barancas/Pensacola Lighthouse

In an area occupied by several historical forts, this national historic site is an excellent stop for the little soldiers in your family battalion. Located atop a strategic bluff—*barancas* means bluff in Spanish—Fort Barancas guarded Pensacola Bay from pirates and raiding French and English sailing ships. The earliest-known fortification existed in the late 1600s. The fort you see today features an octagonal armory and chapel that date to 1845. Exhibits point out other features dating to 1797. A ranger program on artillery is held daily at 9:30 A.M. and is sure to get your attention.

Fort Barancas is a fine place to stretch your legs. It offers a picnic area, nature trails in the nearby woods, and riveting history to boot. One of the many compelling details about this site is that during the Civil War this fort was held by Confederate troops while Fort Pickens, which still stands across the bay, was under Union control.

Fort Barancas is part of Gulf Islands National Seashore, but visitors are often confused by the fact that the fort sits within a U.S. Naval Air Station complex. Also at the air station, you can see but not tour the Pensacola Lighthouse. This black-and-white light tower was built in 1858, replacing one built in 1825. There is no public campground here, but there is a national seashore campground at the Fort Pickens site (see Site 19).

Location: From downtown Pensacola, follow Gulf Beach Highway (State Road 292) west to Navy Boulevard and the entrance to the Pensacola Naval Air Station. At the gate, get directions to the fort and lighthouse.

Important information: The fort is open daily from 9:30 A.M. to 5 P.M. from April to September. Call for operating hours in other months or for more information, 850-934-2600. Free admission.

17. National Museum of Naval Aviation

The seven-story atrium with its four Blue Angels Skyhawks suspended upside down in formation is only one reason that the little pilots in your family will thank you for landing at this museum. Created in 1914, this free attraction at the Pensacola Naval Air Station is one of the three largest aviation museums in the world and the largest in the nation. It is on a par with the Smithsonian National Air and Space Museum in Washington, D.C. Through

World War II, every Navy pilot who took off into the wild blue yonder first trained here at the air station, which is also home to the Blue Angels.

Kids line up to jump into the motion-simulation cockpit and take a fighter for a spin. You can show them blimps, wooden biplanes, and the Skylab Command Module, all the more fun if you take a free tour with one of the personable retired pilots who volunteer here. Don't leave without walking the deck and landing strip of an

aircraft carrier, seeing "The Magic of Flight" in the IMAX theater, or strolling a replica of a Main Street from the 1930s and 1940s. This is one of the most appealing museums to children in all of Florida.

Location: From downtown Pensacola, follow Gulf Beach Highway (State Road 292) west to Navy Boulevard and the entrance to the Pensacola Naval Air Station. At the gate, get directions to the museum.

Important information: Open 9 A.M. to 5 P.M. daily except on Thanksgiving, Christmas, and New Year's Day. Admission is free except to the IMAX theater. For information on Blue Angels shows, contact the Blue Angels Public Affairs Office at 850-452-4784, 850-452-SHOW (7469), or 850-452-2583, extension 125. Or visit <www.blueangels.navy.mil>. For museum information, call 800-327-5002, 850-452-2389, 850-453-2024, or 850-452-3604, or visit <www.naval-air.org>.

18. National Scenic Byway/U.S. Highway 90

● ●

On its way to the Gulf of Mexico, the winding Escambia River has carved 100-foot-high red cliffs that today support a highway. Like many old Florida roadways, U.S. Highway 90, which runs along the west shore of Escambia Bay, probably began as a Native American footpath. Later, as the Spanish Trail, it was used to carry trade goods between Jacksonville and El Paso, Texas. Red clay from the bluffs was used to make bricks for buildings in the region. The wreck of a 1559 Spanish galleon was discovered at English Point, while Gull Point is where the Florida Territorial Council met in 1822. Wooden stairs and a boardwalk allow you to descend the only scenic cliffs in Florida, at Bay Bluffs Park.

Location: From Pensacola, take U.S. Highway 90 north about 12 miles for the scenic drive.

Important information: For more information, call 850-477-7135.

Pensacola Beach Area

With grand dame Pensacola and her beautiful old homes just 15 minutes across the bay, travelers to Pensacola Beach often expect it to be a waterfront town of Victorian mansions in the tradition of Cape May, New Jersey, or Charleston, South Carolina. If this village on Santa Rosa Island ever had such veranda-wrapped beach estates, they are long gone. But compared to some coastal resorts, Pensacola Beach is an appealing enclave. It has its condominium towers, to be sure, but it also has real neighborhoods and low-key motels.

On the side of the island facing Santa Rosa Sound are 8 miles of recreation trail leading directly to Gulf Islands National Seashore at the island's western end. This trail, which parallels Via de Luna Drive, makes it easy to ditch your car. Every summer—which is high season—a free beach trolley also attempts to cut down on traffic and give sand-scorched feet a break. You can hop aboard between 10 A.M. and 3 P.M.

19. Gulf Islands National Seashore, Fort Pickens Unit

Gulf Islands National Seashore shelters shorebirds, preserves dune habitat, and protects significant historic sites. It has six separate units, all of which are miles apart. Its campground is popular, so arrive early to be placed on the daily waiting list; no reservations are accepted.

This is the site of pentagon-shaped Fort Pickens, built by slaves between 1829 and 1834. One of the fort's many claims to fame—the one that most interests kids—is that the Apache leader Geronimo, his family, and his followers were imprisoned here from 1886 to 1888 under sideshowlike conditions. Portions of the fort and its moat remain for you to climb over and walk through. Interpretive exhibits, an aquarium, bike paths, nature trails, a fishing pier, and a sparkling gulfshore beach make this unit of the national seashore a must-see destination.

Although it is exceptionally hot here in the summer, creative park rangers dress up in soldiers' uniforms on summer Sundays and re-enact daily life at the fort in the 1860s. There are three sections of beach between Pensacola Beach and the fort. Laguna Beach has restrooms and showers, and lifeguards are posted in the summer. You can rent bikes at the campground and travel a 6-mile round-trip path that is paved with crushed oyster shells, a valuable coastal fill material.

Location: From Pensacola Beach on Santa Rosa Island, drive west about 2 miles on Fort Pickens Road to the national seashore entrance and about 4 more miles to the seashore's campground and Fort Pickens.

Important information: The national seashore is open daily from 8 A.M. to sunset, while Fort Pickens is open from 8:30 A.M. to 4 P.M. from November through March, and from 9:30 A.M. to 5:30 P.M. from April through October. Fort tours are available on weekends at 2 P.M. and Mondays through Fridays at 11 A.M. and 2 P.M. The admission pass here and at all other fee areas in the national seashore is good for seven days. For more national seashore information, call 850-934-2600 or visit <www.nps.gov/guis>. For fort information, call 850-934-2635 or 850-934-2622.

To cut down on driving and parking hassles and to enjoy a breezy ride, check and see if the ferry to Fort Pickens from Pensacola is running yet. For more information, call the Pensacola Beach Chamber of Commerce, 800-635-4803.

20. Gulf Islands National Seashore, Naval Oaks Unit

If you want to learn more about the national seashore, visit its headquarters here. The Naval Oaks Unit features a visitor center, a picnic area, and nature

Iron wood for Ironsides

Florida soil nourishes more than 24 kinds of oak, but *Quercus virginiana,* or live oak, is the state's most famous. It is a striking shade tree, with beefy branches that extend horizontally from the trunk. Because of this remarkable sideways growth, 200-year-old **live-oak trees** with 100-foot-high crowns present a regal scene in the rural fields of North Florida.

When dried and cut, live-oak timber was super strong. In 1828, Congress reserved the tree for naval shipbuilding. The USS *Constitution,* known affectionately as Old Ironsides, was built of Florida live oak, as were several other important warships. Vast forests of live oak, at one time growing right down to the coastal shore, were felled in the heyday of Florida's live-oak timber industry, from 1830 to 1860. The Naval Oaks Unit of the Gulf Islands National Seashore presents the story of how even the nation's president once kept track of Florida's live oaks.

trails that lead past red cedars and large blooming magnolia trees. It's nestled in a coastal scrub woods on a peninsula in Santa Rosa Sound. Five thousand years ago, this site was a coastal camp of native Indians of the Temple Mound Culture. The old live-oak forest here was set aside by Congress in 1828 for use in building the country's sturdy warships.

Location: From Gulf Breeze, take Gulf Breeze Parkway (U.S. Highway 98 East) to the seashore entrance on the south side of the parkway.

Important information: Open daily from 8 A.M. to sunset. Free admission. For more information, call 850-934-2600 or 850-924-2600 or visit <www.nps.gov/guis>.

21. Pensacola Beaches

If you want to try a Pensacola-area beach other than the one at Gulf Islands National Seashore, the family-friendly community of Pensacola Beach offers two beaches blessed with restrooms and showers. Casino Beach has summer lifeguards, picnic tables, showers, a concrete boardwalk, and a bustling, holiday feel. The beach accessed via Fort Pickens Gate also has showers, restrooms, and picnic tables, but it has no lifeguard. Its atmosphere is less commercial, as it is only a quarter-mile from the entrance to the Fort Pickens Unit of the national seashore, allowing you to stroll there easily. When Florida is deluged with college spring-break revelers, Pensacola Beach always seems less inundated with rowdy students than other coastal resorts. It courts the family crowd.

Location: Casino Beach is at the southern end of Pensacola Beach Road in Pensacola Beach. The gigantic parking lot makes it hard to miss. Fort Pickens Gate beach is west of Casino Beach on the south side of State Road 399, just a quarter-mile before the entrance gate to Gulf Islands National Seashore.

Important information: Both beaches are open 24 hours a day and parking is free. For more information, call 850-932-2257.

22. Gulf Breeze Zoo and Botanical Gardens

Your kids can hand-feed a giraffe (with necks as long as this, do they ever feel full?) at this 30-acre zoo in a garden setting. There's a must-see nursery and incubator room for zoo babies. A safari train will carry you through this reserve where 700 animals of the world roam.

Location: From Gulf Breeze, west of the Naval Oaks Unit of the Gulf Islands National Seashore, take Gulf Breeze Parkway (U.S. Highway 98 East) to the zoo and gardens at 5710 Gulf Breeze Parkway.

Important information: Open from 9 A.M. to 5 P.M. daily. Children under age 3 are admitted free. Fees are $5.75 for ages 3 to 11 and $9.75 for all others. For more information, call 850-932-2229 or visit <www.the-zoo.com>.

23. Gulf Islands National Seashore, Santa Rosa Unit

This glistening, 7-mile-long beach encompasses a portion of the Florida National Scenic Trail. Opal Beach in this unit has showers, restrooms, and picnic shelters. The name Opal comes from the 1995 hurricane that destroyed the national seashore pavilion that once stood here. It is a reminder of the fragility of Florida barrier islands such as this beauty.

Location: On Santa Rosa Island, travel east from Pensacola Beach on State Road 399. The road goes directly through the national seashore, and you can choose one of several parking areas to pull into.

Important information: For more information, call 850-934-2600.

24. Panhandle Butterfly House/Navarre Park

At this small county park, a nonprofit community group incubates and releases native butterflies in the summer. There are also swans, turtles, and ducks at the park's pond, a playground where your kids can pretend to walk the plank on a pirate ship, and even a beach on a bay where the water is just deep enough for splashing. This is an ideal place to picnic and stretch your legs.

Location: In Navarre Beach, on U.S. Highway 98 at Navarre Park.

Important information: The park is open year-round. The butterfly house is open from May 1 through Labor Day from 11 A.M. to 4 P.M. daily. There is no entry fee, but donations are accepted. For more information, call 850-939-3267 or 850-623-1930.

25. Blue Dolphin Kayak Tours

If your family likes kayaking, this outfitter can quietly bring you to beautiful beach and bay areas. Instruction is provided.

Location: In Navarre Beach at 9225 Quail Roost Road.

Important information: For detailed directions, reservations, or more information, call 800-871-5833, extension 83, from outside Florida or 850-939-7734 from within the state.

26. Navarre Beach Family Campground

If there's a space available at this popular, shady, private camp, you'll welcome this waterfront location on Santa Rosa Sound. It features a swim beach, pool, playground, and pier. The water is shallow and relatively calm here.

Location: In Navarre Beach at 9201 Navarre Parkway (U.S. Highway 98).

Important information: For more information, call the campground at 850-939-2188.

Fort Walton Beach Area

This May-to-September beach resort had its modern origins as Camp Walton, a Civil War outpost. Today, it attracts families from South Florida and nearby military bases for fun in the sun, including fishing from its 1,261-foot-long pier. Expect an unpretentious and sometimes overdeveloped swath of shore. The main part of the community is surrounded on three sides by water. It sits at the western end of Choctawhatchee Bay along a narrow section of Santa Rosa Sound. Cinco Bayou separates it on the north from Ocean City. Part of the town spills over onto the eastern end of Okaloosa Island and fronts on the Gulf of Mexico. Fort Walton Beach and nearby Destin are renowned for their sugar white beaches and emerald green waters, which earned this area the nickname Emerald Coast.

27. Indian Temple Mound Museum

Just when you don't want to look at another flashing neon sign for a restaurant, bar, or condominium or see another beach trinket shop, this museum in the middle of a gaudy coastal-highway commercial strip will zip you back in time. Step under shady live-oak trees, see the grassy mound, and imagine the lives of families who lived here as long as 10,000 years ago.

The mound, a national historic landmark, is one of countless mounds that once dotted the region but were flattened during development. Most of the mounds were garbage heaps—ancient piles of scallop, clam, oyster, and conch shells left over from early beach picnics. But this mound, dating to about A.D. 1400, was used for political and religious purposes by a highly evolved civilization.

This city museum tells the little-known story of these pre-Columbian peoples. It features a large projectile point collection, a burial urn, effigy vessels, and other artifacts unearthed within 40 miles of here.

Location: In Fort Walton Beach, on the north side of U.S. Highway 98 (Miracle Strip Parkway) at 139 Miracle Strip Parkway.

Important information: Small entrance fee. Open from 11 A.M. to 4 P.M. Tuesdays through Saturdays. For more information, call 850-243-6521.

28. Focus Science Center

• •

This is a good indoor destination where children can plot the path of a hurricane, try on a space suit, make giant bubbles, experience the "hair-raising" Van de Graaff generator, enter a castle of mirrors, and more. The center is operated by a nonprofit group called Families of Okaloosa County Understanding Science.

Location: In Fort Walton Beach, a half-block south of U.S. Highway 98 (Miracle Strip Parkway) at 139 Brooks Street.

Important information: Open from noon to 4 P.M. Sundays, from noon to 2 P.M. Tuesdays and Fridays, and from 11 A.M. to 4 P.M. Saturdays. The fee is $2.50 per person. For more information, call the center at 850-664-1261.

29. Gulfarium

• •

Visit one of the oldest performing-porpoise shows around, open to the public since 1955. This is also a 10,000-gallon aquarium, where sharks, stingrays, and a loggerhead turtle cruise by. There are performing seal shows, too. The Gulfarium has a captive breeding program and is part of a dolphin-rescue network.

Location: Just east of Fort Walton Beach on U.S. Highway 98.

Important information: Open daily from 9 A.M. to 5 P.M. Children under age 4 are admitted free. Fees are $10 for children 4 to 11, $12 for seniors, and $14 for all others. For more information, call the Gulfarium at 850-244-5169.

30. Liza Jackson Park

A large playground, a fishing pier on Santa Rosa Sound, and a picnic area help make this local park a fine rest stop.

Location: On U.S. Highway 98 on Santa Rosa Island at Fort Walton Beach.

Important information: Free.

31. Brackin and John Beasley Wayside Parks

These two coastal swimming and picnic stops, almost next door to each other, are good to know. They are near the eastern end of the coastal island that farther west is called Santa Rosa Island but here is called Okaloosa Island. *Okaloosa* is thought to mean "pleasant place" in a local Native American language. Brackin Wayside Park has a large pier, summer lifeguards,

Porpoises and dolphins with a dilemma

Sleek, gray **dolphins** and porpoises are related but biologically separate species of marine mammal that fish and breed in Florida's salt water. Dolphins (*Tursiops truncatus*) are larger than porpoises *(Phocoena phocoena)* and more common off the Florida coast. Unlike the porpoise, the dolphin has a 3-inch-long bottlenose snout. Both animals race through the waves, rounding up schools of fish for their lunch. There are few sights more breathtaking to witness than the leap of a wild dolphin.

Don't approach these creatures in the wild. To try to touch, swim, and mingle with them—a folly that unfortunately has become a venture of some coastal captains—is unwise. Not only have state marine protection officers identified this as a significant problem, but it's just plain stupid to attempt it. Let me count the ways. These lively, 150-pound creatures are small whales, and they can accidentally hurt you. Dolphin researchers know this, because they have the broken bones to prove it. Porpoises and dolphins engage in frequent sex, and they have been known to nudge at swimmers in an attempt to mate with them. They have sharp teeth and can nip, even bite. They have no natural immunity to upper-respiratory infections, so your viruses and bacteria can harm them.

It's so tempting for sea captains to attract them with food so that tourists can swim with them, but feeding wild marine mammals is a stupid thing to do if you really like them. They need to go fish. So control yourself—don't swim with wild dolphins or porpoises.

(The dolphin fish, also known as mahi mahi, is a true fish hooked for its tasty meat. It's an entirely different, ah, kettle of fish.)

restrooms, showers, picnic tables, and a beachside restaurant, Harpoon Hanna's. Just a quarter-mile east, John Beasley Wayside Park also has summer lifeguards, restrooms, and showers. Just east of Beasley Wayside is the Visitors Welcome Center, a good place to ask questions and load up on free maps, brochures, and discount coupons.

Location: Across Choctawhatchee Bay from Fort Walton Beach on Okaloosa Island, at 1 mile and 1.25 miles east of Fort Walton Beach.

Important information: Free beach parking. For more information, call 850-651-7131.

32. Gulf Islands National Seashore, Okaloosa Unit

The easternmost section of Gulf Islands National Seashore, the Okaloosa Unit is a beach ideal for families because of the calm, shallow water. It fronts Choctawhatchee Bay. There are paddleboat rentals, a snack bar, restrooms, and showers, but no lifeguard at this fine picnic and swimming spot.

Location: On the eastern end of Okaloosa Island, along U.S. Highway 98.

Important information: For more information, call 850-934-2600.

33. Rocky Bayou State Recreation Area

With a nature trail along Puddin' Head Lake, red cedars to provide a great aroma, bluffs to admire, and Rocky Creek to splash in, this mainland fishing place and campground is a welcome bayside retreat.

Location: On State Road 20 about 5 miles east of Niceville, across Choctawhatchee Bay from Destin.

Important information: For more information, call 850-833-9144 or visit <www.dep.state.fl.us/parks>.

34. Destin Diner

Take your kids to a real 1950s diner for an ice cream float or a stack of pancakes, anytime. This place is affordable and very family friendly.

Location: In Destin on U.S. Highway 98 at Airport Road.

Important information: Open 24 hours a day. For more information, call the diner at 850-654-5843.

35. The Back Porch/The Candymaker

You can sit outside at the beach, munch on a fish sandwich, and watch the water where your lunch may have been swimming just hours ago at the Back Porch, a seafood shack popular with families visiting nearby Henderson Beach State Recreation Area (see below). After lunch, watch out for cars as you head across the street to the Candymaker, where you can watch before you sample, as saltwater taffy, fudge, and caramel apples are created.

Location: In Destin at 1740 Old U.S. Highway 98 East.

Important information: There is a kids' menu. For more Back Porch information, call 850-837-2022. You can reach the Candymaker at 850-654-0833.

36. June's Dunes

Biscuits with sausage gravy for breakfast and hamburgers for lunch are kid-pleasers at this picnic-table café on the beach. Unlike some area eateries, this one is easy on the pocketbook and full of local flavor.

Location: In Destin at 1780 Old U.S. Highway 98 East.

Important information: Not open for dinner. No credit cards taken. For more information, call the café at 850-650-0455.

37. Henderson Beach State Recreation Area

This 208-acre recreation area offers excellent beach access, including boardwalks to the glistening sand. The dunes are stunning and so are the upland magnolias, scrub oaks, and wildflowers. Families also appreciate the lovely campground, picnic shelters, restrooms, and showers. This is an exceptionally wonderful beach parkland. The campground is new.

Location: In Destin at 17000 U.S. Highway 98 (Emerald Coast Parkway).

Important information: Open daily from 8 A.M. to sunset. For more information, call 850-837-7550 or visit <www.dep.state.fl.us/parks>.

38. James Lee County Park

Here's another handy gulfshore picnicking and swimming destination that has restrooms, showers, and picnic shelters. There is also a restaurant, the Crab Trap, that specializes in all kinds of crab dishes. This family-friendly

An inland passage

In Florida, boaters have their own highway: the **Intracoastal Waterway.** It's the reason you might have to wait in traffic at a bridge crossing. Boats on this marine highway have the right of way. Bridge tenders stop auto traffic to let tall-masted sailboats and large yachts and ships pass through—again and again, to the dismay of some drivers.

East of the fishing mecca of Destin, the Intracoastal Waterway makes two unusual jaunts. Much of the famous route passes through the bays and sounds that separate barrier islands from the mainland. But in the Panhandle at Choctawhatchee Bay, the marine highway becomes an inland passage from Point Washington on Tucker Bayou to West Bay. It does this again through Gulf County, at one point leading almost 12 miles inland. The purpose of the Intracoastal Waterway is to provide boaters with smooth cruising on a passage sheltered from storm-tossed gulf or ocean waters.

hangout offers breezy dining in a gazebo, super-sized ice cream cones, and an on-site candy shop.

Location: On Old U.S. Highway 98 in Destin about a quarter-mile east of Henderson Beach State Recreation Area (see above).

Important information: For more information, call 850-651-7131.

39. Topsail Hill State Preserve

No one knows how high Florida's dunes once reached, because the great old ones are long gone. But 40-foot-high sand hills here at this 1,600-acre state preserve help us envision the ancient coastline. The stunning dunes shelter a string of freshwater lakes.

The amenities at the preserve are simple: a parking area, picnic shelter, and restrooms. In contrast, there is a well-manicured, public RV campground nearby that features a camp store, a pool, tennis courts, a clubhouse, and a golf driving range. It makes a unique gulfshore destination if you'd like to spend the day on a wild beach and then return at night to a country-clublike campsite.

Location: The state preserve is on Santa Rosa Beach at 7349 U.S. Highway 98, east of Destin. The RV campground is farther east, at 7525 West Scenic Highway 30A.

Important information: For detailed directions, campground reservations, or more information, call the campground at 850-267-0299. Call the preserve at 850-267-1868 or visit <www.dep.state.fl.us/parks>.

40. Donut Hole II

Your family will thank you for stopping at the Donut Hole II to pick up a bag of fresh pastries—tarts, muffins, Danish pastries, and homemade doughnuts. If you can rinse the sand off little legs, you might even want to sit down here for a family meal. The menu includes country breakfasts, homemade bread, milkshakes, burgers, dinner specials, and more—all at affordable prices.

Location: In Santa Rosa Beach on the north side of U.S. Highway 98, almost 1 mile west of where US 98 meets Florida Scenic Highway 30A.

Important information: For more information, call the Donut Hole II at 850-267-3239.

41. Gulf View Heights Beach/Goatfeathers

This is another two-in-one stop. Gulf View Heights is a beach park with restrooms, showers, and picnic tables. It's tucked behind what is more readily seen from the road: the fun Goatfeathers café. Goatfeathers is an open-air, family-friendly place. It offers food baskets for kids with uncommon side dishes such as applesauce and fried pickles. It also has a seafood market on the premises, so you know the fish sandwich is fresh.

Location: On Florida Scenic Highway 30A, between Dune Allen and Blue Mountain Beach. The park is hidden from the road behind Goatfeathers, which is at 3865 West State Road 30A, Scenic 30.

Important information: The park is open all the time. For more park information, call 850-267-1216. Goatfeathers takes cash only, as do several places on this part of the coast. Call before you go in December, because the café closes for vacation part of the month. The number is 850-267-3342.

42. Baywoods Vacation Homes

This friendly family resort offers seven shaded cottages, a sailboat, a canoe, fishing rods, a pier, a children's playhouse, a putting green, two pools, a gym, a tennis court, playgrounds, a treehouse, and a sheltered beach on Choctawhatchee Bay. It's situated on a quiet street near Eden State Gardens, and you can travel to the gardens aboard the Baywoods pontoon boat. Baywoods welcomes pets; if you'd like to bring yours, ask for a cottage with a fenced back yard.

Location: From U.S. Highway 98 north of Grayton Beach, take Bay Drive north a few blocks to Choctawhatchee Bay and turn right onto East Mitchell Avenue. Baywoods is at 221 East Mitchell Avenue.

Important information: For more information, call 888-999-4229 or visit <www.baywoods.com>.

43. Patrone's

This funky, ramshackle stop in the low-key village of Grayton Beach is one part Sno-Cone shop and one part petting zoo, with a good measure of artists' colony, café, and pontoon/canoe rental business comfortably thrown in, too. It's a fun diversion and a place to buy quality work by area artisans.

Location: In the village of Grayton Beach at 307 DeFuniak Street.

Important information: Open daily from 10 A.M. to 5 P.M. For more information, call Patrone's at 850-231-1606.

44. Grayton Beach State Recreation Area

Explore a nature path through the dunes at this mile-long gulfshore swimming park. Despite the park's tiny size, it preserves some of the best dunes along the Panhandle coast. The dunes and talcum-powder-soft beach sand helped earn it a ranking as a top national beach in a 1994 survey. Grayton is a family favorite. It features a campground nestled among pines and a small lake that attracts feeding herons and wintering ducks. The interpretive path up and down the dunes has several intriguing stops, such as markers pointing out how the sand is drifting over magnolia trees and smothering them alive! Although the preserve is crowded in the summer, you'll have the chance to stay up at night and perhaps catch a glimpse of giant, endangered sea turtles lumbering ashore from the Gulf of Mexico to lay their eggs.

Location: On Florida Scenic Highway 30A just east of the village of Grayton Beach, on the south side of the road at 357 Main Park Road.

Important information: The campground is popular, so call for reservations at 850-231-4210 or visit <www.dep.state.fl.us/parks>.

45. Seaside

● ●

This gulfshore community offers a mix of open-air markets, including a book-store with a good kids' selection and a sneakers store to encourage walking and bike-riding. The development is privately owned, but the public is invited to check out the shops, galleries, gingerbread-trimmed cottages, restaurants, bike paths, and grassy amphitheater, where storytelling events and festivals are frequently held. The closet-sized post office and two-room schoolhouse are also worth a peek. The visitor center provides an overview of this award-winning development. The accommodations here are pricey, but rates are halved in the chilly winter, when Seaside fireplaces glow.

Location: On Florida Scenic Highway 30A, about a quarter-mile east of Grayton Beach State Recreation Area (see above).

Important information: Car use is discouraged in Seaside, so find a parking place—a challenge on crowded weekends and midday in the summer—and prepare to stroll. For more information, call 850-231-2201.

46. Eden State Gardens

● ●

Who can resist lingering a moment in Eden? This 12-acre picnic spot comes with a great lawn for children to tumble upon, an oak-draped view of Tucker Bayou, and a furnished, two-story 1897 mansion to tour. The small garden of purple azaleas and red and white camellias is a quiet place to contemplate the vanished timber industry that once supported this port. Each February, the site hosts the Annual School of the Soldier, a living history event of old-time military drills and period cooking.

Location: From Florida Scenic Highway 30A about 1 mile east of Seaside, take County Road 395 north through the Point Washington State Forest to the end of the road. The sign marking the entrance to the state gardens is on the left.

Important information: The park and gardens are free and open daily from 8 A.M. to sundown. House tours cost $4 and are offered on the hour from 9 A.M. to 4 P.M. For more information, call 850-231-4214 or visit <www. dep.state.fl.us/parks>.

47. Deer Lake State Park

This preserve shelters a small lake and stretches from the gulf shore and a small beach across Florida Scenic Highway 30A to an inland wildlife area. This little-known picnic and nature-study site has restrooms and picnic tables.

Location: On State Road 30A about 2.5 miles east of the village of Seagrove Beach.

Important information: For more information, call the Grayton Beach State Recreation Area office at 850-231-4210 or visit <www.dep.state.fl.us/parks>.

Panama City Area

This crowded coastal zone is inundated with students during spring break. Most families give it a wide berth from March 1 through the Easter holiday. Expect a barrage of beach bars, arcades, tattoo parlors, T-shirt shops, band contests, bumper-car rides, bungee-jumping concessions, and endless other amusements. The area has an anything-goes, 24-hour-a-day, Surf City feel during break time that makes college students (not always fully clothed) yell P-A-R-T-Y! But beyond the annual beer-chugging ritual, there's another side to Panama City, so named because it's on the same meridian as part of the Panama Canal Zone. Perfectly normal families live here year-round and like it. If you are in the area, take a look and decide for yourself.

48. Raccoon River Resort/Magnolia Beach RV Park

Because the campground at St. Andrews State Recreation Area is often filled in the summer and on weekends, here are two shaded, commercial camping sites nearby that also can be fun. Raccoon River Resort has a playground, pool, and pond, and restrooms that resemble log cabins. Magnolia Beach is a lovely bayshore camp graced with large magnolias. It has a fishing pier and pool.

Location: Raccoon River is at 12405 Middle Beach Road at Panama City Beach. Magnolia Beach is at 7800 Magnolia Beach Road at Panama City Beach.

Important information: For more information on Raccoon River Resort, call 850-234-0181. For Magnolia Beach RV Park, call 850-235-1581. Both are part of the GoodSam Club network.

49. Museum of Man in the Sea

See what it was like to don a sponge-diver's suit and explore the sea bottom at this small site devoted to underwater adventures dating back 5,000 years. This vast collection of old diving equipment and underwater exploration devices isn't for everyone, but do visit if you have snorkelers and divers in your crew.

Location: In Panama City Beach at 17314 Panama City Beach Parkway (Back Beach Road).

Important information: Children ages 6 and under are admitted free. Fees are $2 for children 7 to 12 and $4 for older children and adults. Seniors get a 10 percent discount. For more information, call the museum at 850-235-4101.

50. Sea School Trip

View underwater creatures up close, visit Shell Island, and learn something important about the area's ecology along the way by taking this glass-bottom boat on its Sea School Trip.

Location: In Panama City Beach at Treasure Island Marina, 3605 Thomas Drive, behind the Treasure Ship (see below).

Important information: Half-day trips are offered daily from 9 A.M. to noon and from 1 to 4 P.M. Children under 2 are admitted free. Fees are $6 for ages 3 to 12 and $9 for everyone else. For more information, call 850-234-8944.

51. Gulf World

Here's a newly renovated aquarium where you can see sharks and sea turtles, enjoy a porpoise show, and learn about the need to preserve the residents of the gulf waters.

Location: In Panama City Beach at 15412 West Highway 98A.

Important information: Children 4 and younger are admitted free. Fees are $7.95 for ages 5 to 12, $13.95 for all others. For more information, call the aquarium at 850-234-5271.

52. Zoo World

Once a run-down collection of cages, this longtime zoo has transformed itself by adding a sweet petting zoo, a fun place to feed a giraffe, a lush garden, a bat exhibit, and a walk-through aviary. Alligators are among the 350 animals displayed here.

Location: In Panama City Beach at 9008 Front Beach Road.

Important information: Children ages 3 and under are admitted free. Fees are $6.50 for ages 4 to 11 and $8.95 for all others. For more information, call the zoo at 850-230-0096.

53. Treasure Ship

Climb aboard a replica of a 17th-century square-rigged sailing ship to walk the planks of this extravagant but touristy restaurant, bar, and gift shop. You are less likely to dent your vacation budget if you eat lunch or a very early dinner rather than waiting until the pricey dinner hour. Climb your way through this four-level seafood shop, and if you want breezy dining, look for the outside seating area, way up high, known as the Decks. Peter Pan fans might like Hook's Grill. Those who visit in the evening or load up at the Sunday brunch will most likely be visited by marauding Treasure Ship pirates. They'll astound your little mateys, so have the camera ready.

Location: In Panama City Beach at 3605 Thomas Drive (impossible to miss!).

Important information: No reservations are accepted, and there can be a long wait for a table on summer nights, most weekends, on holidays, and on

Some other time

Central standard time, not eastern, is the correct time in the Panhandle, from a point west of the Apalachicola River to the Florida-Alabama border. North of Apalachicola, the Apalachicola River is the dividing line. But a community of people who work and play together extends from east of the river in Eastpoint to west of the river in Port St. Joe. So to accommodate them, the zone boundary does a jog along the Intracoastal Waterway. Most maps show this quirk. It means that the town of Apalachicola is in the eastern time zone, although most Floridians firmly believe otherwise, having learned all their lives that the river is the dividing line.

other crowded resort occasions, such as when area festivals attract throngs of visitors. Lunch is available in one area of the ship. There is a kids' menu. Call ahead for tips on when you can avoid the crowds, 850-234-8881.

54. St. Andrews State Recreation Area

Alligators sunning on a lagoon, dolphins swimming in the gulf, and herons feeding in the marshes help to make this 1,260-acre campground a great place for wildlife watching. Sea creatures are attracted by the clear water and rocks and jetties here. Families crowd the park in the summer to enjoy its two piers, a gulfshore beach, camping near Grand Lagoon, Gator Lake, nature trails, a seasonal ferry to and from nearby Shell Island, and a reconstructed turpentine still. There are even narrated snorkel trips through the grassy flats. In a 1995 survey by *Travel* magazine, this was named the best beach in the United States.

To avoid the crowds, try to visit in the fall or winter off-season. If you are here in the summer, try to come midweek and early in the day. Late summer visitors will have a chance to watch sea turtle hatchlings struggle from their nests on the beach, cross the sand, and slip into the gulf waters— a heartwarming launch to witness.

Location: About 3 miles east of Panama City Beach off State Road 392 (Thomas Drive).

Important information: Concessions such as the ferry to Shell Island and the snorkel tour are offered only in spring and summer. For concession information, call Pier Concession at 850-235-4004, or Jetty Concession at 850-233-0197. A variety of combination tickets and park passes are sold. Campsite fees are steeper here than in other public campgrounds, averaging close to $20. Reservations are recommended and should be made well in advance. For park information, call 850-233-5140.

55. Pine Log State Forest

Unfurl your sleeping bag in an isolated forest setting between two lakes. One is for summer swimming (no lifeguard) and the other lake, fringed with tall cypress trees, is for canoeing and fishing. A 3-mile nature trail lets you tramp through the stunning sandpine forest. There is no office or staff on site.

Location: About 20 miles north of Panama City Beach on County Road 79, south of the crossroads of Ebro.

Important information: For more information, contact the state forest office at 850-747-5639 or visit <www.fl-dof.com/fm/recreation>.

56. Junior Museum of Bay County

Duck into a Native American tepee, enjoy a puppet show, visit a pioneer village populated with chickens and ducks, try hands-on science activities, walk through a swamp, and otherwise take a break from the beach at this ideal site for preschool and grade-school kids.

Location: In Panama City at 1731 Jenks Avenue.

Important information: Open from 9 A.M. to 4:30 P.M. Mondays through Fridays and from 10 A.M. to 4 P.M. Saturdays. Children under age 2 are admitted free. Fees are $2.50 for ages 2 to 12 and $4 for all others. For more information, call the museum at 850-769-6128.

Apalachicola Area

As you tour this small river town, imagine what it must have been like in the 1830s, when the wharves were so busy with ocean-going commerce that Apalachicola rivaled New Orleans as the most prosperous port on the Gulf of Mexico. The wealth of those boom times financed a district of estates and cozy gardens. Several two- and three-story mansions are open today as inns, which makes the town a popular getaway for couples who linger in the antiques shops, jewelry stores, and galleries, looking for unique souvenirs, such as the famed tupelo honey produced in this region.

As Apalachicola's maritime history is brought more to life through hands-on museums and living-history presenters, this charming village will appeal to children much as historic Pensacola does. They will also appreciate the seafood snacks, the chance to study nature, and the smaller pleasures, such as a 19th-century sloop in which you can go for a sail—a thrill especially when dolphins escort the ship. A small museum shows how a local doctor invented air conditioning to relieve the suffering of patients with yellow fever. A state park on an offshore island provides a chance for bay-to-gulf recreation and family camping. An isolated national wildlife refuge, located nearby but accessible only by boat, is a breeding grounds for the red wolf. As you unfurl your sleeping bag at night, can't you just hear the howls from across the bay?

57. John Gorrie State Museum

His patients got no relief as they lay dying from yellow fever, so Dr. John Gorrie came up with a new way to cool their rooms. He's now considered the inventor of modern refrigeration and air conditioning. This solid citizen of Apalachicola, who also served as city treasurer and postmaster, is celebrated at this unique stop. It's fun to see how his contraptions worked and how Florida got cool.

Location: In Apalachicola at the intersection of Sixth Street and Avenue D.

Important information: Open from 9 A.M. to 5 P.M. Thursdays through Mondays. Fee is $1. For more information, call 850-653-9347 or visit <www.dep.state.fl.us/parks>.

58. *Governor Stone* Sloop

Bask in a copper sunset under a glorious full sail on the 1877 sloop *Governor Stone*. Sixty-three feet of glistening white-painted wood, it's said to be the oldest operating sailboat in the southeastern United States and is a registered National Historic Landmark. You and your mates may want to ship out for good.

Location: Docked along Water Street in Apalachicola. (You can't miss it!) The office is at the Apalachicola Maritime Museum, 268 Water Street.

Important information: For more information, call 850-653-8700.

59. Scipio Creek Park/St. Vincent Island National Wildlife Refuge

This park is a small picnic place and a picturesque setting in which to stroll along a short dockage. The pile of gray and white disks across Scipio Creek is a stack of oyster shells to be used for fill. This quiet, dead-end spot on the water is also the location of the headquarters of St. Vincent Island National Wildlife Refuge. Stop here for a good briefing about this little-known federal preserve. The 12,350-acre barrier island, about 20 miles southwest of Apalachicola, is the site of an unusual red wolf breeding program. The best way to see the isolated island—daytime only—is with a local guide. The island has no facilities.

Location: In Apalachicola, take Market Street away from downtown to its end at the waterfront. The refuge has its headquarters in a two-story, wood-frame building on the right.

Important information: The refuge headquarters is open weekdays from 9 A.M. to 4 P.M. To book a trip to the island, contact Jeanni's Journeys at 850-927-3259, an ecotourism guide whose services are available from March through September, or Broke-A-Toe Tours at 850-229-9283, which is open year-round and based at Indian Pass near the refuge island. For more information, call refuge headquarters at 850-653-8808 or visit <www.fws.gov/r4reao>.

Something to howl about

Flamingos and dolphins are the animals many visitors think of when dreaming of a Florida vacation. But in North Florida, two wild canines are creatures to howl about. The endangered **red wolf** historically ranged in Florida. It's being bred southwest of Apalachicola at the St. Vincent Island National Wildlife Refuge and also in Tallahassee at the Museum of History and Natural Science. The howls you hear when camping in North Florida are most likely from **coyotes** that have migrated here from the West and scattered throughout the rural parts of the region.

60. Apalachicola National Estuarine Research Reserve

Apalachicola Bay, nearby East Bay, the delta wetlands, and the region where the Apalachicola River meets the Gulf of Mexico comprise an incomparable natural fish and shellfish hatchery. It's nature's nursery for everything from birds that breed here to shellfish and finned fish that spawn here. To keep this highly productive anchor of the gulf seafood industry humming, a 240,000-acre research preserve has been set aside. Its staff studies what must be done to keep the estuarine ecosystem functioning. The reserve headquarters features educational exhibits about Native American history, some of the animal species that thrive here, the traditional marine uses of the area, and the future of this fragile niche.

Location: In Apalachicola at the end of Market Street in Scipio Creek Park.

Important information: For more information, call the reserve at 850-653-8063 or visit <www.nos.noaa.gov>.

61. Jeanni's Journeys

Jeanni McMillan is a nature guide with a gift for sharing the wonders of natural science with children. She can take you to a variety of kid-pleasing places, including shell-strewn beaches on outer islands and St. Vincent Island National Wildlife Refuge, or on an adventure trip up the Apalachicola River. In the summer, students are devoted to her campouts.

Location: In Apalachicola at 320 Patton Street.

Important information: You can book one of Jeanni's Journeys from March through September. Call 850-927-3259.

62. St. George Island State Park

You can camp here under the whistling pines on the north, or inland, side of St. George Island, which overlooks the calm waters of St. George Sound. Boardwalks lead to the glistening gulfshore swimming and fishing beach and to sandy nature trails where you might spot rabbits, foxes, or bobcats. In the fall, raptors fly over in significant numbers, and butterflies flit through on migration to Mexico.

Although the temptation is great to pull over anywhere and park your car, you should park only in designated areas. Tow trucks are kept busy pulling stranded cars out of the sand.

Location: From Apalachicola, travel east on U.S. Highway 98 across the 5-mile-long John Gorrie Memorial Bridge and causeway system that spans the mouth of the Apalachicola River and East Bay. When you reach East Point, continue on about three-quarters of a mile and turn right (south) onto State Road 300. There is a small brown sign for St. George Island State Park. Continue on SR 300 over a bridge and causeway system to St. George Island. The park is at the eastern end of the island. Follow the signs, bearing left with SR 300, which on the island is called East Gulf Beach Drive. The road dead-ends at the park.

Important information: On summer weekends, the park can get crowded, so arrive early or go later in the day, when the "first shift" is leaving after too much sun. For more information or campground reservations, call 850-927-2111 or visit <www.dep.state.fl.us/parks>.

Panhandle Interior

Drive up and down a few red-clay hills under longleaf pines, past a few lakes full of largemouth bass, and your back-seat navigators will ask if you've left Florida. The interior of the Panhandle is often said to be Georgia and Alabama using an alias.

This is a hunting and fishing region, with tree-shaded cabins perched by lakes and rivers. Country roads flanked by stands selling local honey and boiled peanuts take you through villages with quaint town squares. Increasingly, bird watchers and ecologists flock to the region for year-round plant study and fall raptor migration. Stunning bogs of carnivorous plants and

Green and gooey flesh-eaters of the forest

You might expect the subtropical climate of Florida's southern tip to spawn exotic, **carnivorous plants**. But it's actually North Florida that has the perfect conditions in which these plants can chow down. There are several different genera represented here, and all are endlessly fascinating.

All insect-eating plants grow in easily trampled wetlands, so view them only from roadsides or from boardwalks designed to protect their habitat. Pitcher plants (*Sarracenia* sp.) come in six varieties here. Bugs climb downward into their sticky, tubular leaves until they get stuck. Passersby can sometimes see a wiggling beetle, spider, or even a small frog struggling inside. Sundews (*Drosera* sp.) take five forms in Florida. All have hairy, tentacle-like leaves that act like flypaper to trap insects.

There are five kinds of butterworts (*Pinguicula* spp.) in Florida. They have flat, greasy leaves that curl slightly inward around the edges, and they lure insects into the leaves with a funguslike scent. When struggling bugs try to fly home, the leaves actually move some, curling up a bit to form a slight trough that keeps the bug trapped. The similar-sounding bladderwort (*Ultricularia* spp.), which comes in 14 varieties, looks very different from the butterwort. Bladderworts, as the name implies, are actually small aquatic bags, sacs, or bladders, with a trap door that opens when a tiny tadpole, fish fry, or protozoan brushes against it.

Finally, the most famous of the carnivorous plants is the Venus flytrap *(Dionaea muscipula)*, which likes to grow near other carnivorous plants. It produces a sugary substance that appeals to bugs. The flytrap part of the plant is like a tiny, green, fringed clamshell. It opens and closes—for good—on its protein-rich meal.

Carnivorous plants can be found in season (usually April and May) in the Blackwater River State Forest, the Apalachicola National Forest, and at Big Lagoon State Recreation Area. Ask rangers for plant-viewing tips.

cool, steep river ravines sheltering species native to the Appalachian Mountains are remarkable features of Panhandle parks. Geological features—ravines, a cavern you can walk through, a waterfall—are centerpieces of the Panhandle. Clear, flowing springs are more common east and south of here, but there are a few in this region that are well known.

63. Blackwater River State Forest

The largest state forest in Florida, Blackwater preserves habitat of the once-dominant longleaf pine and wiregrass. It borders the Conecuh National Forest in Alabama, providing a wildlife corridor for black bears, bobcats, the endangered red-cockaded woodpecker, foxes, river otters, gopher tortoises, and more. You can take a scenic drive through this 183,000-acre forest via the Old Spanish Trail (U.S. Highway 90), which takes you past fragile bogs of pitcher plants. These insect-eating plants are endlessly fascinating to children.

Do not walk through the bogs. You will sink into them and your weight will damage these protected plants, which can easily be seen from the roadside during peak bloom time, April and May.

The forest visitor center, just north of Milton, is a good place to learn more about the plants, forest fishing holes, swimming spots, excellent canoe trails, and hiking paths, including a portion of the Florida National Scenic Trail and an old Native American footpath. If your family likes to camp, this state forest is an excellent destination. But in the summer be prepared for frequent thundershowers, biting bugs, and extremely high temperatures. Spring is the best season in which to visit.

There are four campgrounds with restrooms in the state forest: Krul is in the woods near a tiny lake. Bear Lake offers camping on a grassy slope, as does Karick Lake. Hurricane Lake has sunny sites. To camp near the Blackwater River, head to Blackwater River State Park (see below). Commercial cabin resorts, such as Adventures Unlimited, are nearby, as are canoe outfitters. Ask for information at the forest headquarters.

Location: From US 90 in Milton, take State Road 191 northeast about 9 miles to the forest visitor center. It will be on the right (east) side of the road. The main roads through the state forest are SR 191, a north-south route, and SR 4, an east-west route.

Important information: The center is closed weekends and open from 7 A.M. to 4 P.M. weekdays. For more information, call 850-957-6140 or visit <www.fl-doc.com/fm/recreation>. For outfitting services, contact Adventures Unlimited at 850-623-6197, Bob's Canoes at 800-892-4504 or 850-623-5457, or Blackwater Canoe at 800-967-6789 or 850-623-0235.

64. Blackwater River State Park

Surrounded by Blackwater River State Forest, this 590-acre state park features campsites close to the Blackwater River, as well as canoeing access. The river isn't actually black; it's see-through clear, stained by the tannin of leaf litter. It is said to be one of the cleanest, clearest sand-bottom rivers (as opposed to mud-bottom rivers) in the world! The sandy bottom makes it tempting to pull over at river bends and splash on the beaches. The sand has been deposited here through the eons, ground down from Appalachian quartz in far-off mountains. It eventually will end up downstream along the gulf shore. The river is a fascinating geology lesson and a good place to watch for wildlife. Otters swim in the river.

Location: From Milton, take U.S. Highway 90 east about 12 miles to Deaton Bridge Road. Head north on Deaton Bridge Road for about 8 miles, directly into the state park.

Important information: For more information, call 850-623-0235 or visit <www.dep.state.fl.us/parks>.

65. Milton

After camping in the Blackwater wilds, bring the family to Milton, known as the Canoe Capital of Florida, where you can watch canoeists drift through town on the Blackwater River. The village once was a stagecoach stop. Today, you can visit the 1912 Milton Opera House, now the town museum, and also the 1909 Milton Depot, which features kid-pleasing model train displays. Or sample the 8.5-mile Blackwater Heritage State Trail, a paved recreation path for bicycling, inline skating, or walking.

Location: Milton is on U.S. Highway 90, about 12 miles northeast of Pensacola. Parking is free throughout town.

Important information: For more information, call the Opera House at 850-623-4433, or the Santa Rosa Chamber of Commerce in Milton at 850-623-2339. Or visit <www.flausa.com>.

66. Adventures Unlimited

This creekfront, family-friendly ecotourism resort sits in the woods at an old mill site. Amenities include cabins with hammocks and rocking chairs on their porches, campgrounds, a playground, hay rides, and country cooking. The focus is on kayak, canoe, and tubing trips on the area's clean creeks and on the Blackwater River, where glass containers aren't allowed and littering is not tolerated. This resort is popular with youth groups, which can book dorm-type lodging in one of several group cabins. There are no TV sets, but nature will keep you entertained.

Location: About 12 miles north of Milton via State Road 87. You'll get detailed directions when you make your reservation.

Important information: For more information, call 800-239-6864, 850-623-6197, or 850-626-1669. Or visit <www.adventuresunlimited.com>.

67. DeFuniak Springs

· ·

This village of 19th-century Victorian mansions is a good place to stop and stretch your legs if you're making the long drive between Pensacola and Tallahassee. Walk around an oval, spring-fed lake. Astound the kids with a shiny collection of medieval armor and weapons dating back, some say, to the Crusades. The collection is on permanent display in the tiny, charming Walton-DeFuniak Library, built in 1887. Then consider filling tummies at the H&M Hotdog Stand, which dates to the 1920s, or munch a sandwich at the Busy Bee Café.

DeFuniak Springs is the site of the historic winter camp of the Chautauqua cultural association, which first met here in 1885, attracting thousands to learn about Hawaiian dancing and more. A revival of Chautauqua storytelling, talks, theater, music, and more is held each February. If you are charmed by DeFuniak and want to know more, Diane Pickett, dressed in her Victorian best, gives lively walking tours.

Location: About 35 miles north of Seaside on U.S. Highway 90.

Important information: For more information, call the DeFuniak Springs Visitor Bureau at 850-892-2566, or the Pickett's People Parade and Chautauqua Center at 850-892-4300.

68. Ponce de Leon Springs State Recreation Area

· ·

No one can say for sure, but perhaps the famous Spanish explorer Juan Ponce de Leon was attracted to the flowing water here, 14 million gallons of which burst from the ground each day. The 443-acre recreation area is a fine place to stop for a picnic. It features two nature trails and a crystal-clear, 68-degree F spring—a local summer swimming spot. Rangers also conduct nature talks during the summer.

Location: From DeFuniak Springs, drive about 20 miles east on U.S. Highway 90. Turn south onto County Road 181A and travel about 1 mile to the recreation area.

Important information: No camping. For more information, call 850-836-4281 or visit <www.dep.state.fl.us/parks>.

69. Vortex Spring

Some people can't spend too much time splashing in springs. If your family likes to chill out this way, here's another large spring basin with a private resort. There is camping, a lodge, and swimming, so you can enjoy the water even if you aren't an underwater diving family. This place is extremely busy in the summer.

Location: Near Ponce de Leon Springs State Recreation Area (see above).

Important information: This is a privately owned park. For more information and detailed directions, call 850-836-4979.

70. Morrison Springs

It's an amazing story of marine biology, but eels from the Atlantic Ocean swim all the way inland to underground caves in Florida, and this is one location to which they are widely known to journey via the Choctawhatchee River. This privately owned park is popular with divers. There is no camping, but it's an interesting and lovely picnic and swimming destination, shaded with cypress trees.

Location: South of Ponce de Leon Springs State Recreation Area (see Site 68) via State Road 81 and then County Road 181.

Important information: This is a privately owned park. For more information or detailed directions, call 850-836-4223.

71. Cypress Springs

Set amid lovely cypress trees, this privately owned park has one of the state's prettiest spring basins. There is a campground, and you can rent canoes to paddle Holmes Creek and the Cypress Springs run.

Location: On State Road 79 about 4 miles north of Vernon.

Important information: For more information or detailed directions, call the park at 850-535-2960.

72. Falling Waters State Recreation Area

No one is ever likely to write a guide to Florida waterfalls; there are so few of them. But this one is stunning, falling as it does *down into the earth.* The water drops almost 70 feet into a sinkhole, one of many odd openings into Florida's highly porous limestone base. Where it eventually goes, nobody knows. With a campground, a scenic overlook trail, a small lake, and a host of dogwood and beech trees, this 177-acre recreation area is a small jewel.

Location: From U.S. Highway 90 in Chipley, take State Road 77 south and turn east onto SR 77A to the park. It's about 3 miles south of Chipley.

Important information: For more information, call 850-638-6130 or visit <www.dep.state.fl.us/parks>

73. Florida Caverns State Park

On a summer's day, head for this cool, dark underground wonderland. You can walk through several rooms of one cavern on a ranger-guided tour. Kids will be fascinated by the calcite formations, which are millions of years old, including stalactites, which hold tight to the ceiling, and stalagmites, which project upward from the ground. The 1,800-acre park also features delightfully wooded nature tails, picnic areas, a campground, and the disappearing Chipola River, which is spanned by a natural bridge that Andrew Jackson crossed in 1818. It's possible that the Native Americans he was hunting were hiding in smaller caves nearby. Some of the caves served as homes for early natives and later for pioneers.

Location: From Marianna, drive north on State Road 166 for about 3 miles to the park at 3345 Caverns Road.

Important information: For more information, call 850-482-9598 or 850-482-1228 or visit <www.dep.state.fl.us/parks>.

74. Bear Paw Canoe Trails

This outfitter can get you set up for some fine paddling hereabouts.

Location: In Marianna at 2100 Bear Paw Lane.

Important information: For detailed directions and more information, call the outfitter at 850-482-4948.

75. Torreya State Park

Try to follow along. This is Florida, but here you'll be walking through ravines reminiscent of those in the Appalachian Mountains. The reason dates to the Ice Age, when glaciers swept the seeds of northern tree species to the south. The trees survive here because the steep river ravines keep them dark and cool. A stunning feature of this park is the 150-foot-high bluffs overlooking the Apalachicola River. That's a long way down for Florida, which is most often flat and at sea level. On one bluff, you can tour the restored, furnished 1840s Gregory House. Nearby nature trails lead through magnolia and oak woods. The River Bluffs and Rock Creek Units of the park are especially wild, and the terrain is challenging. The park is named for the Torreya tree, a rare species of evergreen that grows here.

Location: About 13 miles north of Bristol, off State Road 12 on County Road 1641.

Important information: For more information, call 850-643-2674 or visit <www.dep.state.fl.us/parks>.

BIG BEND REGION

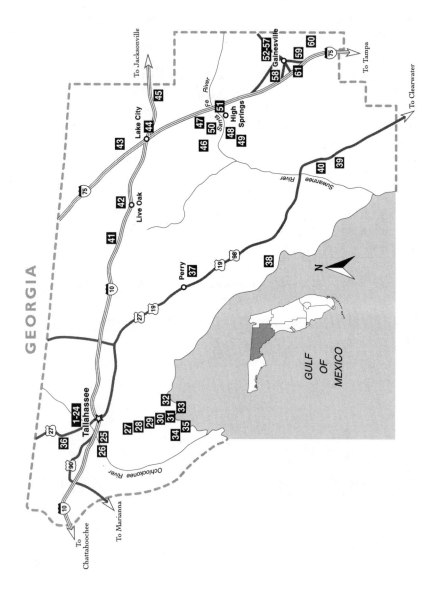

Big Bend
Region

In the Big Bend Region, the marshes bordering the Gulf of Mexico curve like a wide smile. Then the region marches northward from the shore, encompassing fields and forests, until it reaches its topographical zenith at Tallahassee. A thousand years ago, the site of this tree-lined city was a ceremonial and religious center for temple-building Native Americans. Later, the site became the capital of a Spanish mission colony that was destroyed in wars with the British in the 1700s. Today, Tallahassee is Florida's capital city. Its leafy neighborhoods perch among seven red-clay hills just 40 minutes from the Georgia border.

In the Big Bend, Florida reveals some lesser-known aspects of its personality. Bobcats and bears roam two national forests. Puffs of cotton dot the fields in October. Bison, reintroduced to their native home on the wet prairies of Florida, crunch grass in a state park. Children play at three pioneer farm museums and attend traditional sugar-cane grinding events. Restored plantations, once worked by slaves, stand amid the hills and live oaks along red-clay roads. Occasionally the temperature plunges to 27 degrees F.

Visitors ask, is this Florida? The region is sometimes referred to as the First Florida, or the Other Florida. Native Americans who farmed here long ago gave way to European explorers and cattle ranchers. They, in turn, were followed by American pioneers who arrived by wagon train and ox cart in the 1700s and early 1800s.

There are plenty of science centers and museums here, including the Challenger Learning Center, which celebrates space exploration. That is quite appropriate, since space heroes Norm Thagard and Winston Scott, who actively support the center, work at Florida State University in Tallahassee.

Near Tallahassee, you can cool off in a junglelike pool or drift in a float boat over fossilized mastodon bones at Wakulla Springs, where Paleo-Indians once hunted. Fringed by palms and cypress trees, Wakulla served as the setting for 1930s Tarzan movies and for the 1950s horror flick, *Creature from the Black Lagoon.*

Also in Tallahassee, Florida's early Spanish heritage comes alive. Visit the archaeological dig of a 17th-century hilltop village, San Luis, where Native Americans and Spanish families worked and played together, even intermarried, in a communal mission center. On another hill on the other side of town, a small office building site in the woods marks the only known camp where Hernando de Soto and his invading entourage—as cruel as the meanest pirates ever were—lived during the winter of 1539–1540.

Farther east, near Gainesville, folks say they are in the Original Florida partly because they live on top of old Native American villages, one of which was called Alligator. In this area, you can camp at a manatee refuge, at the spot where a river disappears, or at a site where bison roam. You can visit a folklife park or float in a string of springs, including one of the clearest multiple-springs rivers in the world, the Ichetucknee.

At Gainesville, explore a hole in the earth—the only sinkhole in Florida that has steps leading to its bottom. At dusk, visit a lake full of wild alligators on the leafy University of Florida campus and watch a bat colony emerge from its bat house to munch mosquitoes and other insects.

Good family resort cottages aren't as plentiful here as in other parts of Florida, so you may want to consider your favorite chain motel. One popular family resort/outfitter that offers horseback riding and ecotours is Steinhatchee Landing, located on the Steinhatchee River between Tallahassee and Manatee Springs State Park. The Wakulla Springs State Park Lodge, built just outside Tallahassee in 1937, features a marble-topped soda fountain and an 11-foot-long stuffed alligator holding court in the lobby. While rambling in the Big Bend and North Florida area, you might also check into Old Fenimore Mill Resort at Cedar Key or the rustic cabins in Gold Head Branch State Park northeast of Gainesville.

For more information contact:

- Alachua County Visitors and Convention Bureau (Gainesville)
  352-374-5231
  <www.co.alachua.fl.us/acvacb>
- Cedar Key Chamber of Commerce
  352-543-5600
  <www.crestcomm.com/cedarkey/>
- Nature Coast Coalition
  800-257-8881
  <www.naturecoastcoalition.com>
- Original Florida
  800-226-0690
  <www.originalflorida.org>
- Tallahassee Area Convention and Visitors Bureau
  800-628-2866
  <www.tallahassee.com> or <www.co.leon.fl.us/visitors/index.htm>
- Wakulla County Chamber of Commerce
  850-926-1848
  <www.freenet.tlh.fl.us/-wakullac/>
- The Wilderness Way
  850-574-4445

Tallahassee Area

· ·

In downtown Tallahassee, a lassie or a laddie can forecast a hurricane, meet a mastodon, gaze at Spanish gold, wander through a sculpture garden, or ride to the top of a tower for a 360-degree view. And there are still plenty more capital ideas, such as a lively walking tour or a downtown marketplace.

Two outstanding universities, a community college, and employment with state government attract young people to Florida's capital city. The National High Magnetic Laboratory conducts research at Florida State University, and Florida A&M University holds the Florida Black Archives, a national collection of memorabilia that reflects the intertwined heritage of blacks and whites in this former plantation region. The latter school was home to a student-led civil rights movement.

Kid-appealing sites here include the best pioneer farm and zoo of native species in the state, a hands-on science museum, the brand-new Challenger Learning Center, living-history events at a 1656 village site, and one of the friendliest touch-tank marine science centers in all of Florida.

A famous natural attraction here is Wakulla Springs, a clear swimming hole with fossilized mastodon bones lying on its bottom. A manatee visitation zone is located downstream. Also just down the road are campgrounds, lakes full of largemouth bass, and a forest trail that leads past a series of sinkholes. There's a state park in prime eagle nesting territory, a national wildlife refuge where migrating monarch butterflies amass each fall, and clear-water canoe trails. *Tallahassa Talofa* is thought to be an earlier Creek name for the area, and the words may have meant old town. It's been the head village and town of one or more important groups of people for at least 1,000 years.

In downtown Tallahassee, the best parking bets during the spring legislative session or at other busy times include 1) a small lot tucked behind the Union Bank building at the southeastern corner of Apalachee Parkway and South Monroe Street, the intersection where the stately Old Capitol sits; 2) visitor parking levels (only use visitor-labeled spaces) at the two parking garages bordering Bronough Street near the R. A. Gray Building and the Museum of Florida History; and 3) the underground public parking garage behind Tallahassee City Hall, hidden under Kleman Plaza.

I. Old Capitol

· ·

Even folks who don't visit the inside of this beautiful Victorian-era museum are likely to wonder about it as they pass by. Built in 1902 to serve as the state capitol, the building has peppermint-stick awnings that replicate the originals, a grand staircase inside, and imposing front steps outside. It features displays on the state's political history, including an old-time black-and-white photograph of gentlemen in frock coats throwing snowballs on the steps. Paradise does chill out now and then.

Location: On a hill at the intersection of South Monroe Street (U.S. Highway 27) and Apalachee Parkway (US 90) in Tallahassee.

Important information: For more information, call 850-187-1902 or visit <www.floridaheritage.com>

2. New Capitol

Whoosh! An elevator deposits you 22 floors above the ground for a panoramic view and a visit to an art gallery and Artists' Hall of Fame. Back downstairs on the western side of this modern tower, sometimes called the New Capitol, the official Florida Welcome Center provides state maps, regional directories, camping and parks information, and brochures about state attractions. The Welcome Center faces a striking James Rosenquist mural interpreting Florida's official and unofficial symbols, such as its fresh air. Nearby, a Women's Hall of Fame features color portraits of U.S. Attorney General Janet Reno, a Miami native who once worked as a staff director for the Judiciary Committee of the Florida House of Representatives, and Betty Mae Jumper, a leader of the Seminole Tribe of Florida. If you like Florida lore, there's more to see, so wander to the nearby chapel and giant state seal or take a full tour. A basement cafeteria is open in the spring when the legislature is in session.

Location: Between South Monroe Street and Duvall Street. Park at the Tallahassee City Hall parking garage, behind city hall on Duvall Street.

Important information: Open from 9 A.M. to 4:30 P.M. Mondays through Fridays, from 10 A.M. to 4:30 P.M. Saturdays, and from noon to 4:30 P.M. Sundays. For more information, call 850-891-5200.

3. Union Bank

This powder-blue building, the size of a one-room schoolhouse, was built by "Money" Williams in 1840 and has served several purposes since. It was once a bank for regional slave owners and then it served after the Civil War as one of the first banks ever for freed slaves. Today, it's the downtown branch of the Black Archives of Florida A&M University. The excellent displays are sure to engage children, especially if their studies have covered equality issues. A Ku Klux Klan robe, signs from the era of segregation designating "White" and "Colored" amenities, leg chains from a slave ship, and an African drum are thoughtfully shared by Professor James Eaton, a longtime educator in the South.

Location: At the intersection of South Monroe Street and Apalachee Parkway, on the southeastern corner opposite the Old Capitol in Tallahassee.

Important information: Admittance is free. Open from 9 A.M. to 4 P.M. weekdays. For more information, call 850-487-3903.

4. Old Town Trolley

• •

This free weekday trolley takes a loop through downtown along Adams Street and passes the Capitol, Florida Supreme Court, Kleman Plaza and Odyssey Science Center/Museum of Art, Museum of Florida History, Florida State University Law School, Civic Center, Park Avenue Historic District, city bus depot, and Governor's Mansion. It's a way to orient yourself to the city and give tired little feet a rest. Some of the drivers are willing tour guides.

Location: Trolley signs are scattered along the route, including one in front of City Hall on Adams Street in Tallahassee.

Important information: Free. The trolley operates from 7 A.M. to 6 P.M. Mondays through Fridays.

5. Governor's Mansion

• •

In December and during the spring legislative session, this elegant brick home is popular with school kids. Even if you don't get inside to see the pelican-decorated silver service, the frisky sculpture in the vest-pocket park across Adams Street—of kids and a dog balancing on a log—is dedicated to children and brings a chuckle.

Location: At 700 North Adams Street, north of the New Capitol in Tallahassee.

Important information: For tour information, call 850-488-4661.

6. Historic Tallahassee Walking Tours

• •

Step back in time with a lively, costumed guide. These excellent downtown walks offer fun peeks into the frontier days, when settlers feared Indian attacks, and bears and panthers prowled.

Location: Your meeting place downtown is arranged when you make a reservation. The tour office is at 610 West Call Street.

Important information: For reservations or more information about various theme tours—Florida history, ghost stories, frontier days, tours especially for children, even buggy rides—call 850-222-4143.

7. Tours with a Southern Accent

• •

You can learn about black heritage, plantation life, and other Southern themes by visiting such wide-ranging locations as Thomasville, Georgia; Apalachicola; and points closer to Tallahassee. This guide's tour office and welcome center is a wealth of information.

Location: The welcome center is at 209 East Brevard Street, one block east of the Governor's Mansion in Tallahassee.

Important information: For reservations and tour details, call 850-513-1000.

8. Knott House Museum

• •

Riddles and rhymes abound at Luella Pugh Knott's grand three-story house, built in 1843 and located in the Park Avenue Historic District. Children enjoy reading aloud the ditties this talented former resident wrote and playfully attached to her antiques, such as "If you love an ancient book, stop and give us a look." Be sure to look at the 1923 kitchen and the antique toy collection. Your kids will soon be coming up with their own rhymes.

This mansion was also the site of the reading of a significant Emancipation Proclamation, an event that is re-enacted every year. The house was designed and built by George Proctor, a free black man. A post–Civil War owner of this mansion was so impressed with the African-American buggy driver who worked here that he sent him to school. The driver, William Gunn, went on to become Florida's first black physician. From all perspectives, this is a fantastic stop.

Location: At 301 East Park Avenue, two blocks north and one block east of the New Capitol along the Chain of Parks (see below) in Tallahassee.

Important information: Open Wednesdays through Fridays from 1 to 4 P.M. and Saturdays from 10 A.M. to 4 P.M. Fees are $1.50 for children, $3 for adults, and $7 for families. For more information, call 850-922-2459 or visit <www.floridaheritage.com>.

9. Park Avenue Chain of Parks/DowntownMarket

Downtown Tallahassee's historic Chain of Parks offers a cool fountain, a shady place to stretch your legs, and picnic sites in several blocks along Park Avenue. Located between Bronough and Duvall Streets on Park Avenue, the LeRoy Collins Leon County Public Library features an engaging children's department, with a tree-house reading perch for the littlest ones. On Saturday mornings from March through November, visit the Chain of Parks for the outdoor DowntownMarket, a mini-festival under tent canopies with special events such as sidewalk chalk drawing, storytelling, live music, artists' booths, toy makers, a literary café, specialty foods to go, fresh bread, fresh flowers and herbs, a farmer's market, elegant handmade soaps, and more.

Location: On Park Avenue, mainly between Monroe and Bronough Streets, in Tallahassee.

Important information: Free. DowntownMarket is open daily from March through November, from 8 A.M. to 2 P.M. when the weather is warm and from 10:30 A.M. to 1:30 P.M. in cooler weather. For more information, call 850-297-3945 or 850-980-8727 or visit <www.downtownmarket.com>.

10. Museum of Florida History

Mastodons and the ancient people who hunted them lived in Florida during the Ice Age, when the peninsula was cloaked with dry prairie that extended almost 100 miles farther out into what is now the Gulf of Mexico. The remains of one of the giant tuskers, which died at Wakulla Springs, greets visitors to this fine museum. My daughter's favorite spot is Grandma's Attic, where she and pals climb upstairs to enjoy costumes and trunk treasures. But also don't miss the real gold recovered from a Spanish shipwreck, a two-story Florida steamboat, a diorama depicting a 16th-century Timucuan Indian family, a real Timucuan canoe, or the tourist "motor home" of the 1920s.

Location: In Tallahassee at 500 South Bronough Street, underground in the R. A. Gray Building, which sits between the Florida Supreme Court and the Civic Center. From the plaza entrance on Bronough Street, you can take the steps leading down to the museum or enter the building at plaza level and take the elevator one floor down. Other floors hold the Florida Photographic Archives, other state archives, and the state library and program offices.

Important information: Free. Open from 8 A.M. to 4 P.M. Mondays through Fridays and limited hours on Saturdays and Sundays. For more information, call 850-488-1484 or visit <www.floridaheritage.com>.

11. Challenger Learning Center

Many families plan their Florida trip around a space-shuttle launch and a tour of the massive Kennedy Space Center. But if your itinerary doesn't include a zoom over to the east-central Florida coast, you can still achieve liftoff in downtown Tallahassee. Young astronauts will give a thumbs-up to the mission control, space shuttle, and space station re-created here, and they're bound to enjoy the hands-on activities. Two space-shuttle heroes— Norm Thagard and Winston Scott—are on the staff of Florida State University here, so the space story is especially personal. Planetarium star shows and more are part of this stellar science lesson. The IMAX Theater rockets you into other worlds via prize-winning 3-D movies that take full advantage of the space-sized screen.

Location: In downtown Tallahassee on Kleman Plaza between Duval and Bronough Streets.

Important information: Scheduled to open in late 2000 or early 2001. For more information, call 850-410-6370 or visit <www.eng.fsu.edu>.

12. Odyssey Science Center/Museum of Art

Bring the camera to capture your young TV personality forecasting a hurricane here in a miniature TV studio. The hands-on science activities on the second floor delight kids. The first floor features rotating special attractions. The third floor is the Mary Brogan Museum of Art, with changing exhibits that the mannered young artists in your family might enjoy.

Location: On Kleman Plaza in Tallahassee at 350 South Duval Street. Park under the plaza in the public parking garage.

Important information: Fees are $3.50 for students and $6 for adults. Open from 10 A.M. to 5 P.M. Mondays through Saturdays and from 1 to 5 P.M. Sundays. For more information, call 850-671-5001 or 850-671-0800 or visit <www.omoa.org>.

13. LeMoyne Art Gallery/Sculpture Garden

This small, venerable gallery, housed in a cottage that once served as a Civil War hospital, stages special exhibits such as an annual display of Caribbean carnival costumes and another of art by high school students. A variety of classes are held for adults and children. Mannered young artists will be at home here. The Helen Lind Sculpture Garden out back is a quiet place to stroll or sit.

Location: In the Park Avenue Historic District of Tallahassee at 125 North Gadsden Street.

Important information: Open from 10 A.M. to 5 P.M. Tuesdays through Saturdays and from 1 to 5 P.M. Sundays. Fee is $1 for nonmembers. To check on current exhibits or to get more information, call 850-222-8800 or visit <www.lemoyne.org>.

14. Claude Pepper Museum

This new interactive museum, which celebrates the work of former Florida congressman Claude Pepper, offers an uplifting patriotic experience and may even inspire your children to public service. It includes a replica of the floor of the U.S. House of Representatives, as well as reconstructed House and Senate offices where Pepper served. The farm boy turned national leader was known for his advocacy, especially for better labor conditions and a strong military defense against threats to freedom, such as Nazi aggression. My daughter, who has enjoyed the sophisticated Smithsonian museums in Washington, D.C., returned from her visit here insisting that it be included in this book.

Location: At 635 West Call Street on the Florida State University campus in Tallahassee.

Important information: Open from 8:30 A.M. to 5 P.M. Mondays through Fridays. Parking is extremely limited. For more information, call 850-644-9309.

15. Lake Ella

Waddling ducks, diving turtles, gliding carp, strolling people, and fun shops populate this leafy park that surrounds a round, midtown lake. The Black Dog Café, friendly Joe's Bicycles, and other small emporiums help create a festive mood. This is a shady picnic spot with covered tables, a gazebo, and lakeside benches. Bring bread for the ducks.

Location: About a three-minute drive north of downtown Tallahassee, on the eastern side of North Monroe Street behind the Tallahassee Police Department.

Important information: On Wednesday mornings, the Black Dog Café sponsors a mother-toddler playgroup. For more information, call 850-224-2518.

16. Dorothy B. Oven Park

Something pretty is often blooming in the garden of this shady park on a main Tallahassee thoroughfare. There's a short boardwalk through a swamp, a small fountain and pond, and picnic tables. And it's next door to a kid-pleasing fire station.

Location: At 3205 Thomasville Road, north of downtown Tallahassee.

Important information: Open daily from sunrise to sunset and for special events. For more information, call 850-891-3915.

17. Maclay State Gardens

Refresh tired little feet with a splash at Lake Hall. Picnic under live oaks. Hike on paths in the Lake Overstreet section. Tour the lakeside ornamental gardens. This is a breathtakingly beautiful park.

Location: At 3540 Thomasville Road (U.S. Highway 319) about a half-mile north of Capital Circle in Tallahassee.

Important information: Park admission is $3.25. Admission to the Maclay House and gardens is $3 during peak bloom time, from January through April. Otherwise the gardens are included in park admission. No camping. For more information, call 850-487-4556 or visit <www.dep.state.fl.us/parks>.

18. Tallahassee Museum of History and Natural Science

This is the best of Florida's native-species zoos and re-created pioneer home-steads. A tree-lined boardwalk winds through enclosures holding native wolves, bobcats, Florida panthers, black bears, and alligators, allowing you to see the animals in their native habitats. At the fox enclosure, look in the limbs of the live oaks, where these bushy-tailed hunters often curl up. Skunks and river otters, roaming white squirrels, and an aviary featuring birds of prey are all kid-pleasers. An open-air reptile house provides close but not claustrophobic encounters with a rare, nonpoisonous indigo snake; a non-poisonous, orange-tinged corn snake; a cottonmouth water moccasin; and some rattlers. An outdoor pond next to the science center is home to turtles and small alligators.

Each weekend, at the shady farm homestead, re-enactors guide your kids in dipping candles, churning butter, grinding corn, and other chores of the 1870s. A talented smithy frequently fires up the working forge. In the fall, the homestead mule is harnessed to grind sugar cane. Visit other farm animals, play checkers on the porch, see what's ready for harvest in the gar-den, and peek at outbuildings, including the fruit and vegetable house and the privy. Village life is re-created, too. Learn about the life of royalty by touring a 19th-century plantation cottage that once belonged to Princess Catherine Murat, who was related by marriage to Napoleon Bonaparte.

Your kids can also climb through a real red caboose, hold class in a one-room schoolhouse that was used from the 1870s until 1968, pray in one of the oldest African-American churches in Florida (complete with organ), and visit a country store. A family environmental education center, an art gallery, and a wall-sized bird window through which to quietly observe feathered wildlife feeding, a shady playground, and a comfortable café help to make this an outstanding destination. The complex is in the woods at the edge of Lake Bradford and Lake Hiawatha.

Location: At 3945 Museum Drive in Tallahassee. Take Capital Circle south-west past Innovation Park to Museum Drive and turn left into the museum grounds.

Important information: Children under 4 are admitted free. Fees are $4 for ages 4 to 13 and $6 for all others. For more information and a schedule of specific seasonal events, call 850-576-1636 or visit <http://tallahass eemuseum.org>. The grounds are quite shady.

An American princess

Catherine Daingerfield Willis, grandniece of George Washington, moved with her family from Virginia to a log house in Tallahassee. There she met the nephew of Napoleon Bonaparte, Achille Murat, prince of Naples. People say that to catch her attention the flamboyant Prince Murat drank from her shoe. They married in July 1826, when Willis was 22.

Now this daughter of American "royalty" (her great-grandmother was the first president's only sister) became Princess Murat. The prince swept his princess off to Europe, where the French royal family welcomed her. The young couple lived a charmed, extravagant life, traveling and then entertaining in Tallahassee. In this frontier outpost of Florida, their gold serving pieces bore Napoleon's crest.

Prince Murat died almost 20 years after they married, leaving his wife many unpaid bills. Napoleon III asked Princess Catherine to live at court in Paris, which must have been tempting. But she only visited, returning to Tallahassee with a small fortune that the royal family gave her. She bought slaves and a plantation that she called Bellevue. In ten years of operating this small cotton farm, she was able to repay the huge debts. She also raised money to honor her great-uncle, George Washington, by helping to preserve his historic Virginia home, Mount Vernon.

During the Civil War, Catherine sided with the Confederates and embraced the cause of slave owners. She even fired the ceremonial cannon at the state capitol to announce the decision by Florida officials to declare war against the United States and secede from the Union. She died of typhoid fever in Tallahassee on August 6, 1867, just 11 days before her 64th birthday. Her small log home at Bellevue was moved to the Tallahassee Museum of History and Natural Science and restored, giving visitors a glimpse of her unusual life.

19. Tallahassee–St. Marks Historic Rail Trail

Rent a bicycle or skates on site or bring your own to enjoy this popular paved path that's fun for walkers, too. It leads about 16 miles to the gulf coast at St. Marks, or you can begin at St. Marks and venture into Tallahassee. It also links with other paths.

Location: There is more than one place to access the trail, but the bike rental station and main parking area are in Tallahassee. From the Old Capitol, take South Monroe Street (State Road 363) to just south of Capital Circle. The parking lot and rental office are on the right (west) side of the road.

Important information: Free. For more information, call 850-922-6007.

20. Antique Car Museum

This indoor car lot is about 4 miles from downtown but worth the ride if your family brakes for old autos. It boasts beautiful four-wheelers that date to 1915. And holy hornblower! The Batmobile alights here.

Location: About 4 miles east of Capital Circle in Tallahassee on U.S. Highway 90.

Important information: For ticket information, call 850-942-0137.

21. De Soto Site

Just a three-minute drive from downtown Tallahassee on a hill in the Myers Park neighborhood, you'll find this memorial to Spanish attempts to conquer the New World. Spanish conquistador Hernando de Soto, governor of Cuba and a cruel conqueror of the Incas of Peru, halted for several months here in the winter of 1539–1540 during his bloody search for New World gold. This is the only site in America conclusively connected to his expedition.

Each January, a re-enactment of this winter camp and the camps of the natives is staged, enthralling kids who can watch rabbits being roasted over a spit and try on chain-mail vests. Year-round, you can see exhibits in a former governor's home on the site. The exhibits explain the excavation of the site by famed Florida archaeologist Calvin Jones. At least 40,000 camp artifacts were found, including 16th-century Spanish copper coins and chain mail.

Location: From one block east of Apalachee Parkway (U.S. Highway 27) on Lafayette Street, behind Parkway Shopping Center in Tallahassee, turn onto De Soto Park Drive. The visitor center is in the brick mansion directly ahead, at 1022 De Soto Park Drive.

Important information: Free, but parking is limited. No road sign identifies the site, which is also an upscale office complex. For re-enactment information, detailed directions, or other information, call 850-922-6007 or visit <www.dep.state.fl.us/parks>.

22. Lake Jackson Mounds State Archaeological Site

Walk in the footsteps of native Floridians at this lakeshore site where two low ceremonial temple mounds stand as reminders of a culture that thrived in North Florida about A.D. 1200. Three elaborate copper breastplates and other relics have been found here with the remains of important leaders. Interpretive exhibits tell the fascinating story of these people, whose descendants farmed here when Hernando de Soto explored the area in 1539–1540. There are picnic tables and a nature trail at the 165-acre park.

Location: In Tallahassee, take U.S. Highway 27 north over Interstate 10 to the intersection with Crowder Road. Turn right onto Crowder Road and follow it about a half-mile to Indian Mounds Road. Turn right onto Indian Mounds Road, which dead-ends in the park.

Important information: Free. For more information, call 850-922-6007.

23. Lichgate on High Road

• •

This charming house with its small butterfly garden and one of the largest and oldest oak trees in the region is like a fairytale cottage. It's currently undergoing restoration but is open for special events, such as Storytime at the Cottage, that will enchant the little tea-time folks in your family.

Location: From U.S. Highway 90 (Tennessee Street) in Tallahassee, turn north onto High Road. The cottage is at 1401 High Road.

Important information: Call 850-383-6556 or 850-877-7220 for a schedule of special events or to arrange a group visit.

24. San Luis Archaeological and Historic Site

• •

On a strategic hill in Tallahassee, archaeologists discovered the foundations and artifacts of an Apalachee Indian/Spanish village of the mid-1600s. As early as 1608, the prosperous, corn-farming Apalachees invited friars from St. Augustine—then a struggling Spanish outpost dependent on supplies from Cuba—to this verdant region. Some natives resisted the missionaries' new faith in a bloody uprising, but thousands of Apalachees converted. The bustling community became the Mission of San Luis, a successful trading center and fort with 1,500 Spanish and Apalachee residents farming together and intermarrying. In 1704, after nearly 100 years of communal living, the residents torched and abandoned the community to keep it from falling into the hands of the British, who were trying to win control of this part of the New World.

The mission church, built by the Apalachee in 1656, is re-created in detail, including its palm-frond roof. You can also walk into a replica of a round, high-roofed Apalachee council house. As the most studied Indian mission site in Florida and the only re-created one, San Luis offers a unique opportunity to immerse yourself in another culture. It is listed as a National Historic Landmark. Volunteer re-enactors creatively clothed as Apalachees and Spaniards provide hands-on activities, such as period cooking, on the third Saturday of every month. Excellent tours are conducted daily.

Beyond its rich cultural significance, this site is a fine place to have a picnic and stretch your legs under magnolia and pecan trees. It even offers a geology lesson. The site's steep and beautiful Ravine Trail, which features interpretive markers, takes you to a sampling of Florida's seep springs and swallow areas. The seep springs are locations where underground water slowly pushes its way to the surface. The swallow areas are depressions in the ground where the water collects before percolating down to the bedrock. In drier times, the swallow area is muddy and crisscrossed with countless tracks of local wildlife.

The Indians of Tallahassee play ball

The Apalachee Indians are infamous for a fierce game they played. The Catholic friars who lived among them at the San Luis Mission called it simply **jeugo de pelota**, the ball game. The games unfolded only in summer in the midafternoon, when the temperature was hottest. Each team was made up of 40 or 50 men who used their bare feet to hurl a tiny ball, probably about the size of a walnut. The goal was to hit a tall, decorated post topped by wooden pegs and an eagle's nest. The noisy action basically resembled a mob scene. You could kick your opponents, even in the face. You could pull an opponent's arm or leg. Many players fell down from exhaustion and were trampled. Injuries, one friar said in a written complaint, included broken legs, broken ribs, maimed hands, and loss of vision. At least two deaths occurred on the San Luis ball field. People gambled on which village would win, sometimes betting a family's entire winter provisions.

Why did the Apalachee play such a vicious game? We won't ever know for sure, but researchers believe it was part of an important pattern of rivalry between villages. One theory is that the game served as a substitute for war. Before the game, participants held several uninhibited ceremonies that included dancing, drinking specially brewed drinks, eating a putrid stew, beating drums, and even howling like a wolf. These rituals were supposed to create either good luck for the home team or bad luck for the other village. The ceremonies were faithfully followed. In Tallahassee, some people believe that the goalpost was associated with gods of rain and thunderstorms, and the game was intended to bring enough rain for crops. Players who caught the ball during the game were then believed to be blessed with the speed of a deer. Whatever the true nature of this bloody game, can you imagine the sight of it, right here, 300 years ago?

Location: In Tallahassee, take U.S. Highway 90 (Tennessee Street) west past its intersection with Ocala Road (this is the exit route from the park) to White Drive. Turn right onto White Drive and go one block to the intersection with Mission Road. Turn right onto Mission Road. The entrance to the site is on the left at 2020 West Mission Road.

Important information: Free. Open from 9 A.M. to 4:30 P.M. Mondays through Fridays, from 10 A.M. to 4:30 P.M. Saturdays, and from noon to 4:30 P.M. holidays and Sundays. Free tours are offered at noon Mondays through Fridays, at 11 A.M. and at 2 P.M. Saturdays, and 2 P.M. Sundays. Gates are closed promptly at 4:30 P.M. For more information, call 850-487-3711 or visit <www.flaheritage.com>.

25. Silver Lake Campground

Tallahassee-area parks and preserves are beautiful, but they offer few public campgrounds. So this scenic, lakeside home-away-from-home is popular. There's a sandy beach and a footpath among the cypress trees that fringe spring-fed Silver Lake. This fully developed campground is in 569,000-acre Apalachicola National Forest, the largest of Florida's three national forests.

Location: From Tallahassee, take State Road 20 west through the forest for about 8 miles to the intersection with SR 260. Turn left (south) onto SR 260 and go about 4 miles to the campground.

Important information: For more information, call 850-942-9330.

26. Lake Talquin State Recreation Area Campgrounds

Two public campgrounds on the south shore of this popular fishing lake, created by a dam on the Ochlockonee River, are woodsy sites to make camp. Hall Landing Park is a fine picnic place, with a waterfront nature trail/boardwalk. It offers tent camping only. Coe Landing has sites for recreational vehicles and tents.

Location: From Tallahassee, take State Road 20 west for about 10 miles to reach Coe Landing on the north side of SR 20. Continue about 5 miles farther and turn right (north) to reach Hall Landing Park.

Important information: For more information, call 850-922-6007.

27. Natural Bridge Civil War Battlefield

For Civil War buffs and geology fans, this remote and unadorned picnic place at the end of an unpaved country lane is a good detour. On March 6, 1865, after receiving advance warning of a Union attack on the state capital, Confederate forces successfully defended this site in a battle that is re-enacted yearly. Some earthworks can still be seen. This woodsy area is a natural land bridge over the St. Marks River, which flows through a cavern beneath it. The 15-mile-long river is one of several in Florida that disappear underground through the peninsula's porous limestone. It re-emerges just south of here at St. Marks Spring.

Location: The park is on State Road 363 about 4 miles south of Tallahassee. At the village of Woodville on SR 363, take Natural Bridge Road east for 6 miles, most of it unpaved, directly to its dead end at the state historic site.

Important information: There are no facilities at this site, other than picnic tables. For more information, call 850-922-6007 or visit <www.dep.state.fl.us/parks>.

28. Leon Sinks Geological Area

Florida's sinkholes are wondrous openings into the earth that attract worldwide attention when new ones nibble at portions of roads, parking lots, yards, and even homes. This region of woods and cypress swamp, located in Apalachicola National Forest, features sinks both wet and dry that are accessible via 4 miles of nature trails. Big Dismal, with trickling water and cascading ferns, is the most stunning of about 20 named sinks along a loop path. If you pack a backpack, this is an excellent half-day adventure for families who like longer hikes and geology. If time is short, I recommend walking about 1 mile to Big Dismal Sink and then retracing your path back to the trailhead.

Don't set out on a walk without studying the large permanent trail map and estimated walking times posted at the entrance. Distracted by side paths and the beauty of the place, you can lose your way and take a path too long for tiny legs to comfortably complete.

Location: Drive about 6 miles south of Tallahassee on U.S. Highway 319 and turn west into the well-marked site.

Important information: If you can't take the time to hike the full round-trip path, this is still a lovely picnic spot, with restrooms and interpretive exhibits. For more information, call 850-942-9300.

Not your basic kitchen sink

Perhaps you've read in the newspaper about a **sinkhole** opening up. Many sink-holes are small, maybe a few feet across. Many are just shallow depressions in the ground about the depth of a plastic kiddie pool. Sinkholes are made when the land very gradually sinks, and then sinks some more, into a small hole that is underground. Large sinkholes can occur more quickly and dramatically and can be 50 feet across. When a large sinkhole suddenly appears near buildings or parking lots or roads, you can imagine that it would attract a lot of interest. One famous sinkhole in Central Florida, the Winter Park Sinkhole of 1981, eventually swallowed cars, houses, and part of a swimming pool.

Florida has a lot of sinkholes, and it will continue to have more because of its unique geology. Under the soil, Florida is mainly made of limestone. This is a very porous foundation commonly riddled with underground caves and other holes. We don't see them because they're covered by a rather thin crust of earth. Rain filters into the holes through cracks in the earth's surface, creating natural under-ground reservoirs called aquifers, from which Florida gets most of its drinking water. (Florida doesn't have many above-ground reservoirs.)

Rain seeping into the ground also causes cracks and underground caves to get larger. If a heavy rain puts a lot of weight on the thin limestone roof of a cave, this can cause the earth to fall in. This is called a collapse sinkhole. Sinkholes occur year-round in all parts of the state, but especially in North and Central Florida. Climb into the Devil's Millhopper in Gainesville (see Site 58), and walk a forest path edging sinkholes at Leon Sinks (see Site 28).

29. Wakulla Springs State Park

This green jewel, nestled among pines and live oaks, is a destination in itself, so try to book a room at the charming 1937 Wakulla Springs Lodge. From there, you can enjoy fresh fish and country meals in the airy dining room, snacks at the marble-topped soda fountain, guided ranger walks, nature trails, a bike path, guided boat tours, historical exhibits, picnic areas, a swimming hole, a white-sand beach, and an expansive lawn that slopes down to a clear springs. A bird festival and other special events are held here, too.

When you are in the white lodge, you are actually standing over a giant underground system of caverns, partially explored during a 1998 expe-dition sponsored by the National Geographic Society. Check out the cut-away map of the caverns and other exhibits in the boat-basin ticket office. On one boat tour, you can float over the mouth of the mammoth Wakulla Cave and learn a portion of the 10,000 years of human history at this cave site. It probably once served as a home to mastodon-hunting Clovis people during the Ice Age, when Florida extended about 100 miles farther out into the Gulf of Mexico, the cave was high and dry, and the springs was a fresh-water trickle. From the glass-bottomed boat, you can see fossilized mastadon bones lying near the cave entrance. Because of the long history preserved here, this state park is also listed on the National Register of Historic Places.

A second boat tour takes you for a 3-mile glide on the Wakulla River. You pass a jungle of wildlife and lush trees, including 300-year-old cypresses. Resident birds include the endangered limpkin, a brown bird with a curved bill and stiltlike legs that mainly eats plump, brown-shelled apple snails; the black anhinga, which perches with its wings outstretched to dry them; the purple gallinule, which seems to run across the water before launching into flight; and the majestic bald eagle, which nests here. Expect to see alligators of all sizes. If you are lucky, you may spot a large mamma floating in the water with her babies on her back.

In the 1930s, while filming six movies, Tarzan swung through this jungle on real vines. If you are bold, plunge from the high dock with a Tarzan yell into the 70-degree F water. You'll emerge absolutely tingling. At night, take a flashlight with you to walk the path to Sally Ward Spring and look for glowing eyes—perhaps an opossum, raccoon, or skunk. Your family won't want to leave Wakulla.

Location: About 14 miles south of Tallahassee on State Road 267.

Important information: Open from 8 A.M. to sunset daily. Boat tours generally run from about 9 A.M. to 4 P.M., but call 850-224-5950 for specific times, reservations, or more information, or visit <www.dep.state.fl.us/parks>.

30. TNT Hideaway

This popular canoe outfitter is perched on the scenic Wakulla River just outside Wakulla Springs State Park. In the summer, paddling in these clear waters will bring you near endangered manatees, giant but gentle marine mammals with few defenses—so be careful not to disturb them.

Location: At 6527 Coastal Highway in Crawfordville, almost 2 miles west of State Road 363.

Important information: For reservations and more information, call 850-925-6412. On summer weekends, the river is crowded.

31. Gulf Marine Specimen Laboratories

Tickle a starfish and watch an endangered sea turtle surface and dive at the friendly, 25,000-gallon touch tanks of Jack and Anne Rudloe. Their non-profit, walk-through nature center is one of the best introductions for children to creatures from the Gulf of Mexico, especially when you take a guided tour. You'll be amazed by close-up access to jellyfish, octopuses, sharks, horseshoe crabs, small rays, and fish fry. After a visit, there's no way you can look at Florida's coastal marshes—often inscrutable to visitors—without a greater appreciation of what's out there.

Be sure to hold on to little hands at tanks where touching is not allowed. These are marked with large signs. You don't want to give the sharks your germs!

Location: At 300 Clark Drive in Panacea. From U.S. Highway 319, follow the signs to the laboratories, which are two blocks east of US 319 on Clark Drive via Palm Street or Rock Landing Street.

Important information: For detailed directions or to ask about special events, call Gulf Marine at 850-984-5204 or visit <www.adsul.com/gulfspecimen/>. This is a small site compared to major Florida aquariums, so a visiting school group can occupy the staff entirely. You might be able to tag along on a school tour, but your family might want to visit during a less hectic time. Call ahead to find out what times are best.

32. St. Marks National Wildlife Refuge, Headquarters Unit

This 70,000-acre coastal preserve for aquatic and upland waterfowl has several entrances. It also has wild regions where black bears roam and bobcats hunt. The Headquarters Unit is the best family stop. It features hands-on interpretive exhibits, an orientation video, a wooden deck overlooking a pond, family events such as songbird and butterfly festivals, easy loop trails, a 7-mile scenic drive that winds past alligators cruising in pond impoundments, picnic spots, and an 1829 lighthouse perched over the Big Bend's marshy gulf shore. If your family likes nature unmanicured but likes a bit of comfort on the side, this site is excellent. The birders in your family can add the roseate spoonbill, wading birds such as herons, and more to their life lists. Have your binoculars handy. We've seen wild hogs here, too.

Location: About 30 miles south of Tallahassee via State Road 363, U.S. Highway 98, and SR 59.

Important information: Expect biting insects in warm months. The visitor center is open from 8 A.M. to 4 P.M. Mondays through Fridays and 10 A.M. to 5 P.M. Saturdays and Sundays. For more information, including a schedule of special events, call 850-925-6121 or visit <http://saint-marks.fws.gov>.

The manatees of summer

Since **manatees** need water of about 70 degrees F or more to thrive, they collect in the warm waters of South Florida in the winter. (Some locales are Manatee Springs State Park near Chiefland and utility discharge watercourses near Tampa, Fort Myers, Turkey Point, and Fort Pierce.) In the summer, they return to the Big Bend Region, where they customarily visit the same locales every year. They migrate slowly, making about 3 to 5 miles per hour, and they share busy waterways with speedboats, commercial ships, and fishing boats. Being mammals, they need to swim near the surface in order to breathe air. As a result, they are often cut by boat propellers. It's a rare manatee that isn't healing from one cut or another. In fact, boat accidents are one of the leading causes of death for this endangered species, which may number only 2,400. The manatee has no natural enemies, yet about 95 die every year.

Near Tallahassee, the St. Marks and Wakulla Rivers usually attract a small group of manatees in summer. In fact, a manatee festival is held in the vicinity of the town of St. Marks every May. It's hard to see these gray giants beneath the water. Look for swirls of water or muddy wakes. Polarized sunglasses may help you see below the surface more easily.

Although the entire state of Florida has been declared a manatee sanctuary, some Big Bend boaters haven't embraced the concept of manatee protection. Perhaps when state and local officials put more observation decks and education centers in boating areas, manatee harassment—which includes speeding, touching or hurting the animals, or otherwise interfering with their feeding and natural movements—will subside.

Any Florida marine enforcement problem can be reported by calling 800-342-5367 (800-DIAL-FMP). The special manatee hotline is 800-342-1821. The U.S. Coast Guard offers a boating safety hotline at 800-368-5647. The national hotline for oil spills is 800-424-8802.

To learn more about preserving these gentle giants, contact the Save the Manatee Club at 800-432-5646 or <www.savethemanatee.org>.

33. San Marcos de Apalache State Historic Site

Most little explorers can't resist climbing around a fort, so this small historic site near the confluence of the Wakulla and St. Marks Rivers is a great place to stretch your legs. Adults will soak up the historical saga, which dates to 1528, when the Panfilo de Narvaez expedition camped here during a march from Tampa. A log fort was first established here in 1679, but pirates burned it. Another log fort was built and then a stone fort. Exhibits tell the story of the controversial double hanging of two British traders who were popular with the Native Americans. General Andrew Jackson ordered the execution in 1819, after invading the territory to put a stop to Indian raids. The incident led to an international political crisis.

During the warm (but buggy!) summer, manatees move through the area waters, and visitors often can see them from the fort site. The HuManatee Festival, held each May on the fort lawns, celebrates the annual migration of the slow-moving marine mammals.

Location: In St. Marks, off State Road 363 at 148 Old Fort Road.

Important information: Open from 9 A.M. to 5 P.M. daily. Entrance to the grounds is free, but there is a small fee to enter the museum. For more information, call 850-922-6216 or 850-922-6007 or visit <www.dep.state.fl.us/parks>.

34. Ochlockonee River State Park

This riverfront park in a pinewoods on the coastal plain encompasses 392 acres of greenery in the middle of prime eagle-nesting territory. Bobcats hunt here, and the endangered red-cockaded woodpecker finds the only sort of tree it will nest in: tall, dead pines. Ask park rangers for wildlife sighting tips. A scenic drive and footpaths take you past some of the best wildflower displays around.

Location: On U.S. Highway 319 about 4 miles south of Sopchoppy and about 40 miles south of Tallahassee. The park is about 11 miles from the gulf shore.

Important information: For campground reservations, recommended in the popular warm-weather months, or for more information, call 850-962-2771 or visit <www.dep.state.fl.us/parks>.

35. Bald Point State Park

This beach on Ochlockonee Bay is one of the newest day-use parks in the state. It has long been a favorite fishing spot, and the sandy beach is a nice place to picnic and build sand castles.

Location: About 45 miles south of Tallahassee. Take U.S. Highway 319 south to US 98 and then follow US 98 south across the wide bridge over

Ochlockonee Bay to State Road 370. Follow SR 370 eastward to the shore and bear left. The park entrance is about 2 miles farther, on the left.

Important information: This park is brand new, so be sure to visit <www.dep.state.fl.us/parks> for current information and the new telephone number.

36. Nicholson Farmhouse Restaurant

About 35 minutes north of Tallahassee and west of a small antiques district in the town of Havana, this collection of Florida farm buildings and an 1828 homestead sit prettily in a field of wildflowers. Weekend diners are offered a free mule-drawn cart ride. Stroll around, examine the old gas pumps, and wait your turn to be seated in one of several distinctive dining buildings where country cooking (with city prices) is served.

Location: From U.S. Highway 27 in Havana, turn west onto State Road 12 toward Quincy and drive about 2 miles to Nicholson's, on the north side of SR 12.

Important information: No reservations are taken; open weekends only. For exact hours, call 850-539-5931.

Suwannee River Area

East of Tallahassee, rolling rural vistas lead to river floodplains. Cypress swamps ring clear-water springs. Small crossroads communities sprout roadside stands selling boiled peanuts and handmade quilts. On the Gulf of Mexico, you find a marshy coast fringing waters famed for fishing and scalloping.

37. Forest Capital/Cracker Homestead

The town of Perry hosts a state museum that is a fine 13-acre picnic place with exhibits about Florida's timber commerce. Kids will marvel at the 1864 farmhouse out back. It has a dirt yard so that snakes and other varmints could be readily seen and a gourd house for insect-eating purple martins.

Location: In Perry, on U.S. Highway 27 at 204 Forest Park Drive.

Important information: Free. Open from 9 A.M. to 5 P.M. Mondays and Thursdays through Sundays. In October, this site hosts a free fish fry. For more information, call 850-584-3227 or visit <www.dep.state.fl.us/parks>.

38. Steinhatchee Landing Resort

In the middle of beautiful nowhere, on the Steinhatchee River near a marsh on the Gulf of Mexico, this woodsy family resort and canoe outfitter offers a host of excellent ecotourism trips. You can take a guided canoe trip to a small river rapids—a rare feature in Florida—or to sites where you might see river otters, large pileated woodpeckers, or, at Hagen's Cove Preserve, vast armies of the tiny fiddler crabs. Horses, a fishpond, meandering King's Creek, and a nature trail delight children. The new buildings are two-story, Victorian-style cottages with porches and balconies—popular settings for family reunions. Summer finds the region busy with scallop harvesting. Fishing for tarpon (April–June) and redfish also attracts visitors.

Location: From Tennille Crossing on U.S. Highway 98, about 80 miles south of Tallahassee and 20 miles south of Perry, take State Road 51 west for about 8 miles to Steinhatchee Landing, on the left.

Important information: For more information, call 800-584-1709 or visit <www.SteinhatcheeLanding.com>.

39. Manatee Springs State Park

In 1774, naturalist William Bartram wrote with wonder about this Eden of woodland springs, which he called an admirable fountain. The springs flow into the nearby Suwannee River. In winter, you can easily see manatees from an observation area above the spring bowl or from a boardwalk that runs through the surrounding cypress swamp. The perfectly clear water is one of Florida's natural treasures. With its bike paths, hiking paths, picnic areas, and summer swimming in the 72-degree F springs, this longtime campground park of 2,075 acres is one of the most popular on Florida's west coast. Deer are abundant, and you might see an endangered swamp bird, the limpkin, feeding on apple snails.

Location: From U.S. Highway 98 in Chiefland, take State Road 320 west about 6 miles to its dead end at the park entrance.

Important information: For more information, call 352-493-6072 or visit <www.dep.state.fl.us/parks>.

40. Fanning Springs State Recreation Area

In the cool months, manatees feed at this small and lesser-known park on the Suwannee River. This wayside picnic spot features two 72-degree F springs, a playground, a volleyball court, and a nature trail, making it a 188-acre gem.

Location: On U.S. Highway 19/98 in Fanning Springs, about 9 miles north of Chiefland.

Important information: For more information, call 352-463-3420.

41. Suwannee River State Park

If you're traveling along Interstate 10 near Live Oak, this campground and fishing place on the famous Suwannee River awaits your family. The Suwannee, immortalized in song by Stephen Foster, meets the Withlacoochee River here amid limestone river bluffs. Ask park rangers about viewing the beaver dams. Walk along nature trails lined with longleaf pines. Learn about the ghost town, where only a cemetery remains. Look at the Civil War earthworks.

Location: From the intersection of U.S. Highway 90 and Interstate 10 about 13 miles west of Live Oak, follow the signs west along US 90 to the park.

Important information: For more information, call 904-362-2746 or visit <www.dep.state.fl.us/parks>.

Cooters catch some rays

The **Suwannee cooter** is a fairly common kind of turtle that loves to sunbathe. You are likely to see one in a spring or spring-fed river in this region. The reptile can also tolerate mildly salty water, and some feed near river mouths along the Gulf of Mexico. At midday, dozens of cooters will crowd on a log to catch some rays. In the early morning and late afternoon, they chow down on aquatic plants. They are one of the few turtle species that eats only plants.

42. Suwannee County Historical Museum

Into every vacation some rain may fall. So it's good to know that this former railroad depot can hold your family's attention with such curiosities as an antique dental chair, pony cart, moonshine still, farmhouse exhibit, extinct-animals exhibit, and Native American dugout canoe.

Location: In Live Oak at 208 North Ohio Avenue.

Important information: For more information, call 904-362-1776.

43. Stephen Foster State Folk Culture Center

Located upstream from Suwannee River State Park in the former 19th-century resort village of White Springs, this event-oriented destination features a Craft Square where old-time skills are demonstrated during the school year. Storytelling festivals, sugar-cane grindings, fiddle contests, and the annual Florida Folk Festival (held over the Memorial Day weekend) are among the many spirited events. The site offers a welcome, shady respite for interstate travelers.

Location: In downtown White Springs, just north of the intersection of Interstates 10 and 75.

Important information: For more information and a schedule of events, call 904-397-2733 or visit <www.dep.state.fl.us/parks>.

44. Sports Hall of Fame/Welcome Center

If your highway-weary troupe needs a stop, let young sports enthusiasts try this museum near the intersection of Interstates 10 and 75. Chris Evert, Babe Didrikson Zaharias, Frank Shorter, Larry Csonka, Red Barber, and even Needles, winner of the 1956 Belmont Stakes and Kentucky Derby, are among the Floridians enshrined here. There is an official tourist Welcome Center here, too, with free samples of citrus juice and a live baby gator to meet, so you really can't go wrong.

Location: In Lake City at 601 Hall of Fame Drive, at the U.S. Highway 90 exit of I-75, on the north side of US 90.

Important information: For more information, call 904-758-1310, 904-758-1312, or 800-352-3263.

45. Ocean Pond/Olustee
Battlefield State Historic Site

When you see this round lake in Osceola National Forest, you'll understand its name. The wind can whip up waves on this 1,700-acre "pond," making it look like an ocean. The sandy day-use beach, a boardwalk interpretive trail, picnic pavilions, swings, and a fishing pier are on the south shore, called Olustee Beach. The main campground in the forest, Ocean Pond Campground, is on the north shore. It has its own swimming beach.

Nearby, there's a small visitor center and Olustee Battlefield State Historic Site, where a widely attended re-enactment every February not only re-creates an 1864 Civil War battle in which 2,800 troops lost their lives but also presents a fascinating sutler's camp, where participants dress, talk, and act as if it were 1864. Since much of the forest is used primarily by hunters, this stop is a good way for family vacationers to visit the cypress swamp and pinewoods of this national forest.

Location: From Lake City, drive east on U.S. Highway 90 for about 11 miles to the crossroads of Olustee. Take County Road 231 north about 1 mile to Olustee Beach. To reach Ocean Pond Campground, drive about 1.5 miles east of Olustee on US 90 to its intersection with CR 250A. Take CR 250A north for about 12 miles to its intersection with graded but unpaved Forest Road 268. Take FR 268 1 mile to the campground.

Important information: For more information, call 904-752-2577 or 904-758-0400. For more information about the historic site, visit <www.dep.state.fl.us/parks>.

High Springs Area

The historic railroad and mining town of High Springs, about 12 miles northwest of Gainesville on the Santa Fe River, is a fun place to eat, shop, and stay overnight in North-Central Florida. There are several private springs resorts here that welcome campers, as well as cabin resorts, fish camps, and country inns that also are appealing.

46. Ichetucknee Springs State Park

Looking at the Ichetucknee River is like gazing into a deep, clear, natural aquarium. It is a national natural landmark with a reputation worldwide.

The park encompasses a 6-mile stretch of the river. It's easy to see fish and occasionally fish-eaters such as river otters. In the summer, a park tram returns visitors to the parking lot after they have floated downstream on inner tubes or rafts. The river is fed by nine crystal-clear springs that connect to underground caverns. When you're not on the river, two trails are worth exploring. The 1-mile Trestle Point Trail, in the south entrance area, is the easiest for little feet. It follows the river for a while and then leads to an old railroad trestle. The 2-mile Pine Ridge Trail, near the north entrance, skirts sinkholes.

Location: From Fort White, about 10 miles northwest of High Springs, follow U.S. Highway 27 north to the park's south entrance.

Important information: The park reaches capacity on summer weekends, so arrive early or plan a weekday visit. For more information, call 904-497-2511 or visit <www.dep.state.fl.us/parks>. There is no route all the way through the park. If you want a longer river float, check the map or with a park ranger to find out how to reach the north entrance on State Road 238.

Fountains of youth

While some of Florida's **springs** are manicured tourist attractions, others are still wild. A plunge into either kind is welcome on a hot day. Stay in them for 20 minutes and you'll emerge tingling, alert, and feeling more alive than you have in many days. Some say that this energizing "springs rush" is the experience that led 16th-century explorers, primed to expect great discoveries in the New World, to believe that one particular spring might be a fountain of everlasting youth.

Unknown to the Spanish, French, British, and other explorers, this peninsula has one of the largest concentrations of springs in the world: 300 known springs. You can find your own fountain of youth in a state park or national forest, at a commercial springs attraction, or along a river canoe trail. If you travel the length of the Suwannee River, you'll pass more than 20 springs that add to the river's forward push of 200 miles to the Gulf of Mexico. Before the Santa Fe River empties into the Suwannee, it is fed by dozens of springs, including the unusually pure Ichetucknee Springs and River, a designated national natural landmark.

Through the ages, visitors have been spellbound by Florida's springs, including William Bartram, who was commissioned by the king of England to explore the region in the 1700s. He said they were like a "crystal flood, which flows down with an easy, gentle, yet active current, rolling over its silvery bed...." Several springs, such as Wakulla Springs near Tallahassee and White Springs near Lake City, were so important to early Indian tribes that they declared them sacred zones, places of peace that all tribes would share, even during war.

47. O'Leno State Park

Kids are fascinated by the disappearing Santa Fe River. It winds beautifully through the woodlands and fields that make up this park—and then disappears into the earth. It flows underground for more than 3 miles before it surfaces again. Your campers will also like the swaying suspension footbridge over the river. The fact that this is the site of a ghost town just adds to the allure. A group camp with cabins and a dining hall help make this a popular place for family reunions and youth groups. It's also an ideal picnic spot. There are several nature paths and small sinkholes in the vicinity.

Location: From High Springs, take U.S. Highway 41/441 north about 6 miles to the park entrance.

Important information: For more information, call 904-454-1853 or visit <www.dep.state.fl.us/parks>.

48. Poe Springs Park

Have a picnic, fish or swim in the Santa Fe River, and hike a nature trail at this regional park that shelters the fast-flowing and crystal-clear Poe Springs. There's a boardwalk, an avenue of giant oak trees, and a rustic meeting hall with fireplace for group events.

Location: From High Springs, take U.S. Highway 27 south a quarter-mile to the intersection with County Road 340. Turn right (west) onto CR 340 and drive about 2.5 miles to the park entrance on the right.

Important information: Free. For more information, call 904-454-1992.

49. Ginnie Springs Resort

This private campground and outfitter overlooking stunning Ginnie Springs is well known among accomplished cave divers. The resort offers instruction in scuba diving and rents diving equipment, canoes, inner tubes, and snorkel equipment for use in the 72-degree F springs. Located in the woods along the Santa Fe River, this resort is popular.

Location: From High Springs, take U.S. Highway 27 south a quarter-mile to the intersection with County Road 340. Turn right (west) onto CR 340 and drive about 4.5 miles. Turn right (north) onto Ginnie Springs Road, a rough-graded road that winds through fields for about 1 mile to the resort gate.

Important information: There is an admission fee to enter the resort grounds; other fees are based upon rentals, usage, etc. For more information, call 800-874-8571.

50. Santa Fe Canoe Outpost

• •

This excellent longtime outfitter arranges 3-mile to 3-day floats down the Ichetucknee and Santa Fe Rivers and brings you back afterward to the outpost and your car. One rental chalet is available.

Location: On U.S. Highway 441 at the Santa Fe River, about 1 mile south of O'Leno State Park (see above) and about 5 miles north of High Springs.

Important information: Fees vary, but this family-oriented outpost offers free trips with paying adults to Ginnie and Poe Springs for children 6 and younger and other free trips for children 12 and younger. For more information, call 904-454-2050.

51. Great Outdoors Trading Company/ High Springs Opera House

• •

Two restored buildings, including the 1895 High Springs Opera House, comprise this fun destination. A café serves fresh-baked muffins, gourmet hamburgers, pasta, vegetarian dishes, and rich desserts, while a toy shop is guaranteed to get your kids' attention.

Location: In High Springs at 65 North Main Street.

Important information: For more information, call 904-454-2900.

Gainesville Area

• •

The woodsy region around Gainesville was once farmed by Native Americans and ranched by Spanish immigrants. It also is renowned for a necklace of crystal springs and winding rivers. Other worthwhile sites include the only sinkhole in the state where you are encouraged to climb down to the bottom and a vast prairie where native bison have been reintroduced. The prairie is a prime wintering ground for red-capped sandhill cranes, which are easily viewed. One of the nation's most outstanding spring-fed rivers, declared a national natural landmark by the U.S. Department of Interior, lures families who delight in floating it every summer. The oldest college in the state, the University of Florida, dominates the region with a campus in Gainesville that boasts a lake preserve where it's almost guaranteed you'll see alligators. Visitors stop at the lake's bat house every dusk to watch these insect-eaters swoop out and dine.

52. Florida Museum of Natural History

Walk through a replica of a Florida cavern, measure yourself against the giant jawbone of a prehistoric shark, stare up at an 18,000-year-old mammoth skeleton recovered from a Florida riverbed, check out artifacts from early native cultures, and find answers to your questions about alligators, manatees, pelicans, and other native fauna and flora. This is a very kid-pleasing place. The airy halls were designed by the same architect who did the Smithsonian's National Air and Space Museum in Washington, D.C. This may be the largest natural history museum in the South. Go see!

Location: On the western edge of the University of Florida campus at the intersection of Hull Road and SW 34th Street in Gainesville.

Important information: Free. Open from 10 A.M. to 5 P.M. Mondays through Saturdays and from 1 to 5 P.M. Sundays. For more information, call 352-846-2000 or visit <www.flmnh.ufl.edu>.

53. Samuel P. Harn Museum of Art

Budding artists will be inspired by this small and thoughtful art collection in a new building that lifts the soul with its pyramid of glass.

Location: Next to the Florida Museum of Natural History on SW 34th Street in Gainesville.

Important information: Free. Open from 11 A.M. to 5 P.M. Tuesdays through Fridays, from 10 A.M. to 5 P.M. Saturdays, and from 1 to 5 P.M. Sundays. For more information, call 352-392-9826 or visit <www.arts.ufl.edu/harn>.

54. University of Florida/Lake Alice

Here's a place right in Gainesville where you can easily see wild alligators from a lakeshore. The best views are from small parking areas along Museum Road near its intersection with Southwest Radio Road. Although this is a picnic spot, don't throw your crumbs to the gators, no matter how many tourists you see doing this. It's dangerous, bad for the reptiles, and illegal to boot. Across Museum Road, the Gainesville Bat House is a popular attraction every evening at dusk, as the colony flies out to scour the air for insects.

Location: Along the far west section of Museum Road, which runs from Hull Road on the west side of the University of Florida campus to SW 13th Street on the east side of the campus in Gainesville.

55. Morningside Nature Center/Pioneer Farm

A good time to visit this site is late afternoon, when the animals get their dinners and your little farmhands may be asked to help milk the goats or hand out barnyard treats. This is a lovely picnic place featuring a re-created Florida pioneer farm of 100 years ago, with a log barn, heirloom garden, and nature paths through woods of longleaf pine.

Location: From downtown Gainesville, drive about 3 miles east on East University Avenue to 3540 East University Avenue.

Important information: Fees are $1 for children under age 10 and $2 for all others. Open from 9 A.M. to 5 P.M. daily. For more information, call 352-334-2170 or visit <www.natureoperations.org>.

56. Book Lover's Café

Have your kids select a good used children's book or two for vacation reading, order them a peanut butter and jelly sandwich from the family-friendly health-food menu, pick a room of used books with lunch tables that suits you, and enjoy some quiet time.

Location: At 505 NW 13th Street, just a few blocks from the University of Florida campus in Gainesville.

Important information: For more information, call the bookstore at 352-374-4241 or the café at 352-384-0090.

57. Santa Fe Community College Teaching Zoo

This is an unusual chance for young animal-lovers to see what animal handlers need to learn to work in zoos and nature centers. It's a fun stop and quite educational for any child thinking about zoo work.

Location: In Gainesville near Interstate 75 at 3000 NW 83rd Street.

Important information: Open Mondays through Sundays from 9 A.M. to 2 P.M. Appointments are necessary on weekdays. For more information, call 352-395-5604 or visit <www.santafe.cc.fl.us>.

58. Devil's Millhopper State Geological Site

The centerpiece of this 63-acre park is a huge sinkhole, 120 feet deep, which formed when the roof of an underground cavern collapsed. Listen to small waterfalls trickle down the sinkhole's lush walls. Be sure to hold little ones' hands as you descend the slippery wooden steps to the floor of this leafy place. It's an amazing journey into the earth, 221 steps down—and back! You may spy frogs and salamanders hiding among the tree limbs and the ferns. Fossilized shark teeth and other ancient fossils recovered from the bottom of the sinkhole indicate that this was once part of the ocean floor.

Location: Two miles northwest of Gainesville off State Road 232 at 4732 Millhopper Road.

Important information: The fee is $2 per car. Open from 9 A.M. to 5 P.M. daily. Be especially cautious on the steps; they are almost always wet and slippery. For more information, call 352-955-2008 or visit <www. dep.state.fl.us/parks>.

59. Paynes Prairie State Preserve

This 21,000-acre preserve encompasses land farmed and ranched by both Native Americans and Spanish colonialists. A Seminole chief, King Payne, ruled here. Another Seminole leader, Osceola, ambushed a supply caravan here, too.

A herd of bison roams the preserve, so ask a ranger about likely places to see them. These mammals, more commonly associated with the American West, were once hunted here by Native Americans and were reintroduced. The preserve is also a prime winter feeding ground for great flocks of red-capped sandhill cranes; listen for their loud and distinctive calls. Eagles and hawks soar, bobcats hunt, and white-tailed deer are frequently seen.

As you look down over this vast prairie basin, it's hard to imagine that from 1881 to 1891 it was a lake where busy paddlewheelers traveled. Then a natural plug opened and the water quickly drained, returning the land to prairie.

On the last weekend of February, the preserve hosts the Paynes Prairie Primitive Art Festival, which features food, crafts, primitive games, and demonstrations of arrowhead making. Nature trails, excellent guided tours, a visitor center, observation towers, a recreation lake, and a playground are some of the features of one of the most historically interesting parks in Florida. The campground is also popular.

Location: From Gainesville, drive south about 10 miles on U.S. Highway 441. The preserve is on the eastern side of the road.

Important information: For more information, call 352-466-3397 or visit <www.dep.state.fl.us/parks>.

60. Marjorie Kinnan Rawlings State Historic Site

Rawlings was the Pulitzer Prize–winning author of *The Yearling,* a poignant coming-of-age tale about a boy and his pet deer. The book has become a children's classic. Even children who don't know the book like to visit this furnished country house, listed on the National Register of Historic Places. Ducks waddle in the yard. There's a 1930s car parked in the barn, an outhouse to peek into, a garden, and more. An accomplished eccentric, Rawlings hunted, loved to cook and eat, knew author Ernest Hemingway, and was friends with author F. Scott Fitzgerald. There is a picnic site on nearby Orange Lake and a nature trail in a nearby woods.

Location: From Gainesville, drive south about 11 miles on U.S. Highway 441. Turn left (east) onto County Road 346 and go about 4 miles to a T intersection with CR 325. Take CR 325 east about 3 miles to the historic site, which is on the right (west) side of the road.

Important information: The site is closed every August and September. The rest of the year, the farmyard and trails are open from 9 A.M. to 5 P.M. daily. Guided tours of the house, limited to the first ten visitors, are available at 10 and 11 A.M. and hourly from 1 to 4 P.M. Thursdays through Sundays. The house may be viewed only via a guided tour.

This site has become a literary mecca, so you may have to wait your turn, especially in the afternoon. School groups and other youth groups are urged to make special reservations in advance. For more information, call 352-466-3672 or visit <www.dep.state.fl.us/parks>.

61. Historic Micanopy

This leafy community was a Timucuan Indian village in the 1600s, a Seminole town called Cuscawilla in the 1700s, and a trading post after 1821, when Florida became a U.S. territory. Well-mannered children like to listen to Native American lore in the small museum and stop at the ice cream and sandwich shops. Parents look for rare used books and collectibles. The town was named after a Seminole leader.

Location: From Gainesville, drive south about 10 miles on U.S. Highway 441. Micanopy is just a quarter-mile west of US 441.

Important information: Walking tours are conducted by the Micanopy Historical Society on the second Saturday of each month. For more information, call 352-466-3200 or 352-466-3121.

NORTHEAST REGION

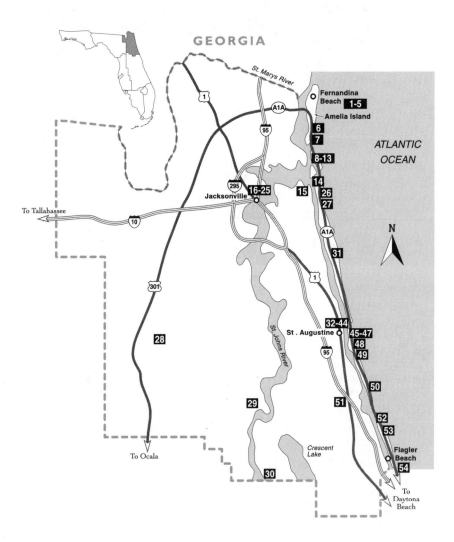

Northeast
Region

Early tourists in Florida entertained themselves by cruising the north-flowing St. Johns River and watching the wildlife along its banks. In the late 1800s, paddlewheel steamboats carried Victorians upriver to a junglelike winter paradise. John James Audubon, William Bartram, and Harriet Beecher Stowe helped entice people here with their published impressions of Florida.

Today, you can still see alligators, magnificent birds, and rare right whales in this region. Stroll in the footsteps of 19th-century tourists along the narrow streets and through the 17th-century Spanish fort in St. Augustine—a community established 42 years before Jamestown and 55 years before Plymouth. The historical site of Fort Mose, the nation's oldest community of free African-American families, is also located there. In a city brimming with "oldest" sites, kids especially like to peer in the windows of the Oldest Wooden Schoolhouse.

The many Atlantic beaches in this region, some ringed with barrier dunes, are ideal for bird watching, shelling, and surf fishing. A little-known, multi-habitat national preserve at Jacksonville features the ruins of slave cabins made of coquina, a soft, porous rock composed of shell fragments. A national park memorial in Jacksonville is the only fort reconstruction from the time when Florida was known by some as New France, a prize possession of the French Crown. Jacksonville is a popular family destination, with a vibrant science museum, maritime museum, river walk, and zoo. At several scenic coastal state parks, you can lull your little ones to sleep with the sounds of the surf. There's also a car ferry ride to take, lighthouses to visit, an alligator zoo, the first marine mammal park, and two state gardens.

If you're on a driving tour of the eastern seaboard but don't have time to venture far into Florida, you and your family can still collect a treasure chest full of vibrant Florida experiences if you make some carefully selected stops in the Northeast Region. Of course, you'll want to return later to explore what you missed the first time around.

You'll find lots of family cottages in the region's many beach towns, but you might especially want to consider staying at the 1735 Lighthouse and Amelia Island Plantation, both on Amelia Island; Holiday Inn Sunspree, with free kids' activities and some free meals, in Jacksonville; Sea Turtle Inn, Ruby Inn by the Sea, and Fig Tree Inn, all at Jacksonville Beach; the stylish River Suites, originally a Palmolive family estate in Orange Park; Ponte Vedra Resort at Ponte Vedra Beach; Saragossa Inn, Secret Garden, Segui Inn, Historic Casa Monica Hotel, and Anastasia Inn, all in St. Augustine; and Topaz Inn in Flagler Beach. Coastal state parks with camping include Fort Clinch at Fernandina Beach, Little Talbot Island south of Amelia Island, Anastasia Island State Recreation Area at St. Augustine, and Faver-Dykes State Park near St. Augustine. Private campgrounds popular with families include North Beach Camp Resort and Ocean Grove, both northeast of St. Augustine near Guana River State Park.

For more information contact:

- Amelia Island Tourism
  800-226-3542, 904-277-0717
  <www.ameliaisland.org>
- Flagler County Public Library
  <www.flaglercounty.org>
- Jacksonville and the Beaches Visitors Bureau
  904-798-9148, 800-733-2668
  <www.jaxcvb.com>, <www.coj.net>
- Putnam County Chamber of Commerce
  904-328-1503
  <www.putnamcountychamber.org>
- St. Augustine, Ponte Vedra, and the Beaches
  800-653-2489
  <www.oldcity.com>

Amelia Island Area

In the northeastern corner of the state sits Amelia Island, an important barrier beach that shelters the mainland from hurricanes and other storms. The island's only town, Fernandina Beach, is a charming fish and shrimp seaport. Its 19th-century buildings comprise a leafy, 50-block historical district of cafés, toy shops, bookstores, and inns. Amelia Island's Atlantic beaches feature a famed resort. A state recreation area offers horseback riding on the beach.

I. Fort Clinch State Park

Your little soldiers will salute this 1840s red-brick fort. It's fun to scramble through, with its passageways, bastions, cannons, and small museum. Enthusiastic rangers dress up in Civil War costumes to re-enact the period when Union troops held the fort. They wear wool uniforms—not often a comfortable outfit in hot Florida—present their armaments, and cook hardtack. At night, they keep handmade candles burning, so try to take the nighttime tour. They welcome questions about their lives; ask how they kept food cold!

This 1,110-acre park is also a haven for wildlife watchers. You may be able to spot right whales, which were once almost hunted to extinction for their oil and are still extremely rare. It's thought that only 350 exist in Atlantic waters. They migrate every winter from Nova Scotia to offshore calving grounds here. Among the many birds that land here, you'll see brown pelicans, double-crested cormorants, several kinds of gulls, royal terns, and other shorebirds. Alligators are often seen in the park interior at freshwater Willow Pond. Summer brings glimpses of the vibrant painted bunting in tree branches. This park is an excellent base from which to explore.

The park's fishing pier is a great place to spot shore life but not always the best place to fish, because the water is shallow and a rock jetty keeps marine life at bay. Fish for flounder, spotted seatrout, redfish, and sheepshead from the shoreline or the jetties, but watch your footing on the jetties, which are slippery when wet.

Location: From the mainland, take State Road A1A across the Amelia River to the island and stay with it as it turns north to Fernandina Beach. The entrance to the park is at 2601 Atlantic Avenue on the northern end of Amelia Island.

Important information: Open daily from sunrise to sunset. The candlelight tour of the fort by costumed rangers is held on Friday and Saturday nights. On the first weekend of each month, a group of re-enactors inhabits the blacksmith and carpenter's shops, kitchen, surgeon's office, and other areas. For more information, call 904-277-7274 or visit <www.dep.state.fl.us/parks>.

2. Kayak Amelia

This outfitter can take you on guided adventures around the sheltered waters of the Amelia River, including a paddle to a bird rescue sanctuary.

Location: A meeting location will be decided when you make reservations.

Important information: For more information and reservations, call 904-321-0697.

3. Fernandina Beach Historic District/ Amelia Island Museum of History

With 50 blocks of restored Victorian mansions—some of them bon-bon colored, others with lots of white "gingerbread" trim—Amelia Island's only

What's wrong with
the right whale?

The **right whale** is the whale of *Moby Dick* fame. Whalers called it the "right" or best whale to hunt and kill for oil because it swam near shore and easily floated after death. The right whale is considered extremely rare. In fact, it is the rarest whale in the world and in danger of becoming extinct. Hunting reduced the herds of great right whales, and water pollution, entanglement in fishing nets, and injuries from ships' propellers further aggravated their situation. There are perhaps 300 to 350 right whales left in the Atlantic Ocean and maybe 2,000 worldwide. Once, there were probably 300,000.

Right whales can weigh up to 70 tons. They can be as long as a telephone pole, a small car can fit into their mouth, and an adult's heart can be about the size of a living room chair. Every winter, the females yield to a centuries-old genetic call. They swim south from Canadian waters and give birth off the coast of northeastern Florida and southeastern Georgia.

The winter calving grounds in Florida are also dense with military and commercial ship traffic. With increased awareness of the whales' plight, some commercial and private boat operators have joined the Right Whale Watch. When they see a group of right whales—or even an individual—they call a federal tracking team. The whales travel slowly, sometimes moving forward, sometimes going back to the previous days' feeding location. So information about them can be passed along, and captains can make slight alterations in their vessels' courses to minimize the chance of hitting them. If you see low-flying planes in this area during the winter, they may be part of the Right Whale Watch.

Right whales swim surprisingly close to shore, frequently just beyond the surf line. This may account for their occasional stranding along the Florida coast as far south as Cape Canaveral. It certainly accounts for a winter ritual among northeastern Florida newspapers, especially the *Daytona Beach News Journal*. Photographers publish excellent photographs of the whales swimming close to shore. Readers delight in knowing when "their" right whales have arrived. Because the females are giving birth and then watching over newborns while avoiding ship traffic and trying to feed, what the whales need most is to be left undisturbed. Whale-watching tour-boat rides aren't the best way to show appreciation for the species.

Observation towers, such as those at Little Talbot Island State Park and Guana River State Park, along with other coastal viewing spots, such as boardwalks over the sand dunes and fishing piers—even your condominium rental apartment—are perches from which to watch whales. With these tips and with luck, your young whale watchers might be able to shout, "Thar she blows!"

town is a charming place to visit. Several different nations, as well as lawless pirates, have at times ruled this little outpost, so help your family imagine the intrigue hatched along these old streets. The Amelia Island Museum of History, like most coastal museums in Florida, is really a world-history stop, too. Prior to Florida's statehood, strategic ports like this one were highly regarded prizes in the international contest for dominance in the New World. On the waterfront at the western end of Centre Street, join the crowd as it collects to watch shrimp boats return with their catch. Later, you can watch the sun set from this same spot or take a horse and buggy ride through the old streets. Part of the old movie *Pippi Longstocking,* based on the classic children's book, was filmed here.

Location: Once you find your way to Centre Street, which connects with Atlantic Avenue, just pick a free parking space and stroll. The Amelia Island Museum of History is at 233 South Third Street in Fernandina Beach.

Important information: The Amelia Island Museum of History offers guided walking tours as well as a brochure outlining a self-guided walk. For more information, call 800-226-3542 or 904-261-7378.

4. Florida House Inn

I don't often recommend that families stay at small historical inns, because they're usually best suited to a quiet, mature clientele. But why not set young imaginations loose by treating them to a stay in historical lodgings at least once in a childhood? This unpretentious inn is a good pick. Built in 1857 and listed on the National Register of Historic Places, it's the oldest continuously operated hotel in Florida. The dining room offers family-style seating and bowls of country cooking at long wooden tables. For your kids' nightly bubble bath, ask for a room with an old-fashioned claw-foot tub. Florida House is a short walk from the shops and activities of Centre Street downtown.

Location: In Fernandina Beach at 22 South Third Street.

Important information: For more information, call 904-261-3300 or visit <www.floridahouse-inn.com>.

5. 1735 Lighthouse

How would your children like to spend the night in a lighthouse? The rooms in this four-story replica perched at water's edge are circular, one sea-worthy room per floor. From the top of the tower, you'll get a 360-degree view that, at high tide, will make you feel like you're out to sea. This overnight adventure is fun for little lightkeepers, one they'll talk about for years. Bring your spyglass. If the lighthouse is booked, put your young mateys to bed in wooden ship bunks in the adjoining nautical-theme inn known as 1735 House.

Location: South of downtown Fernandina Beach at 584 South Fletcher Avenue.

Important information: Reservations are a must for the popular lighthouse, and the high season in the Northeast Region is summer. For more information, call 904-261-5878 or visit <www.ameliaislandlodging.com>.

6. Amelia Island Plantation

With its own nature center, staff naturalist, and extensive nature programs covering everything from sea turtles to crabbing expeditions, this lush Atlantic beachfront resort on 1,300 acres is a fine place for junior naturalists. There are plenty of children's activities, as well as restaurants and poolside cafés on site.

Location: On Amelia Island at 6800 First Coast Highway.

Important information: For more information, call 800-874-6878 or 904-261-6161 or visit <www.aipfl.com>.

7. Amelia Island State Recreation Area/ Seahorse Stables

Here's a chance to see the beach as European soldiers did: from the saddle, riding through the surf and sand of a barrier island. Seahorse Stables operates guided tours on horseback through the dunes of an undeveloped beach at Amelia Island State Recreation Area. The horses are brought here from off site. Bring carrots.

Location: At the southern tip of Amelia Island, about 7 miles south of Fernandina Beach.

Important information: Beach access is free, but parking is limited. Seahorse Stables requires reservations and charges a fee. This area is supervised from Little Talbot Island State Park, and there is no ranger office on site. There also are no facilities here, such as restrooms or drinking water, so plan accordingly. For more park information, call 904-251-2320 or visit <www.dep.state.fl.us/parks>. For Seahorse Stables reservations, call 904-261-4878.

8. Little Talbot Island State Park/Geopark

This park extends over four islands. On Big Talbot Island, you'll find two walking trails. One of them, the Bluffs Trail, is unusual for Florida in that it leads to a scenic overlook on an ocean promontory. The vantage is popular with artists. On Little Talbot Island, you'll find nature trails, ranger-led walks, a shady campground, canoe rentals, an observation deck, a picnic area, and more. Ask rangers about opportunities on Long Island, a narrow strip between the two Talbots.

Geopark is an outstanding preserve. You may spot river otters, shorebirds, and even rare right whales during their winter calving season. Endangered loggerhead sea turtles nest along the park's undisturbed beaches in summer, and rangers conduct popular walks with the intention of spotting turtles laying their eggs. In the summer, the area is excessively hot, buggy, and prone to strong afternoon lightning storms, but it's popular nonetheless with Floridians accustomed to these conditions. The ocean currents in this area are exceptionally strong, so heed warning signs about rip tides and undertows. Don't allow your family to swim where park signs prohibit it, or you could be risking a life.

Location: From Fernandina Beach on Amelia Island, drive south about 9 miles on State Road A1A (Coastal Highway). The park office and campground registration are on Little Talbot Island.

Important information: For more information, call 904-251-2320 or visit <www.dep.state.fl.us/parks>.

9. BEAKS Wildlife Rehabilitation

This private, nonprofit animal sanctuary tends to the wounds of 2,000 wild birds a year, including eagles, owls, and other native species. BEAKS stands for Bird Emergency and Kare Sanctuary.

Location: On Big Talbot Island. You will get directions when you call to arrange a tour.

Important information: Donations are accepted. Visits are by appointment only. Call 904-251-2473 for more information.

10. Huguenot Memorial Park

Here's a park that's delightful fall through winter, especially if you don't mind bundling up to enjoy the wide day-use beach on brisk days. In addition to the beach, the park encompasses a regional bird sanctuary, a public campground, an observation tower, picnic shelters, and a boat ramp. In the summer—especially on weekends—expect excessive noise, in part from the young adult sun worshippers who careen around designated portions of the beach in dune buggies. Folks who can't get into the campground at Little Talbot Island State Park, just across Fort George Inlet from this site, sometimes camp here instead.

Location: From the main entrance to Little Talbot Island State Park, drive about 1 mile south on State Road A1A (Heckscher Drive).

Important information: For more information, call 904-251-3335.

11. Kingsley Plantation

One of the most significant and striking stops on Florida's African American Heritage Trail, Kingsley Plantation is also a National Park Service site. It preserves the ruins of slave cabins and a riverfront plantation house, transporting you back to about 1800. Most slave shacks in the South were made of shoddy materials, and they have vanished over the years. But these 23 apartments, which sit in a woodland semicircle, were constructed of a natural seashell concrete called tabby. They are mute and important testimony to the system under which one person in America could own others.

The family sagas here are intricate because plantation owner Zephaniah Kingsley married Anna Jai, a woman from Senegal, Africa, who was his former slave. He also freed other slaves. The interracial Kingsley family and some of their former slaves relocated to Haiti in 1837 when new Florida laws discriminated against free blacks, but not before amassing 32,000 acres on four plantations and about 200 slaves. The planter's house is the oldest remaining plantation mansion in the state.

This site is part of the national Timucuan Ecological and Historic Preserve, an expansive 53,000-acre property that includes units on both shores of the St. Johns River.

Location: Just south of Little Talbot Island, on Fort George Island, take State Road A1A (Heckscher Drive) to Palmetto Avenue and turn west onto Palmetto. Follow the signs to Kingsley Plantation.

Important information: Free. Open from 9 A.M. to 5 P.M. daily except on Christmas. For more information, call 904-251-3537 or visit <www.nps.gov/timu>.

12. Fort George Island State Cultural Site

For at least 5,000 years, people have fished and lived on Fort George Island, including the Timucuan Indians, a corn-growing people who befriended French explorers. This site interprets the many waves of human habitation: native, French, Spanish, British, and pioneer. Take a winding, partly one-way, partly paved 4.4-mile driving tour called Saturiwa Trail. It meanders through lush woods, past stately palms, and along a marshy shore. The numbered stops and informative drive booklet are a good introduction to the history and natural features of the region. Help your children imagine life at the island's Spanish mission, built in 1587 and listed on the National Register of Historic Places. The exact site of the British fort for which the island was named has not yet been discovered, but it may be near Mount Cornelia, said to be the highest point along the Atlantic seaboard south of North Carolina. As you visit here, you are following in the footsteps of naturalist William Bartram, Quaker missionary and shipwreck survivor Jonathan Dickinson, and French sea captain Jean Ribault. This site is part of the Talbot Islands State Geopark.

Location: On Fort George Island, just south of Little Talbot Island along State Road A1A, take Palmetto Avenue and follow signs for the cultural site and the driving tour, called the Saturiwa Trail.

Important information: Saturiwa Trail is extremely narrow; allow room for traffic traveling in the opposite direction to pass. Also, some areas are private property and should be respected. For more information, call 904-251-2320 or visit <www.dep.state.fl.us/parks>.

13. Mayport Ferry

Drive your car onto the Mayport Ferry for a ten-minute push across the strong currents of the St. Johns River. This is the longest river in the state and one of the most commercially used. It was known by Spanish sailors as the River of Currents, or *Rio de Corrientes,* because of the dangerous currents at its mouth. The French called it River of May, *Riviere de Mai,* because they came upon it in May 1562. A 1590 Spanish mission at the river's mouth gave rise to its final name, *Rio de San Juan del Puerto,* St. John of the Harbor

River, or St. Johns River. The river's Timucuan Indian name was Welaka, which is thought to have meant River of Lakes. The river forms many lakes on its north-flowing struggle to the sea from its headwaters west of the town of Melbourne.

When you debark from the ferry in Mayport, you can visit this seaport town, which calls itself the oldest fishing village in the country. Depending upon changing security conditions, there are also weekend tours of the ships berthed at the Mayport Naval Station.

Location: From State Roads A1A/105 on Fanning Island, about 2 miles south of Palmetto Avenue, turn into the well-marked roadside parking lot for the Mayport Ferry. Park your car within a traffic lane and wait for directions to drive onto the ferry when it docks.

Important information: Fees are $2.50 per car or 50 cents per person. The ferry shoves off about every 15 minutes from 6:30 A.M. to 10:15 P.M. daily. For more information, call Hornblower Marine Services at 904-270-2520. To arrange tours of the naval station, call 904-270-6289.

14. Marine Science Education Center and Museum

This is a fine stop in Mayport that features tanks of marine creatures, shark replicas, and a 14-tank wet lab for hands-on learning. The building is an old schoolhouse near the St. Johns River.

Location: In Mayport at 1347 Palmer Street.

Important information: Open from 8 A.M. to 3 P.M. Mondays through Fridays. For more information, call 904-247-5973.

Jacksonville Area

Jacksonville is a vibrant river city. Visitors often return because there's always something fun to do, from visiting a hands-on science museum, exploring a maritime museum, strolling the Riverwalk, watching street performers at a shopping and dining emporium, or watching the antics of the animals at an outstanding zoo. The sprawling city straddles the busy St. Johns River and is connected by at least half a dozen bridges, so it's wise to check a detailed city map before setting out to explore. (Or, try getting around downtown via a water taxi, a bicycle taxi, or the skyway.) The Main Street Bridge leads from points north to downtown Jacksonville. J. Turner Butler Boulevard, an east-west route south of University Avenue, will take you east to the beaches.

Interstate 95 is the north-south throughway, and the beltway that wraps around the city like a gray ribbon is Interstate 275.

Neighborhoods worth exploring include Avondale, with its cafés and eclectic shops, and the adjoining garden district of Riverside. Together, the two comprise one of the largest districts on the National Register of Historic Places in the country. To the east across the river, ride through little-known Ortega, considered one of the wealthiest neighborhoods in the nation. Its streets are lined with mansions. Harriet Beecher Stowe, the famed author of *Uncle Tom's Cabin*, became so enchanted with this area that she bought a commercial orange grove just outside Jacksonville at Mandarin. Her landing on the river became a steamboat tour attraction.

The city is named for President Andrew Jackson, who fought Seminole Indians in North Florida and who served briefly as territorial governor. It was once called Cowford by native residents, because it was considered the best place to ford the river with domestic animals. City founder Isaiah Hart built a log cabin here in 1821, the same year the peninsula became a U.S. territory.

For a quick orientation to the city, check out Visitors TV, a 24-hour information channel about Jacksonville and the nearby beaches. It's available in most cottages, inns, motels, and hotels in the area.

15. Fort Caroline National Monument

Florida might today be called New France if the Spanish hadn't squelched an attempt by French Protestant Huguenots to colonize the region. This reconstructed, triangular fort and memorial are reminders of the brief colonization attempt. The hardy Huguenots came to the New World in the hope of finding religious tolerance, but they were massacred instead by Spanish Catholics. One of the most lasting aspects of the brief French colonialization attempt are the striking engravings of alligators and Indians created by French expedition artist-historian Jacques LeMoyne. This riverfront park, administered by the National Park Service, sits amid live oaks and is a lovely picnic place and engaging world-history lesson. It is part of the 53,000-acre Timucuan Ecological and Historic Preserve.

Location: About 10 miles east of downtown Jacksonville, on the south shore of the St. Johns River at 12713 Fort Caroline Road.

Important information: Open from 9 A.M. to 5 P.M. daily. For more information, call 904-641-7111 or visit <www.nps.gov/parks>.

16. Jacksonville Museum of Science and History/Planetarium

Spend some entertaining time indoors among the vivid painted murals, unique artifacts, and rare photographs on display at this family-friendly museum of history, science, and nature. A favorite attraction among children is Fermata, a 52-foot-long touchable sculpture of a right whale. It's part of an exhibit on endangered marine mammals of Florida. You can also view a 25-pound alligator snapping turtle, enjoy the Alexander Brest Planetarium show, and visit the wreck of the 1860s ship *Maple Leaf,* recovered from the bottom of the St. Johns River. Check out the hands-on exhibits in the Kidspace, a fun stop with a puppet theater, tree house, and more. The Explorer, in the Science Circus area, is a kid-thrilling computerized simulator that takes visitors through the organs of the body or inside an aircraft carrier, using computer programs to move young travelers' seats to correspond with the action on-screen. In front of the museum, the Friendship Fountain is a spectacular 120-foot-high spray of water that is lit at night. You might get sprinkled when the wind blows! Nearby is the popular waterfront footpath known as Riverwalk.

Location: At 1025 Museum Circle in Jacksonville, on the south bank of the St. Johns River.

Important information: Children ages 2 and under are admitted free; fees are $3 for ages 3 to 12, $4 for seniors, and $5 for all others. Open from 9 A.M. to 5 P.M. Tuesdays through Fridays, from 11 A.M. to 5 P.M. Saturdays, and from 1 to 5 P.M. Sundays. For more information, call 904-396-7062.

17. Jacksonville Historical Center/ Maritime Museum

The museum and historical center are next-door neighbors along the Southbank Riverwalk. Model ships are part of the allure at the Maritime Museum. Exhibits on the Timucuan Indians and the great Jacksonville fire of 1901, which destroyed nearly 2,400 buildings, will enthrall young visitors to the historical center.

Location: On the Southbank Riverwalk under the Main Street Bridge.

Important information: Admittance to both museums is free. The historical center is open from noon to 5 P.M. daily. For more information, call 904-398-4301. The Maritime Museum is open from 11 A.M. to 5 P.M. daily except

Tuesdays, when it's open from 11 A.M. to 4 P.M., and Sundays, when it's open from 1 to 5 P.M. For more information, call 904-398-9011. The Maritime Museum has a second location at Jacksonville Landing, across the river in downtown Jacksonville on the Northbank Riverwalk.

18. Water Taxi/Jacksonville Skyway

If you want to get from the attractions on one side of the St. Johns River to those on the other side, why not hop aboard a water taxi for a brisk ride across? For a different river view, ride the skyway, a 2.5-mile airy ride.

Location: Board a water taxi or the skyway from the Riverwalk, near the museum plaza in Jacksonville.

Important information: The water taxi operates from 11 A.M. to 10 P.M. daily, but ask the captain when the last ride of the day will be. Fees are $2 round-trip, $1 one way for children and $3 round-trip, $2 one way for adults. The skyway fee is 35 cents a passenger, one way. It operates from 6:30 A.M. to 7:30 P.M. Mondays through Thursdays, from 6:30 A.M. to 10 P.M. Fridays, and from 10 A.M. to 10 P.M. Saturdays. For more information, call 904-630-3100; for Riverwalk information, call 904-630-0827.

19. Eastcoast Transportation

A range of tours from boat rides to lively walking tours and ghost tours are available.

Location: A meeting place will be decided when you make reservations.

Important information: For more information, call 904-829-7433.

20. Ped-L-Taxi

If you wonder what those bicycle/carriage-seat contraptions pedaling around town are, they're part of the downtown Ped-L-Taxi service. Ride in style, enjoy the fresh air, and avoid parking hassles.

Location: Hail a Ped-L-Taxi from downtown locations, or visit the main office at 421 West Church Street in downtown Jacksonville.

Important information: The service is available from 7 A.M. to 4 P.M. daily, and the fee is $1 per city block. For more information, call 904-354-3557.

21. Cummer Museum of Art and Gardens

The museum's Art Connections gallery is a special place for young artists to learn more about art with hands-on activities such as painting on a prism and mixing colors. Kids love the computerized finger painting. This child-friendly aspect of the lovely Cummer Museum reflects its origins as a memorial to an infant. Ninah M. H. Cummer, a Jacksonville civic leader, began amassing an art collection after the death of her baby. The museum was established at Mrs. Cummer's mansion after her own death. The gardens, created in the early 1900s, are beautiful and quiet sanctuaries with formal pools. A 250-year-old live oak spans 150 feet and is a sight to behold. Even if your troupe doesn't usually do well in art museums, this one is an excellent choice.

Location: On the western shore of the St. Johns River, at 829 Riverside Avenue in Jacksonville.

Important information: Children ages 4 and under are admitted free; fees are $1 for ages 5 to 18, $2 for seniors, and $3 for all others. Open from 10 A.M. to 9 P.M. Tuesdays and Thursdays; from 10 A.M. to 5 P.M. Wednesdays, Fridays, and Saturdays; and from noon to 5 P.M. Sundays. For more information, call 904-356-6857.

22. Animatronics

The Sally Corporation offers limited tours of its robotics factory, where workers create and build mechanical characters and rides for museums and theme parks, such as Walt Disney World. The entertaining tour of the world of animatronics is like a show in itself. This is a great stop for your young inventors, animators, and electricians.

Location: In downtown Jacksonville at 745 West Forsyth Street, two blocks north of the Prime F. Osborn III Convention Center (a prominent 1910 building with Doric columns that was the country's largest railway station once).

Important information: The robotics-creation tour and show are on Wednesdays only, beginning at 10:30 A.M. You should call for details and directions, 905-355-7100.

23. Jacksonville Zoo

Journey to Africa at this zoo. It shelters cheetahs, rhinoceroses, leopards, monkeys, warthogs, crocodiles, giraffes, zebras, and more on the 20-acre Plains of East Africa. The jungly Okavango Village delights little safari trekkers with domesticated African animals in a petting zoo called Mahali Pa Kucheza (the Playing Place). Zulu craftsmen constructed the building with the thatched roof, the largest in North America, for the zoo. Walk through the Birds of the Rift Valley aviary. There's also an elephant enclosure with a 250,000-gallon pool. You may see the celebrity pachyderm, Ali, who was donated by rock superstar Michael Jackson.

Other sites you won't want to miss are the Seronera Overlook, a 275,000-gallon pool and reptile house, and Mahali Pa Simba (Place of the Lions), which offers a close-up look at adult lions and cubs. As an accredited specialist in endangered species, the zoo is helping the rare white rhino endure. Don't leave without putting your youngest ones on board the Okavango Railroad, a 1.3-mile train ride. If your group is game, sign up in advance for the Safari Sleepover and spend the night at the zoo!

Location: From downtown Jacksonville, take the Main Street Bridge across the Trout River. Turn east onto State Road 105 and drive to 8605 Zoo Road. Follow the large billboards.

Important information: Open from 9 A.M. to 5 P.M. daily except Thanksgiving and Christmas. Children ages 3 and under are admitted free; fees are $4 for ages 3 to 12, $4.50 for seniors, and $6.50 for all others. Safari Sleepovers are held on Friday and Saturday nights. For more information, call 904-757-4463.

24. Tree Hill Nature Center

Take a break with nature at this 50-acre, nonprofit wildlife preserve laced with nature trails and exhibits of native animals.

Location: In Jacksonville's Arlington neighborhood on the eastern side of the St. Johns River, at 7152 Lone Star Road.

Important information: Open from 8:30 A.M. to 5 P.M. Mondays through Fridays. For more information, call 904-724-4646 or visit <www.treehill.org>.

25. Loretto Nature Preserve

This is one of three satellite locations of the Tree Hill Nature Center (see above), with similar programs, paths, and nature exhibits.

Location: In Mandarin, a suburb of Jacksonville on the eastern side of the St. Johns River, at 3900 Loretto Road.

Important information: Open from 8:30 A.M. to 5 P.M. Mondays through Saturdays. For detailed directions and more information, call 904-724-4646 or visit <www.treehill.org>.

26. Kathryn Abby Hannah Park

This oceanfront public park with a mile of beach is also a favorite family fishing hole and campground. It features a pond stocked with largemouth and sunshine bass, bluegills, and other freshwater species. Nature trails and an off-road bicycle path meander through the park's 450 acres.

Location: From State Road A1A just south of the Mayport Naval Station and north of Jacksonville Beach, turn onto Wonderwood Road and drive a quarter-mile to the park entrance at 500 Wonderwood Road.

Important information: For more information, call 904-249-4700 or visit <www.coj.net/fun>.

27. Pablo Historical Park

Recall the transportation systems of early 20th-century Florida at this collection of historical buildings, which includes a restored train depot and post office. Climb over Locomotive No. 7, a 23-ton steam engine. The Lindbergh Memorial to Children is also here.

Location: At 425 Beach Boulevard in Jacksonville Beach.

Important information: Open from 10 A.M. to 3 P.M. Mondays through Saturdays. For more information, call 904-246-0093.

28. Gold Head Branch State Park

This longtime family vacation spot has the only public park cabins near Jacksonville. There's swimming in Lake Johnson, nature trails in the cool

Go fish!

In Florida, **young anglers** can try their skills—and luck—in either freshwater or salt water. Because some fish species have come close to being depleted, licenses are required to help protect the resource. Many anglers today routinely catch and release, especially those on vacation who aren't set up to dress and cook a catch. As a quick guideline, children under age 16 are exempt from both saltwater and freshwater fishing license requirements.

Almost every angler needs bait or lures, and bait shops and fishing guides are excellent sources of information about local conditions, state license requirements, seasons, sizes, and limits. This information is crucial; for example, to legally keep a tarpon, which is inedible, you need a $50 special tag. Also, if you want your large catch to be considered for the record books, you must have hooked it legally. The shops have copies of *Fishing Lines,* a free booklet about saltwater species, the *Fresh Water Sport Fishing Guide,* and *Florida Fishing & Boating.* You can also visit <www.floridafishing-boating.com>.

Saltwater licenses are waived for anglers younger than 16 or older than 65. You also don't need a saltwater license if you are saltwater fishing with a licensed saltwater guide or if you are a Florida resident saltwater fishing from land or a structure fixed to land, like a pier. As for freshwater fishing, a stamp is required for residents and nonresidents ages 16 and older. Seven-day freshwater licenses for nonresidents are a good vacation purchase. If you are freshwater fishing in wildlife management areas, you may also need an additional stamp. Also, in some estuary areas, where both freshwater and salt water are present, you must have both licenses. Bait shops sell licenses and can provide local information. An excellent guide featuring hot spots, maps, and insider tips is Kris Thoemke's *Fishing Florida.*

Florida has a DUI law for boaters. If you are suspected of drinking alcohol while operating a boat—unwise anyway, what with currents and channels to reckon with, speed zones to observe, and passengers to bring home safely—you may have to take a field sobriety test. You can be arrested, and your boat can be confiscated.

If you think you have legally landed a record fish, ask your local bait shop where to find the nearest certified scale and marine biologist to certify your record. But keep your finned beauty breathing, so you can release it later.

ravine of the spring-fed stream called Gold Head Branch, 3 miles of the Florida National Scenic Trail, and 2,100 rolling acres in which to roam! Deer are abundant, and you may also see burrowing gopher tortoises and fox squirrels, which have longer, bushier tails than other kinds of squirrels. In the summer, look in the tree branches for the summer tanager, a scarlet beauty that nests here and likes to east wasps.

Location: West of the St. Johns River and about 26 miles southwest of the Jacksonville suburb of Orange Park, just off State Road 21.

Important information: For reservations and more information, call 352-474-4701 or visit <www.dep.state.fl.us/parks>.

29. Ravine State Gardens

Visit one of Florida's prettiest picnic parks in a ravine of the St. Johns River that is lush with oaks, magnolias, and sweetgums. Bananas, jasmine, camellias, and azaleas are among the species planted here by the Civilian Conservation Corps. The floral display, especially in March and April, is abundant. You can ride your bike, walk, or drive along a 1.8-mile paved loop around the 80-acre gardens. This is an exceptionally scenic park and an unusual ravine setting in a state that's primarily flat.

Location: About 35 miles south of Jacksonville in Palatka at 1600 Twigg Street.

Important information: For more information, call 904-329-3721 or visit <www.dep.state.fl.us/parks> or <www.putnam.special/net/chamber>.

30. National Fish Hatchery

Two Florida saltwater species that swim miles up freshwater streams to spawn—shad and the nearly depleted sturgeon—are raised here in hopes of replenishing their populations. Other fish, such as striped bass, are also hatched here. Exhibits tell about the strong upstream swimmers that make the change from salt water to fresh, about declining fish populations, and about the federal effort to save them. Visit the aquarium, where there are also snakes, frogs, and other reptiles and amphibians on display.

About 3 miles south of this headquarters site, a second hatchery area, Beecher Unit, is fed by Beecher Springs. It has an observation tower, the 0.75-mile Beecher Springs Nature Trail, and a picnic area where you might see wild turkeys, rabbits, and river otters. The hatchery is an informative roadside stop, especially appealing if you have ever cast a line. No fishing allowed!

Location: From Welaka, about 50 miles south of Jacksonville, follow State Road 309 south to the main hatchery and aquarium, which straddle the road. The Beecher Unit is also on SR 309, about 3 miles farther south.

Important information: Free. The aquarium and visitor center are open from 7 A.M. to 4 P.M. daily. The hatchery office, where you are welcome to stop and ask questions, is open from 7 A.M. to 4 P.M. Mondays through Fridays. There are restrooms. As you walk around the fishponds, hold on to little hands because the water is deep. For more information or to arrange group tours, call 904-467-2374 or visit <http.//southeast.fws.gov/welaka/>.

Miles of smiles

How far is it? That's a back-seat question you're likely to hear often in this long peninsular state that sprawls across two time zones. Here are some between-town **distances** that might help you plan your drive so your trip is made up of miles of smiles.

As you drive through Florida, think like a scout and be prepared. Refuel before your gas gauge gets too low, and always buckle up! Florida requires car safety seats for little ones under age 4 and for children weighing less than 40 pounds. Check with your car rental company if you need one. If you've arrived in your own car without them, make your first stop a department store to buy one. The number to call to report highway accidents is 911.

Pensacola to Key West	793 miles
Tallahassee to Miami	487 miles
Jacksonville to Pensacola	354 miles
Jacksonville to St. Augustine	38 miles
St. Augustine to Gainesville	73 miles
Daytona Beach to Miami	257 miles
Cocoa Beach to Palm Beach	86 miles
Pensacola to Tampa	424 miles
Orlando to Miami	230 miles
Orlando to Jacksonville	135 miles
Orlando to Tallahassee	245 miles
Jacksonville to Fort Lauderdale	318 miles
Tampa to Naples	156 miles
Sarasota to Miami	214 miles

St. Augustine Area

St. Augustine is the nation's oldest continuously occupied European settlement; Spaniards first settled here in 1565. Before that, the site was the homeland of Native Americans for 10,000 years. It also is the site of the nation's first free black community. Today, St. Augustine remembers its heritage with an ancient castle fort, narrow Spanish-style streets, and vest-pocket parks.

St. Augustine was a winter resort in the 1890s, with tourists arriving overland by stagecoach and then up the St. Johns River by steamboat. Later, people came by railroad. Today, about two million people visit each year, and they throng the narrow streets of the historic district. To avoid wasting your time driving and trying to find a rare parking place, select lodging within walking distance of the historic district. All attractions will be crowded in the summer and on weekends and holidays, so bring a book to read in line.

Some fall and spring weekdays are less crowded, although even then St. Augustine is a popular vacation town.

If you are staying here a couple of days, take an orientation tour, such as a horse-and-buggy ride or trolley trip. These are fun ways to get a quick overview of what can at first seem to be an embarrassment of historical riches. Some tours are like private bus services, allowing frequent boarding and disembarking, so make sure that's what you're getting if you want that.

Commercial historical attractions don't have to follow state or federal research standards. In other words, there is no real Fountain of Youth, but after a couple of days in St. Augustine, it's understandable that you think there is.

If you only have time for a dash through the town, don't try to visit every old thing or you'll have a family uprising on your hands. Some top kid-pleasing sites to select from are the Spanish fort Castillo de San Marcos (a must-see attraction for every visitor), the Oldest Wooden Schoolhouse, the Spanish Quarter, the St. Augustine Lighthouse, and some of the excellent restaurants, bakeries, and shops. Then vow to return on another vacation to conquer some more.

31. Guana River State Park

This is the best and most natural beach in the area. It's wide and covered with shells, great for young specimen collectors. (Live shellfish, including starfish and sand dollars, are for leaving; the empty shell skeletons are for taking.) The 40-foot-high dunes are anchored with stately sea oats, native prickly pear cacti, and other plants. Dune boardwalks and observation towers are ideal perches from which to look for the extremely rare right whale offshore; you may spot one just beyond the surf line during its winter calving season. White pelicans sometimes visit the upland part of this park, at Guana Dam. They land in the water and communally herd fish into a group, then feed in a frenzy that's a sight to behold. The gray-and-white hawklike birds flying overhead with freshly caught fish in their talons are probably ospreys.

Location: On State Road A1A, about 13 miles north of Historic St. Augustine at 2690 South Ponte Vedra Boulevard. The three main park entrances, all on Ponte Vedra Boulevard within a few miles of each other, are the Guana Dam site on the inland or western side of the park, and the two beach areas, South Beach and North Beach. The dam site has no beach.

Important information: Open from 8 A.M. to sunset. No camping. For more information, call 904-825-5071 or visit <www.dep.state.fl.us/parks>.

Sea oats save sand at the seashore

Sea oats are more than pretty stalks of beach grass. They are defenders of the coastal zones, and it's actually illegal to pick them! Sea oats are beach pioneer plants. These pale, graceful, strawlike beauties, which sometimes grow up to 6 feet tall, anchor the beach. Their roots spread into the sand and help keep it from blowing away. Without sea oats, the dunes on Florida's beaches would quickly diminish. And dunes are not only pretty. They also act as barriers against storm tides and floods. They also shelter a world of important shorelife that a flat, denuded beach can't support.

So that's why we say sea oats save sand at the seashore. Don't walk on them, and don't dig them up or pick them. If you want to plant sea oats on beaches in your area, contact a local nursery that specializes in native species, your regional Florida Department of Environmental Protection office, or a coastal state park for resource information.

32. Carousel

In downtown St. Augustine, about a half-mile north of the historic district, the grounds of the St. Augustine public library feature a carousel. So this is a two-for-one stop. This is a popular city park and a good place to ask local families about their favorite places to see and eat.

Location: In Davenport Park at San Marcos Avenue and May Street.

Important information: Open daily from 11 A.M. to 9 P.M. during the school year and from 10 A.M. to 10 P.M. the rest of the year. For more information, call 904-823-3388.

33. St. Augustine Visitor Center

If you need directions to a specific site or want to snare some discount admission coupons, a local map, or some attraction brochures, the visitor center is the place to get oriented.

Location: At the intersection of State Road A1A, San Marco Avenue, and Castillo Drive in St. Augustine.

Important information: Open daily from 8 A.M. to 6 P.M. in the summer and from 8:30 A.M. to 5 P.M. the rest of the year. For more information, call 904-825-1000 or visit <www.oldcity.com>.

34. Castillo de San Marcos National Monument

If you can make only one stop in St. Augustine, this is it. It's free for children ages 15 and younger. Stroll over the 40-foot-wide moat via a double drawbridge and through a dark tunnel to emerge in the late 17th century. It's a compelling walk into world history. A nighttime visit when torches are lighted is even better. If you can, arrive when costumed rangers are re-enacting the 1670s, when the fort was built. They fire a cannon as they try to defend the fort against attack.

This castlelike fort, constructed from 1672 to 1695 at the mouth of the Matanzas River, is where the famed Seminole Indian war leader Osceola was imprisoned with other warriors and their wives and children in the 1830s. You'll see the actual rooms where these unfortunate Floridians lived. The fort served as a hospital and also as home to St. Augustine citizens when the town was under attack by pirates, Native Americans, the British, or others. The gun deck is a good place to imagine patrol duty of 300 years back.

This is the oldest masonry fort in the United States. It took 15 years to quarry and build the fortress from coquina rock; convicts and Timucuan Indians supplied the forced labor. When you encounter a ranger, costumed or not, ask questions: How did soldiers keep their food from spoiling? What were their favorite pastimes? How did they write home? How were they paid? And yes, you should definitely videotape or photograph your kid talking to a Spanish-costumed soldier.

Allow 1.5 hours at the very least to visit this National Park Service site and national historic landmark.

The oldest tourist?

Lovely old St. Augustine isn't the oldest community in the United States. The first named European settlement, according to historian Michael Gannon, was San Miguel de Gualdape, which was established in 1526 at a native village site in what is now Georgia. But it didn't last. The next one was Pensacola, which was settled originally in 1559; a hurricane wiped out that colony. The French set up Fort Caroline near Jacksonville in 1564, but the Spanish arrived to rout the French.

St. Augustine, founded in 1565, is the oldest continually occupied community in the country. Before the Europeans arrived, St. Augustine was a Timucuan village called Seloy, where families grew corn, collected oysters, and had parties on the beach. The Timucuans had been around for thousands of years, and so had their ancestors, who most likely migrated here from colder, snowier points north. That would make them the oldest known tourists.

Location: Just north of the Bridge of Lions in Historic St. Augustine, across from the Old City Gates at 1 Castillo Drive.

Important information: Open from 8:45 A.M. to 4:45 P.M. daily except Christmas. Children 15 and younger and seniors over 61 are admitted free; fee is $4 for all others. Call 904-829-6506 for private tour information and a schedule of the 30-minute ranger talks, special nighttime events, workshops, and re-enactments, or visit <www.nps.gov/casa>. Parking in the fort lot is very limited.

35. Spanish Quarter Museum

This is St. Augustine's first "little Williamsburg," a living-history village of seven historical or re-created buildings where candles are dipped, soap is made, wool is spun, lace is made, and wood is carved. The re-enactors are selected for their enthusiasm and ability to entertain children with lore. This is an excellent stop. Allow about two hours, but don't visit if it's raining, because many demonstrations are outside and you need to walk from building to building.

Location: In the pedestrian open-air mall of St. George Street, just a half-block south of U.S. Highway 1. Enter the museum at Triay House, 33 St. George Street.

Important information: Open daily from 9 A.M. to 4:30 P.M. Children ages 5 and younger are admitted free; fees are $4 for ages 6 to 18, $5 for seniors, and $6.50 for all others. Families are admitted for $13. For more information, call 904-825-6830.

36. Oldest Wooden Schoolhouse

Built before 1763 by Greek carpenter Juan Genopoly, this building made of red cedar and cypress and held together with wooden pegs and handmade nails appeals to the youngest scholars, who can imagine what it was like to learn arithmetic in an austere setting like this. The schoolmaster and his family also lived here, and the kitchen is out back for you to inspect. In a city of sites that can require a two- to three-hour attention span, this is a quick and fun visit.

Location: In the pedestrian mall of Historic St. Augustine at 14 St. George Street, between Orange and Cuna Streets.

Important information: Open daily from 9 A.M. to 5 P.M. Children under age 6 are admitted free; fees are $1 for ages 6 to 12, $1.50 for seniors, and $2 for all others. For more information, call 904-824-0192.

37. Oldest House

Someone's family hearth has been a tourist attraction for about 100 years, and archaeologists can show that this exact spot first became a colonial home-site sometime in the early 1600s. Visit the actual 17th-century homesite, another house dating to the 1720s, the garden, a kitchen separated from the rest of the house to minimize fire damage, and two museums, all interpreted authentically by the St. Augustine Historical Society. Make sure to see the banana trees, the cabbage palm (Florida's state tree), and the grape arbors. Children from about ages 7 to 12 enjoy this best.

Location: About 9 blocks south of the pedestrian-only mall in St. August-ine, at 271 Charlotte Street.

Important information: Open from 9 A.M. to 5 P.M. Children under age 6 are admitted free. Fees are $12 for families, $3 for students, $4.50 for se-niors, and $5 for all others.

38. Ghostly Walking Tour

This tour by lantern-light will keep everyone's attention focused on history. The spooky tales of days gone by are a family pleaser and are designed to be entertaining, not ghoulish. Take your flashlight.

Location: Meet at the Old City Gate in St. Augustine. Get exact directions when you make a reservation.

Important information: The tour begins at 8 P.M. It's free for children un-der age 6 with an adult, $6 otherwise. For more information, call 888-461-1009.

39. Mission of Nombre de Dios Park

In a city of old sites, this is said to be the oldest. It may be part of the Timucuan village site called Seloy, where in 1565 a Spanish priest said a mass for Pedro Menendez de Aviles, the admiral credited with founding St. Augustine. Menendez named it after the saint because he first sighted the coast of Florida on the saint's feast day. The Spaniard is infamous for his massacre of French Protestant Huguenots south of here, an event that lives on in the name Matanzas, or Massacre, River. The first mass site is marked with a large cross in a peaceful park, and it's one of the most visited historical sites in the city. This shrine is a quiet change of pace. Near the park, at the end of Myrtle Avenue, an ancient oak tree known as the Senator spreads its branches to create some welcome shade.

Location: On Old Mission Avenue, just north of Castillo Drive off San Marcos Avenue in St. Augustine.

Important information: Free. For more information, call 904-824-2809.

40. Fort Mose

A century before the Underground Railroad was created to spirit slaves to the North, courageous Africans and their Indian allies risked death trying to escape slavery in South Carolina by fleeing south to Florida. The Spanish freed them in exchange for their conversion to the Catholic faith and their establishment of this site as a forward defense for the Spanish in St. Augustine. Thus, in 1738, this became the first legally sanctioned town for free blacks in the nation. The village, Gracia Real de Santa Teresa de Mose, or Fort Mose (pronounced MOH-say), provided inspiration to slaves around the world.

Location: From U.S. Highway 1 north of State Road 16 in St. Augustine, take Saratoga Boulevard east.

Important information: A plaque commemorates the site, and eventually there will be more educational interpretation. For more information, call 904-461-2033 or visit <www.oldcity.com/mose>.

41. Historic Villages of St. Augustine

With a slightly different emphasis than other living-history sites in the vicinity, this historical attraction includes a re-created, pre-European Timucuan village and a Florida pioneer village of the 1800s.

Location: Inside the Old Sugar Mill Train Station at 254 San Marcos Avenue in St. Augustine.

Important information: Call 904-824-8874 or 800-797-3778 for hours and fee information.

42. Old St. Augustine Village Museum

This living-history site with ten historical buildings focuses on Florida's significant French history, not emphasized at all museums. It also features an illuminating John James Audubon exhibit in the 1839 Dow House. Audubon based himself at St. Augustine while on some of his famed Florida bird-hunting expeditions.

Location: In Historic St. Augustine at 250 St. George Street.

Important information: This historical park is new. For more information, call 904-823-9722 or visit <www.old-staug-village.com>.

43. Pizza Garden

In a district of expensive and elegant eateries with linen napkins and uptown prices, it's helpful to know about an affordable and yummy kid-pleaser that's not a fast-food franchise. Have lunch or dinner outside in the fenced-in courtyard; enjoy pizza by the slice. A hassle-free, delicious local stop.

Location: South of Cuna Street at 21 Hypolita Street in Historic St. Augustine.

Important information: For more information, call 904-471-2332.

44. Lightner Museum

Your children will find quite a few things to amaze them in this eclectic nonprofit collection of collections, so let them tarry where they like. There are mechanical musical instruments, antique toys, oddities of science from the 19th century, coral and shell collections, and real Tiffany glass windows. The elaborate, rambling 1888 Alcazar Hotel, in which the museum is housed, is listed on the National Register of Historic Places. The museum was created in 1948 by the publisher of *Hobbies* magazine, Otto C. Lightner. His diversion is a nice change of pace from the Spanish history sites and a must-see for families who've been bitten by the collecting bug.

Location: In the beautiful St. Augustine City Hall Complex at 75 King Street.

Important information: Open from 9 A.M. to 5 P.M. daily except Christmas. Children under age 12 are admitted free with an adult, whose fee is $6. For more information, call 904-824-2874.

45. St. Augustine Lighthouse and Museum

Take a hike to the top. The 219 steps of the winding staircase reward you with a dizzying view of the region. This 1871 beacon, originally lit with lard-oil lamps, is best for older kids, who are sure to have strong legs and the energy to make it to the top. Be very careful on the way down; take the narrow steps slowly. Even if you decide not to climb, the museum is enlightening. It features such items as a lightkeeper's record of a rare earthquake that shook the tower in August 1886.

Location: Across the Matanzas River from St. Augustine on Anastasia Island at 81 Lighthouse Avenue.

Important information: Open daily from 9 A.M. to 5 P.M. Children under age 7 are admitted free; fees are $2 for ages 7 to 12, $3 for seniors, and $4 for all others. For more information, call 904-829-0745 or visit <www.stauglight.com>.

46. Conch House

Your little castaways will want to climb the couple of wooden steps to the outdoor, palm-thatched dining tables at this family-friendly resort, marina, outfitter, and restaurant that features a bit of everything on its menu. The waterside huts are worth waiting for, so bring the camera for tropical photo ops. The conch (pronounced konk) is a marine snail of several varieties. The Florida fighting conch, a 3-inch light-brown univalve, and the tropical queen conch are both protected in Florida. But imported, commercially raised conch is served here in fritters.

Location: Take the Bridge of Lions across the Matanzas River to Conch Island, just west of Anastasia Island. Signs will direct you on your winding way through a residential neighborhood to 57 Comares Avenue.

Important information: This popular spot has lines on weekends and holidays. For more information, call 904-829-8646.

47. St. Augustine Alligator Farm

With a guidebook like this one in your hand, it's easy to find alligators in the wild. But attractions like this are still fun. There's a lush swamp *full* of alligators and crocodiles and snakes here. This zoo has participated in alligator research featured in *National Geographic*. At times it displays a guest reptile visiting from another zoo, such as an outrageously large croc or gator, or an albino one. I'm especially fond of this homegrown tourist attraction because it dates to 1893, when alligator claws, teeth, and heads were crafted into Victorian canes, lamps, and bric-a-brac. Their hides then were the stuff of great suitcases, like the vintage, burnished brown one here in my office, the likes of which you could only hope to find at a flea market. Purists who only like to see animals in the wild won't want to detour here, but I predict the rest of you will probably enjoy seeing a gator growl.

Location: Across the Bridge of Lions from the Historic St. Augustine on Anastasia Island. Take State Road A1A south and follow the large signs.

Important information: Open daily from 9 A.M. to 5 P.M. Children under age 3 are admitted free; fees are $6.95 for ages 3 to 10 and $10.95 for all others. For more information, call 904-824-3337.

48. Anastasia State Recreation Area

Sleep in the coastal scrub forest among secluded, windswept live oaks and red cedars at this popular beach park. There are 4 miles of Atlantic Ocean beach, a picnic area, a nature trail, and ranger-led programs. Shelling can be good here. You can rent canoes for meandering in the saltwater lagoon.

Location: At St. Augustine Beach, via State Road A1A to SR 3. The park is at the dead end of SR 3.

Important information: For more information, call 904-461-2033 or visit <www.dep.state.fl.us/parks>.

49. Saltwater Cowboys

Here's a casual eatery with local flavor. It perches over a tidal marsh, feels like a friendly fish camp, and is graced with beautiful live oaks. You can order frog legs, gator bites, and key lime pie here, as well as chicken, barbecue, and seafood.

Location: South of St. Augustine Beach off State Road A1A. Turn west off SR A1A at the large restaurant sign at Dondanville Road. Cowboys is at the end of the road at 299 Dondanville Road.

Important information: Open for lunch and dinner. There are lines on weekends and often on weekdays at dinnertime. Try lunch. For more information, call 904-471-2332.

50. Fort Matanzas National Monument

Ride a small National Park Service ferry across an inlet and then climb into the actual watchtower built by the Spanish in the 1740s as a southern defense against pirates, the British, and all other attackers who might be approaching their colonial stronghold at St. Augustine. The name *matanzas* means massacre and comes from the bloody executions of Protestant French Huguenots that Spanish soldiers conducted here in 1565. Kids enjoy the ranger-led ferry ride to and from the watchtower on Rattlesnake Island.

Location: Drive about 10 miles south of St. Augustine Beach via State Road A1A to the park at 8634 State Road A1A.

Important information: Free. For more information, call 904-471-0116 or visit <www.nps.gov/parkslist/fl.html>.

51. Faver-Dykes State Park

This public campground is a woodsy place to stay and a scenic camping option for St. Augustine visitors who can't get a site at Anastasia State Recreation Area. You'll see deer and possibly wild turkeys. Other residents include bobcats and river otters. The park encompasses 1,449 acres on Pellicer Creek, an aquatic preserve.

Location: Drive about 13 miles south of St. Augustine on U.S. Highway 1 to its intersection with Interstate 95.

Important information: For campsite reservations or more information, call 904-794-0997 or visit <www.dep.state.fl.us/parks>.

Flagler Beach Area

It's a wonder this casual beach community with its houses perched on stilts isn't more widely known. Since most of the development is across State Road A1A from the beach, there's an uninterrupted vista for coastal drivers and beach strollers. Flagler Beach is one of several quiet coastal enclaves south of St. Augustine from which you can view stunning sunrises over the Atlantic Ocean.

52. Marineland

A bit off course for the SeaWorld/Walt Disney World crowd, this marine attraction made a splash in 1938 with the first porpoise show in the nation. The pastel Art Deco architecture alone is worth a look. Marineland is listed on the National Register of Historic Places. Although it's small by today's standards, that makes it a breeze to see the whole boatload of marine mammal shows. I met my own Flipper here as a child visiting from New Jersey in the early 1960s. Thirty years later, my daughter Anna giggled often here in her toddler years. A brand-new dolphin encounter program will thrill your animal-crazy kids.

Location: The attraction straddles State Road A1A about 12 miles south of St. Augustine.

Important information: Open Wednesdays through Sundays. Call 904-460-1275 for more information, or visit <www.marineland.net>.

53. Washington Oaks Gardens State Park

Pause for a picnic beside the Matanzas River or look for crabs in the tidepools of the park's Atlantic Ocean Unit. You'll leave refreshed after touring the gardens and spring-fed pond, which were part of a mid-1800s pioneer homestead. This secluded spot, like much of this area, seems like a state secret.

Location: From Flagler Beach, drive north about 7 miles on State Road A1A to 6400 North Oceanshore Boulevard (the local name for SR A1A).

Important information: Open daily from 8 A.M. to sundown. Admission is $3.25 per car, and the parking lot at the beach unit is frequently checked for windshield display of payment ticket. For more information, call 904-446-6780 or visit <www.dep.state.fl.us/parks>.

54. Gamble Rogers Memorial State Recreation Area

The sound of the surf and the golden glow of sunrise over the Atlantic Ocean will greet you every morning at this dunes campground retreat. This is also a super place for picnicking and beachcombing. But think twice about swimming. Strong rip tides and undertows frequently rule here, especially after storms. A beloved Florida troubadour, Gamble Rogers, gave his life rescuing a young man in the surf here.

Location: From Flagler Beach, drive about 2.5 miles south on State Road A1A.

Important information: Open daily from 8 A.M. to sunset. Entrance fee is $3.25. For more information, call 904-517-2086 or visit <www.dep.state.fl.us/parks>.

EAST-CENTRAL REGION

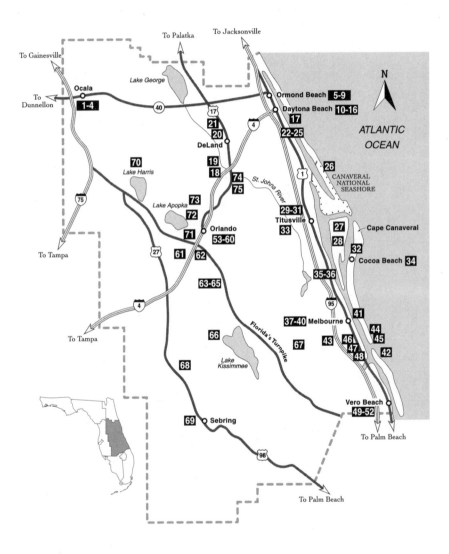

To Palatka
To Jacksonville
To Gainesville
Lake George
To Dunnellon
Ocala
To
1-4
40
17
21
20
DeLand
19
18
70
Lake Harris
74
75
St. Johns River
73
Lake Apopka
72
71
Orlando
53-60
61
62
27
63-65
4
To Tampa
66
67
68
Lake Kissimmee
Florida's Turnpike
69
Sebring
98

Ormond Beach 5-9
Daytona Beach 10-16
17
22-25
N
ATLANTIC OCEAN
26
CANAVERAL NATIONAL SEASHORE
1
29-31
33
Titusville
27
28
32
Cape Canaveral
Cocoa Beach 34
35-36
95
41
37-40 Melbourne
43
44
45
46
47
48
42
Vero Beach
49-52
To Palm Beach
To Palm Beach
75
27
4
To Tampa

East-Central
Region

East-Central Florida is world-famous for Cape Canaveral, where Kennedy Space Center is located. Kids delight in watching shuttle rockets hurtle into space. If you plan ahead, your children might not only see a launch. They also may be able to attend space camp. Even if such special events aren't part of your visit, children are still awed by the towering rockets and many NASA exhibits, as well as other out-of-this-world attractions.

Kennedy Space Center is surrounded by nature preserves, such as a national seashore that shelters endangered manatees and roseate spoonbills. You'll find beaches with high dunes and great fishing opportunities. So you don't have to jettison a palmy, paradise-type vacation to please your young astronauts.

Heritage flavors the region, too. It's quite a goose-bumpy feeling to realize that the site where rockets blast into space is in the same locale where Spanish explorer Ponce de Leon paused offshore in 1513. It was while he was in this region of the New World that he named Florida.

Elsewhere in the lush East-Central Region, a national forest harbors clear springs and black bears. A state park shelters a spring known by school children nationwide who "adopt" members of its winter manatee herd. And there's a state park with a campground on a river island that is an ancient native campsite; you can reach it by ranger-run ferry.

The bustling Orlando area is famous for being the home of Walt Disney World and SeaWorld. But you can also explore the area's state parks, nature preserves, and an excellent science museum. Farther south, you can visit a zoo or check out the swimming beaches along the Atlantic Coast. In fact, swimming, surfing, surf casting, and beach walking are among the region's constant pastimes. Environmental centers will challenge young minds, and historic sites and museums—including the ruins of an early 19th-century sugar mill and ancient Indian mounds—will appeal to a young person's sense of wonder.

The East-Central's coastal areas, from Ormond Beach to Vero Beach, have stretches with little development and are dotted with marshy inlets and sounds and other important wetlands. Indian River Lagoon, an estuary that shelters about one-third of Florida's manatees, flows here. The nation's first wildlife refuge, Pelican Island, can be reached by boat from an oceanfront state park. This stretch of sandy coast and the barrier islands have yielded great pirate and sailor lore. Gold from Spanish shipwrecks glitters in coastal museums.

In the East-Central interior, south of Orlando, vast agricultural lands dominate. You can tour one historical working cattle ranch that is also a wildlife wonderland of caracaras, sandhill cranes, and bobcats. You can also visit a state park where rangers dress and talk like old-time cow hunters who've just come in from riding through the palmetto thickets. Traditionally, Floridians called their wranglers cow hunters and not cowboys because they had to search so hard to find their free-ranging cattle in the swamps and thick forests.

Public campgrounds on the coast, some with campsites almost on the beach, are popular homes away from home. Blue Springs, an inland manatee park in a lush setting of live oaks, offers a campground and rustic cottages. Another lodging option is resorts that arrange nature excursions, such as the oceanfront Disney Vero Beach Resort and the riverfront Refuge at Ocklawaha. The latter is run jointly by the Audubon Society and the National Wildlife Federation. You might also try family-friendly lodging at Tropical Palms in Kissimmee; Sunspree Resort at Lake Buena Vista; Sun Viking Lodge, Perry's Ocean Edge, Beacon by the Sea, Anchorage Suites, Palm Circle Villas, and Pierside Inn, all in Daytona Beach; Coral Sands Inn in Ormond Beach; Islander in New Smyrna Beach; Indian River Bed & Breakfast in Titusville; Surf Studio in Cocoa Beach; Melbourne Harbor Suites in historic downtown Melbourne; Harbor Light Inn Resort in Fort Pierce; Sandpiper Club Med Family Resort in Port St. Lucie; and Driftwood Inn and Disney Vero Beach Resort, both at Vero Beach.

For more information contact:

- Central Florida Visitors and Convention Bureau
  800-828-7655
  <www.sunsational.org>
- Cocoa Beach Visitor Information
  321-459-2200
  <www.cocoabeachchamber.com>
- Daytona Beach Visitor Information
  904-255-0415
  <www.daytonabeach.com>
- DeLand/West Volusia Visitors Bureau
  800-749-4350
  <www.naturalflorida.org>
- Florida's Space Coast Office of Tourism
  800-872-1969
  <www.space-coast.com>
- Kissimmee/St. Cloud Chamber of Commerce
  800-327-9159
  <www.floridakiss.com>
- Lakeland Area Chamber of Commerce
  863-688-8551
  <www.lakeland.net/chamber>

- Melbourne Chamber of Commerce
  800-771-9922
  <www.melpb-chamber.org>
- New Smyrna Beach Resort Information
  800-541-9621
  <www.newsmyrnabeachonline.com>
- Ocala/Marion County Chamber of Commerce
  352-629-8051
  <www.ocalacc.com>
- Orlando/Orange County Visitors Bureau
  800-551-0181, 407-363-5872
  <www.go2orlando.com>
- St. Lucie County Tourism
  888-785-8243
  <www.st.lucieco.gov>
- Sanford/Seminole Chamber of Commerce
  407-322-2212
  <www.sanfordchamber.com>
- Titusville Area Chamber of Commerce
  321-267-3036
  <www.spacecityflusa.com/>
- Vero Beach/Indian River County Chamber of Commerce
  800-338-2678
  <www.vero-beach.fl.us/chamber>
- West Volusia Visitors Information
  800-749-4350
  <www.naturalflorida.org>

Ocala Area

The Ocala area is a green inland region known for its rolling meadows and white horse barns. It is equally renowned for a national forest where black bears roam and for springs that have been attracting tourists since the 1800s, when they arrived by stagecoach and steamboat.

1. Horse Farm Tours

Young equestrians sometimes daydream of owning a horse farm, and they'll have plenty to fantasize about here; there are hundreds of them nearby. At least five Kentucky Derby winners were raised in the Ocala area. Other barns, some air-conditioned, are palaces for elegant Arabians and sturdy draft horses. Drop-in visitors aren't welcome at these competitive operations, part of a $4 million industry. But you can reserve a spot on a two-hour tour sponsored by the Florida Thoroughbred Breeders' Association. Your dedicated riders will like it. Tally ho!

Location: You'll be told where to meet when you make reservations.

Important information: For more information and reservations, call the Florida Thoroughbred Breeders' Association at 352-629-2160.

2. Silver River State Park

Pause at this picnic place, which features a small pioneer village and an environmental education center that presents information about animals and plants from the 14 different habitats represented in the park. You can rent a canoe to glide along the crystal-clear Silver River, which runs through the park. The 2,300 acres are laced with nature paths and springs.

A dark future for Florida's black bears?

Once upon a time in Florida, **black bears** roamed the shores in summer to paw through the sand and dig up sea-turtle nests. Imagine the messy sight they made, as they slurped a slimy meal of turtle eggs.

There are no longer any bears on the Florida coast. Very few visitors or Floridians will ever see a wild one. The animals are hidden in Florida's pinewoods and cypress swamps, where they like to dine on acorns, berries, swamp cabbages, wild honeycombs, and occasionally small animals.

Florida's black bears are quite threatened. At one time, there were perhaps 12,000 in Florida, Georgia, and Alabama. Only about 1,500 to 2,000 remain today. The species has declined due to highway accidents, poaching, and loss of habitat. Some think the black bear is poised to go the way of the Florida panther, which is just about extinct.

Although hunting was stopped in the mid-1990s, poaching continues. There is a market in the Far East for bear paws and claws, and the accidental highway slaughter continues, killing about 80 bears each year. Short sections of select Florida roads and highways that cross known black-bear travel routes are being elevated to create foliage-buffered wildlife travel tunnels, in hopes of reducing the road kill.

For more information about the Florida Black Bear Festival, organized for the first time in 1999, call 352-735-3562 or visit <www.villagecircle.com/flbearfest/>.

Location: From State Road 40 in Silver Springs, take County Road 35 south about 1 mile to the park entrance.

Important information: Call 352-236-1827 for information and to see if plans for a campground or cabins have materialized at this relatively new state park. Or visit <www.dep.state.fl.us/parks>.

3. Ocala National Forest

• •

Two million people visit the national forest each year, a testimony to its appeal. Forest Visitor Center on State Road 40 near Forest Corners will orient you to this 430,000-acre pine forest and cypress swamp expanse, created in 1908 by President Theodore Roosevelt. There are several commercial inholdings and some intensive logging operations. But that said, it's easy to find your way to some of the 600 lakes, 23 spring-fed streams, and two major rivers. The forest shelters a unique habitat of inland sand dunes called Florida scrub, where animals and plants have adapted to parched conditions. Among the species living here, the threatened black bear is the largest mammal. Deer are abundant in the forest; raccoons accustomed to visitors' handouts are real pests. I've been lucky enough to see a bobcat chase a mouse here, fittingly enough near Bobcat Lake on SR 40.

There are seven developed campgrounds in the national forest: Salt Springs, Fore Lake, Lake Eaton, Juniper Springs, Lake Dorr, Alexander Springs, and Clearwater Lake. The campgrounds near springs are the most popular and the hardest to get into. Lines form early in the day for remaining sites; no reservations are taken. Try bedding down instead at the Lake Dorr Campground, an often-overlooked beauty at the southern end of the forest, across from a lesser-known forest visitor center, Pittman, on SR 19. Or consider Clearwater Lake Campground, southeast of Lake Dorr and equally scenic.

From these forest bases, take day visits to the overflowing springs campgrounds to enjoy picnics, swimming, canoeing, and woodland walks, especially on the 1.1-mile Timucuan Indian Trail, an interpreted history path at Alexander Springs. The bus tours you see leaving from the visitor centers from November through May are three hours long and informative. The buses make several stops, but children might not appreciate having to spend more time sitting still. If you take a tour, make sure to bring along kids' activities, such as a drawing pad or favorite book.

The best season to visit the national forest is from fall through spring. In the summer, the area is plagued by frequent lightning storms, excessive heat, and biting insects, although none of these keep locals from splashing in the springs.

Not your everyday backyard bird

The **Florida scrub jay** is not your everyday backyard bird. To most who finally see it, it doesn't seem like a jay at all. It has no crest or black bars, like the more flamboyant blue jay. Acorns from the scrub oak, not worms or bugs, make up its diet. It's colored a beautiful blue—as vivid as a bluebird—and has brown markings on its sides. But the most interesting thing about the scrub jay is its family life.

Scrub jays mate for life. They live communally and help raise each other's young. A baby scrub jay stays with its parents for one to six years after birth, helping to raise the new young and watching out for predators. Although the species is threatened—there are perhaps 3,600 families left in the state—they can easily be seen in the open, hopping along the ground in the scrub. They can be bold about approaching people. Scrub jays are reluctant to move through the forest or over water to find new territory if their scrubland is taken over by development. They are homebodies, staying for life in a small area near their birthplace among the remnants of ancient dunes.

Audubon officials have initiated a campaign to elevate the scrub jay from obscurity by making it the state bird in place of the mockingbird, a fine-feathered friend but also the symbol of several other states.

Location: Forest Visitor Center and Bookstore is on SR 40 near Silver Springs, about 15 miles east of Interstate 75 at 10863 East Highway 40. The Pittman Visitor Center near Lake Dorr Campground is at 45621 SR 19.

Important information: Forest Visitor Center is open from 9 A.M. to 5 P.M. daily; Pittman is open from 9 A.M. to 4:30 P.M. Tickets for the bus tours conducted by the Ocala National Forest Interpretive Association are $3. For more information, call Forest Visitor Center at 352-236-0288, or Pittman Visitor Center at 352-669-7495, or visit <www.fs.fed.us>.

4. Refuge at Ocklawaha

Imagine bringing your family deep into forested wildlands where black bears and bobcats roam and eagles soar—yet retiring each evening to cozy beds, fresh-cooked meals, and sparkling-clean bathrooms. The Refuge at Ocklawaha, a riverfront ecotourism resort at the edge of the Ocala National Forest, offers this appealing combination. It also offers canoeing, horseback riding, bicycling, and programs on such subjects as wildflower identification and tips on how to transform suburban yards into wildlife habitats. At night, a blanket of stars glistens overhead with no bright lights to dim their luster. A frog chorus fills the night with song, competing only with the voices of guests and an occasional guitar.

Lodging is in cabins, some recycled from the property's colorful days as a ranch, others built to resort specifications. The resort is self-sustaining whenever possible, generating some of its own electricity, for example. The Audubon Society and the National Wildlife Federation are involved and so is a successful developer of environment-friendly resorts in the Virgin Islands.

Location: Get detailed directions when you make your reservation. The resort is east of Ocala via State Road 40 and County Road 314A.

Important information: For more information, including schedules of family and student programs, call 352-288-2233 or 877-862-8873 or visit <www.flrefuge.com>.

Ormond Beach Area

This coastal community in the northeastern corner of the East-Central Region is a low-key retirement mecca. Children build sandcastles on the beach with their grandparents. Unlike Daytona Beach next door, Ormond Beach prohibits all driving on the beaches, so families often detour here from Daytona for a more peaceful beach experience. A riverfront state park sits on the former site of an Indian village and a British sugar-cane plantation.

5. Tomoka State Park

In addition to an abundance of deer, you may see pileated woodpeckers, river otters, marsh rabbits, and alligators at this park near the confluence of the Tomoka and Halifax Rivers. This was once the site of a Timucuan Indian village and, later, a plantation. Fish were once so abundant in this region that artist John James Audubon, who traveled the Tomoka waters by boat, wrote his wife, "Would you believe, if I was to say, that the fish nearly obstructed our head-way?" A small but excellent park museum, the Fred Dana Marsh Center, interprets the rich history of the Timucuans and of the plantation established here circa 1766. The plantation owner, Richard Oswald, a wealthy Scot, grew rice and indigo here using slave labor.

Location: On the mainland in Ormond Beach, about 3 miles north of State Road 40, at 2099 North Beach Street.

Heh-heh-heh-HEH-heh

Woody Woodpecker, the cartoon character, would feel right at home among the **pileated woodpeckers** of Tomoka State Park. The pileated is the largest American woodpecker; it grows to about 17 inches tall, or about the size of a crow. Its red crest, black-and-white striped neck, and large white wing patches help to make it a striking woodland bird. Like the ivory-billed woodpecker, a larger Florida species thought to be extinct, the pileated is losing much of its old-growth woodland habitat. To find one here—a thrilling experience—listen for its loud, ringing call and for the hammering sound it makes drilling tree cavities in search of insects. Also, ask rangers about recent sightings.

Important information: Open daily from 8 A.M. to dusk. For more information, call 904-676-4050 or visit www.dep.state.fl.us/parks>. This is a popular campground with motorcyclists during the annual Bike Week festivities. Be sure to check with rangers about regional special events, so you can avoid visiting when the park is crowded and noisy. Park rangers and volunteers stage a fun living-history festival of native and plantation life the first weekend of every February.

6. Bulow Creek State Park/Fairchild Oak

Walk in the shade of this 800-year-old tree and think of the Indians and pioneers who used it as a gathering place. The tree survived the flurry of timber cutting here in the mid-1800s, when ancient live oaks like this were used to build federal warships for the Civil War. The Fairchild Oak has also triumphed over fires, disease, and the threat of development. Miami botanist David Fairchild, who wrote frequently for *National Geographic* in the 1920s about his exotic experiences traveling the world, recognized it as a rare specimen and helped local residents save it from destruction. It's now the centerpiece of Bulow Creek State Park, which preserves one of the largest remaining stands of southern live-oak forest along the eastern coast of Florida.

Location: Just north of Ormond Beach and west of Flagler Beach at 3351 Old Dixie Highway.

Important information: Free. Open daily from 8 A.M. to sunset. For more information, call 904-676-4050 or visit <www.dep.state.fl.us/parks>.

7. Bulow Plantation Ruins State Park

The coquina ruins of an 1821 sugar mill, the foundation of a plantation house, and some slave cabins are rubble with a cause, and the cause is a vivid history lesson. A scenic walking trail leads through the ruins to an interpretive center, where the dramatic story unfolds. This plantation was burned by Seminole Indians during their unsuccessful fight to continue living in this region. John Bulow, son of the plantation founder, is famous for firing a cannon at territorial militiamen who arrived to take his Indian slaves prisoner and ship them out West. John James Audubon was a guest of the plantation in 1831. This state park is an isolated yet popular spot for picnicking, fishing, and canoeing on Bulow Creek. A state canoe trail winds for 13 miles through a jungly green land.

Location: About 3 miles west of Flagler Beach and just north of Ormond Beach on County Road 2001 (Old Kings Highway).

Important information: Open daily from 8 A.M. to sunset. For more information, call 904-517-2084 or visit <www.dep.state.fl.us/parks>.

Trees with beards

Floridians become accustomed to the sight of grand live-oak trees trailing long gray beards of **Spanish moss,** but visitors are fascinated. They ask: Won't the moss smother the branches? No. What does it live on? Rain and dust. How does it get so high up in the tree? The wind carries its seeds, and the seeds fasten to the tree bark.

Spanish moss is in the pineapple family. It's not a moss or a parasite. It relies on a branch or the trunk of a tree for mechanical support, not nutrients, and so is classified as an epiphyte. Its seeds have feathery parachutes that allow them to float through the air and then grip the bark.

From spring to fall, Spanish moss has minuscule, lilylike blossoms that give off a slight fragrance at night. The Timucuans and other early Indians of the peninsula gathered Spanish moss for a variety of uses, from clothing to cushioning. A product called vegetable hair was made from cleaned and dried Spanish moss and used to stuff automobile cushions and mattresses before synthetic stuffing was developed.

Today, Spanish moss is still collected in Florida and used in flower arrangements and artwork. Many craft shops sell bags of treated Spanish moss, if you want some as a souvenir. You may want to think twice about picking clumps of it up off the ground to keep. Such clumps are appealing homes to chiggers, tiny bugs that dig into your skin and cause excessive itching. This I know from experience.

8. Ormond Memorial Gardens and Art Museum

Here's a local vest-pocket park that will encourage young imaginations to run wild. There are green glades, a manmade waterfall, several small ponds, and short winding trails that lead up and down an Indian mound. My daughter, Anna, enjoys munching a tangerine in the gazebo and watching turtles sunning in the ponds. The small, adjoining art museum is an extra treat for your well-mannered young Picassos.

Location: In Ormond Beach at 78 East Granada Boulevard.

Important information: The gardens are open daily from 8 A.M. to dusk, and admittance is free. There is a small fee to visit the art museum, which is open from 11 A.M. to 4 P.M. Tuesdays through Fridays and from noon to 4 P.M. weekends. For more information, call 904-676-3347.

9. The Casements/Granada Bridge Park

The Casements, on the Halifax River Lagoon at the foot of Granada Bridge, was once the winter home of industrialist John D. Rockefeller. Today, the Beaux Arts mansion and a small museum are open to the public and are the site of children's festivals and other events. The home was named for its tall, distinctive casement windows. The waterfront parks on either side of Granada Bridge are excellent picnic places; there is a fun playground on the east side. At dusk, marsh rabbits emerge from the tall grass to feed. Be sure to see the spring-fed waterwheel in the park.

Location: On the eastern end of Granada Bridge in Ormond Beach at 25 Riverside Drive.

Important information: Admittance is free. Tours are offered from 10 A.M. to 2:30 P.M. Mondays through Fridays and from 10 to 11:30 A.M. Saturdays. For information on special events, call 904-676-3216.

Daytona Beach Area

Daytona is widely known for its racing, and my advice is to avoid visiting when the big NASCAR, sports-car, and motorcyle events are scheduled unless you like lots of noise and crowds. Surprisingly, the London Symphony Orchestra has its summer headquarters here every other year, offering experiences that are soothing to the ears.

It's hard to imagine Daytona as the quiet, woodlands frontier community it was in the late 1800s. Today, driving and parking on some of the community's 18 miles of hard-packed sandy beach is a tradition. To ride in a car at surf's edge can be a thrill for a kid, but it can be dangerous. It's also not an environmentally responsible way to treat Mother Nature in a coastal zone where sea turtles and a host of other creatures and plants are trying to thrive.

Like Panama City Beach, the oceanside Daytona Beach strip along State Road A1A sprouts tacky tattoo emporiums and the like. Many families drawn by the legendary Daytona racing end up gravitating northward or southward to lovelier, calmer beach communities, such as Ormond Beach, Flagler Beach, South Daytona Beach, and Ponce Inlet. If your heart is set on Daytona Beach, I recommend family-friendly resorts such as Perry's Ocean Edge and the Sun Viking Lodge. You can ask local tourism officials for other recommendations.

10. Mary McLeod Bethune Home

Eleanor Roosevelt once stayed overnight at the memorabilia-filled home of Dr. Mary McLeod Bethune, who served as a special adviser on minority affairs to President Franklin D. Roosevelt. A longtime educator, Bethune founded the Daytona Educational and Industrial Training School for Negro Girls in 1904. Today, the school is known as Bethune-Cookman College, and the Bethune cottage, built in 1914 and designated a national historic landmark in 1975, is located on the college campus. Bethune was born in South Carolina to former slaves. She lived an extraordinary life, rising from extreme poverty, standing tall against severe prejudice, and facing down cross-burning racists to empower generations of students.

Location: On the mainland in Daytona Beach at 640 McLeod Bethune Boulevard.

Important information: Admission is free. For information on hours, special events, and more, call 904-255-1401 or visit <www.bethune.cookman.edu>.

11. Halifax Historical Museum

Inside this Beaux Arts–style building, built in 1910 to be a Merchants Bank, collections of everything from old Seminole Indian clothing to race-car memorabilia are ingeniously displayed. This is an engaging diversion from beach fun. Just across the street from the museum, in an attractive downtown district, is a shady waterfront park. See if your children can find a topiary tribute to Brownie, the Daytona Beach town dog.

Location: On the mainland in Daytona Beach at 252 South Beach Street, near Memorial Bridge.

Important information: Open from 10 A.M. to 4 P.M. Tuesdays through Saturdays. For more information, call 904-255-6976.

12. Downtown Daytona Beach

A leisurely stroll here feels worlds away from the oceanside strip. This appealing, mainland historic district centers on Beach Street, which is not on the beach but on the western side of the Halifax River Lagoon, just west of City Island. You'll find sidewalks shaded by palm trees, fountains, tropical flowers, a topiary tree in the shape of Brownie (who was the town dog in the 1940s), and plenty of free parking. Check out the local chocolate shop, which makes its own confections, and the local history museum, which has a surprisingly rich collection (see Site 11).

Location: Beach Street is on the mainland in Daytona Beach.

Important information: For more information, contact the Daytona Beach Area Visitors Bureau at 800-854-1234 or visit <www.daytonabeach.com>.

13. Jackie Robinson Memorial Ballpark/City Island

Across a small canal from downtown Daytona Beach sits the Jackie Robinson Memorial Ballpark, named after the hall-of-famer who played here in 1946 for the Brooklyn Dodgers farm team, the Montreal Royals. Robinson is famous for breaking the color barrier in major-league baseball and paving the way for racial integration of the sport. An engaging sculpture of Robinson with children graces the entrance to the ballpark and can be seen from the street. You can still catch a game in this beautiful park on City Island; the Chicago Cubs have an affiliate here.

Just a fly ball away to the north of the ballpark is the main branch of the Daytona Beach Public Library, which features a creative children's wing. Just west of the ballpark, a colorful farmer's market offers fresh fruit, breads, pastries, vegetables, and more every Saturday. Just across Orange Avenue is the Daytona Beach Area Visitors Bureau, which has maps and brochures of area attractions.

Location: On City Island in downtown Daytona Beach, via Memorial Bridge/ Orange Avenue.

Important information: For a schedule of games at the ballpark, call 904-257-3172. To contact the library, call 904-257-6036. The visitor center is at 800-854-1234.

14. A tiny Cruise Line

"A tiny Cruise Line" offers a breezy ride along the Intracoastal Waterway, ideal for young mates who'll delight in taking the wheel if offered the chance. Meet the enthusiastic captain at the Halifax Harbor Marina for this narrated tour. You may see dolphins. The small boat has a red-and-white-striped awning and is built to resemble an 1890s launch.

Location: In Daytona Beach at Halifax Harbor Marina, 425 South Beach Street.

Important information: To make a reservation or for more information, call 904-226-2343 or visit <www.visitdaytona.com/tinycruise>.

15. Avalon Historical Canoe Tours

This outfitter will guide you on fascinating canoe or kayak history tours.

Location: In Port Orange at 5438 Dubois Avenue.

Important information: For reservations and more information, call 800-929-9854 or 904-322-5352 or visit <www.avaloncanoetours.com>.

16. Museum of Arts and Sciences/Planetarium

Children are very welcome in this small but excellent museum. It features African, Cuban, Chinese, and American art collections along with a hands-on, natural history area that focuses on fossils. The big draw for kids is the skeleton of a 13-foot-long sloth that roamed the Daytona area 130,000 years ago. It's the most complete skeleton of its kind ever found. The Cuban collection is historic for several reasons. Cuban dictator Fulgencio Batista, who used to vacation in Daytona Beach and fled here in 1959, assembled the group of exquisite oils and other artwork. This important collection now attracts expatriate families for a nostalgic look at their heritage. All in all, this is an ideal place to introduce children to art appreciation. And the natural history wing features drawers full of objects that children are encouraged to open and explore. The museum's Center for Florida History is a lively and

Ladies and gentlemen, stop your engines!

● ●

With a lighthouse, an ancient Indian shell mound, a scenic downtown shopping district, an engaging science and art museum, a fascinating creek preserve, tidal salt marshes, a river lagoon, and famous beaches, the **Daytona Beach** area has enormous potential as an ecotourism destination for families. But there are numerous events held here that many families may wish to avoid. An annual motorcycle festival is one of them. It attracts speeding, noisy, drunken motorcycle revelry to the region. Beer-drunk college students on spring breaks are another reality. You can easily avoid the midnight riders and the spring breakers by checking with tourism officials to learn the dates of such events, which vary from year to year.

Beach driving presents a more difficult challenge. Almost every visiting family I know is flabbergasted when, at low tide, two lanes of rolling automobile traffic separate families relaxing on beach blankets on the sand from the water's edge. To me, it's like inviting cars to drive through a sandlot playground. Parents must stay on constant guard to make sure their wee one hasn't wandered into traffic. It's definitely not relaxing. And it's not conducive to marine health, what with the exhaust fumes and leaking oil. Banning cars from the beaches would allow sea oats to spread and dunes to grow, creating the kind of wild beaches where sea turtles choose to lay their eggs.

To cater to families looking for a more sedate vacation, some beaches are now closed to cars. When making reservations, ask whether your cottage or resort is in a car-free beach zone.

interactive invitation to learn vivid stories of the peninsula's past. The planetarium offers a chance to rest weary little feet and travel to the stars. Given its lush grounds and frequent special events, this museum can easily become a half-day adventure.

Location: On the mainland in Daytona Beach, go about two blocks south of U.S. Highway 92 to 1040 Museum Boulevard.

Important information: Open from 9 A.M. to 4 P.M. Tuesdays through Fridays and from noon to 5 P.M. Saturdays and Sundays. Children under age 6 are admitted free; fees are $1 for children 6 and older and $4 for adults. Admission to the planetarium is $2, and shows are offered at 2 P.M. Tuesdays through Fridays and at 1 and 3 P.M. Saturdays and Sundays. Call 904-255-0285 for information on special events or visit <www.moas.org>.

17. Ponce de Leon Inlet Lighthouse and Museum

Older children will want to climb all 203 spiraling steps to the top of this red-orange working lighthouse built in 1887. From the top, you can see south to Kennedy Space Center and its giant Vehicle Assembly Building. Younger children may find the climb too strenuous and could have trouble keeping their balance on the dizzying walk back down. Family members who don't take the sky-high hike will stay busy on the ground touring the seven museum buildings, including the lightkeeper's restored house. The cats that prowl the tidy grounds are believed to bring good luck. This is a fine picnic place, and there's a small, shady playground next door. The fishing docks in the village of Ponce Inlet, where charter boats return with the day's catch before dusk, are just west of the lighthouse across a narrow street. This is a place to stay and explore.

Location: At the southern tip of the Halifax peninsula, about 3 miles south of Daytona Beach, at 4931 South Peninsula Drive in the village of Ponce Inlet.

Important information: Open daily from 10 A.M. to 8 P.M. Fees are $1 for children and $4 for adults. For more information, call 904-761-1821 or visit <www.ponceinlet.org>.

18. Blue Spring State Park

Just 30 minutes west of Daytona Beach lies one of the nation's most popular manatee-viewing sites: Blue Spring State Park. From about November through March, the slow-moving gray mammals leave the colder waters of St. Johns River and congregate in the more comfortable 72-degree F spring. Visitors travel here from around the world to peer into the clear waters at the plant-munching manatees.

This lovely state park among the pines features a visitor center built in the 19th century, a half-mile boardwalk with overlooks along the spring run, and nature trails. In the summer, swimming is allowed and the park becomes a busy splashing place. A campground and six well-equipped cabins help make the park a family destination anytime.

Location: From U.S. Highway 17/92 in Orange City, about 22 miles southwest of Daytona Beach, follow the small, brown state park signs and drive west on French Avenue for about 3 miles. The park entrance is at 2100 West French Avenue.

The Save the Manatee Club

Preventing the extinction of the endangered manatee is what the **Save the Manatee Club** is all about. One way the nonprofit organization, founded in 1981 by singer/writer Jimmy Buffett, tries to achieve this is through manatee "adoptions," which are popular with school students nationwide. Manatees return each winter to the same feeding grounds, where individual animals are named and photographed. For a donation, a classroom or family can adopt one.

About 150 to 200 manatees are killed each year in Florida waters, usually as a result of collisions with boats. It takes three to five years for a female manatee to reproduce. Today, there are only about 2,500 of these wrinkly relatives of elephants left. The mammals are easily weakened by infections, especially those that set in after they've been gashed by a boat propeller. Sometimes the gash itself is enough to kill the manatee. Boating deaths continue to happen despite the fact that the entire state is a manatee sanctuary. As "no-prop" and "no-wake" zones are established and as reduced-speed zones are introduced where manatees are known to congregate, there should be fewer accidents.

To report an injured manatee, call 800-342-5367. You can also get more information about the animals at <www.state.fl.us/fwcc/psm>. You can contact the Save the Manatee Club, which Buffett remains active in, at 407-539-0990 or 800-432-5046 (outside the state) or <www.savethemanatee.org>.

Important information: Open daily from 8 A.M. to dusk. Programs about the manatee are held at 1:30, 2:30, and 3:30 P.M. Mondays through Fridays; there is an additional program at 11 A.M. Saturdays. On winter weekends, the park reaches capacity by noon. For more information, call 904-775-3663 or visit <www.dep.state.fl.us/parks>.

19. Hontoon Island State Park

It's fun to imagine yourself transported back in time 1,200 years to when the Timucuan Indians hunted here on Hontoon Island. They left behind wooden carvings of animals, including a striking owl totem pole, a replica of which stands here while the original is preserved elsewhere. To reach this 1,650-acre marshy island park in the St. Johns River, you must take a ferry. Near the dock are a visitor center, boatslips, a small store, a picnic area, a playground, a campground, and primitive cabins (without kitchens, heat, or bathrooms). The rest of the island is largely a tangled wilderness of live oaks traversed by a nature trail that leads to a giant Indian mound. In wet weather, the path is sometimes boggy or even flooded in patches. If your family likes to rough it without forsaking all comforts, this is a memorable overnight destination. Otherwise, it makes a great day trip and picnic place.

Location: From DeLand, take State Road 44 west and then south for about 6 miles to Old New York Road. Turn onto Old New York Road and then turn south onto Hontoon Road. Follow it as it winds around a verdant residential neighborhood. Just when you think you're lost, you'll see an empty lot along the St. Johns River. The island is directly across the water.

Important information: You can only reach the island by private boat or small park ferry. Some campers arrive in their own boat and spend the night onboard. Rangers take visitors to the island about every 15 minutes, so sit tight until the ferry returns. For camping or cabin reservations or for more information, call 904-736-5309 or visit <www.dep.state.fl.us/parks>.

20. De Leon Springs State Recreation Area

This woodland spring sends forth 19 million gallons of water a day; it collects behind concrete walls to create a swimming area that's busy in the summer. Year-round, people drive here to claim a table in the park's rustic Old Spanish Sugar Mill Grill and Griddle House. Part of the appeal, especially for kids, is that each table has a griddle in the center on which you make your own pancake breakfast. There are lines at the restaurant on weekends, especially Sundays.

Ponce de Leon never visited here, so Spring Garden, the name early naturalists William Bartram and John James Audubon used for this site, is more fitting. De Leon Springs connects to Lake Woodruff, which the St. Johns River flows through. Bartram was enchanted with this place and remarked upon the fish flashing in the spring boil.

Location: At the corner of Ponce de Leon Boulevard and Burt Parks Road in De Leon Springs, next to the Lake Woodruff National Wildlife Refuge.

Important information: Open from 8 A.M. to sunset weekdays and from 9 A.M. to sunset weekends. For more park information, call 904-985-4212 or visit <www.dep.state.fl.us/parks>. The restaurant closes at 4 P.M. For more restaurant information, call 904-985-5644.

21. Pioneer Settlement for the Creative Arts

If this 19th-century village has a special event scheduled during your stay, that's the best time to stop by and see old-fashioned chores being done at the blacksmith shop, woodwright's shop, and barn. The resident peacocks are entertaining, and storytelling events here are a hoot. The old schoolhouse is a small historical museum.

Location: From DeLand, drive 15 miles northwest on U.S. Highway 17 to its intersection with State Road 40. The village is about one block west of the intersection, on the south side of SR 40 in Barberville.

Important information: Open from 9 A.M. to 3 P.M. Mondays through Fridays and from 9 A.M. to 1 P.M. Saturdays. The best time to visit is during an event or festival. Children ages 4 and younger are admitted free; fees are $1.50 for children ages 5 to 12 and $2.50 for all others. For more information, including a schedule of special events, call 904-749-2959 or visit <www.driveflorida.com/pioneersettlement>.

22. Sugar Mill Gardens

This 12-acre site, the ruins of what was once a British sugar plantation, has a surprise for young ones, because the nature footpath leads a short way to concrete dinosaurs. In 1946, this garden site acquired a stegosaurus, a triceratops, and other giant outdoor sculptures to become a homegrown theme park called Bongoland. Today, the lush, forested setting and a couple of remaining 30-foot-tall dinosaurs make this a fun place to stop and stretch your legs. The workings of the old sugar-boiling pot and sugar house are explained.

Location: In Port Orange, about 1 mile west of U.S. Highway 1 at 950 Old Sugar Mill Road.

Important information: Free. Open daily from dawn to dusk. For more information, call 904-767-1735.

23. Spruce Creek Park

Overlooking the marshy north bank of Spruce Creek, this playground and picnic place features a boardwalk that winds through the marsh. The park is also a regional public campground and a scenic wayside stop.

Location: On the mainland, south of Daytona Beach off U.S. Highway 1, just after State Road 5A.

Important information: For more information, call 904-322-5133.

24. Spruce Creek Preserve/Snow White Cottage

The James Gamble family created a quiet winter retreat in the woods on Spruce Creek in 1907. This 150-acre preserve features a tiny log cottage built in 1940, a model for the home occupied by Snow White and the seven dwarves in the original Disney movie. Walt Disney was a family friend of the Gambles.

Location: In Port Orange.

Important information: Visitors to the preserve must make reservations for one of the guided tours, which are offered Wednesdays and Saturdays. Call 904-255-0285 for tour times, reservations, and directions.

25. Harris House/New Smyrna Beach Downtown

Something artsy and intriguing is always happening at Harris House, an outreach gallery, workshop, and gift shop (with creative toys) for the nearby Atlantic Center for the Arts, a nonprofit artists' collaborative. The ongoing children's programs at Harris House might include mobile making, children's theater, and storytelling. At Old Fort Park, a few blocks to the north on Riverside Drive, you can learn the early history of this British outpost. Across the street from Harris House, shady Riverfront Park on Indian River Lagoon features a long waterfront promenade and one of the region's most creative playgrounds. The site of frequent art festivals, including one featuring children's art, the park is adjacent to the New Smyrna Beach Public Library.

Location: Harris House is at 214 South Riverside Drive in New Smyrna Beach, south of Daytona Beach.

Important information: Harris House is open from 10 A.M. to 4 P.M. Mondays through Saturdays. For more information, call 904-423-1753 or visit <www.atlantic-centerarts.org> or <www.newsmyrnabeachonline.com>.

Space Coast

If your family picks only one part of Florida to visit on its first trip to the state, make it this one. Here, you can combine beach play, hands-on lessons on the magic of space travel, and the study of 8,000-year-old artifacts and pirate heritage. You can fish, see manatees, collect seashells, and watch birds.

Historians say this point on the Atlantic coast is where Ponce de Leon, the first known European to explore what is now Florida, landed his expedition in 1513. Now, at this same location, the world watches a select group of modern explorers blast off in fiery rockets launched from Kennedy Space Center on Cape Canaveral. The massive space center is a crossroads for visitors and dignitaries from around the world who throng here seven days a week to watch launches from the sandy beaches. Ponce de Leon didn't know what he was launching!

26. Canaveral National Seashore, North Unit/ Turtle Mound Historic Site

The longest stretch of wild beach on the eastern coast of Florida—24 miles long—begins here in the northern unit of Canaveral National Seashore. The shoreline is steep and the sea here is known for its strong currents, so keep little swimmers splashing near the water's edge. Shelling is often good. The boardwalks over the dunes protect the 20-foot-high sand hills and, from December through March, are good observation points from which to scan beyond the surf line for rare right whales. In the summer, sea turtles crawl onshore at night to dig holes and lay eggs in nests that park rangers protect with fences. The rangers lead memorable night walks during which you might get a glimpse of the turtles giving birth. Egg-stealing raccoons are frequently seen here, even during the day, as are occasional armadillos. Late in the summer, your beachcombers may catch sight of a tiny hatchling turtle as it struggles during the day to shove off into the water.

On the side of the preserve facing Mosquito Lagoon, there are hiking paths to historic spots and a small visitor center. The lagoon is a prized estuary, or fish nursery, sheltering crabs, shrimp, and many other marine species. Turtle Mound Historic Site features a 50-foot-tall, centuries-old shell mound—one of about 100 Indian mounds scattered throughout the 57,000-acre national seashore. It was created by the Ais Indians, who lived here until about 600 years ago.

The northern unit of Cape Canaveral National Seashore gets fewer visitors than the southern unit, but it still reaches capacity on summer weekends and holidays. On winter weekdays, the beach can feel very isolated. The Audubon Society named this one of the ten best seashores in the country.

Location: South of New Smyrna Beach at the end of State Road A1A, at 7611 South Atlantic Avenue.

Important information: Leave valuables locked in your car trunk here and at the southern unit of the national seashore, because car thefts sometimes occur. For more information, call 904-428-3384 or visit <www.nps.gov/parklists/fl.html>.

27. Canaveral National Seashore, South Unit/ Merritt Island National Wildlife Refuge

• •

This is the main access to the 57,000-acre national seashore and also to the adjoining national wildlife refuge, a haven for birds and alligators. From the beaches of the southern unit, you can see the original gantry launch pads of the 1960s space era at Kennedy Space Center. There's a visitor center here and a 7-mile causeway drive through the wetlands. You'll see alligators cruising, roseate spoonbills feeding, wood storks brooding, and, in the winter, ducks paddling. The wildlife is so close you won't need binoculars, but bring them anyway. Merritt Island protects more endangered species than any other refuge in the nation outside Hawaii. The Space Coast Flyway Festival, a four-day event with a contest to see who can spot the most species of birds, is held here the middle of each November.

Location: From Titusville, take State Road 406 east across the Indian River Lagoon and veer left, following signs to the wildlife refuge drive on SR 406, or take a right on State Road 402 and head into the national seashore. The visitor center is on the south side of SR 402.

Important information: Nudists hike from the beach parking areas here to isolated parts of the northern national seashore beach, so be aware of that if your family decides to take a long walk. Make sure to lock valuables in your car

What is 155 miles long and 3 feet deep?

• •

The **Indian River Lagoon,** which separates Merritt Island from the mainland, is an age-old water route that isn't really a river. As a lagoon, it depends on wind and tidal movements to move water and any pollution or litter through it. At 155 miles, it's a long stretch, almost as long as the Chesapeake Bay. Its average depth is only 3 feet. Yet within this shallow world as much as a third of the Florida manatee population lives, feeding on seven kinds of sea grass. Dolphins fish here. The lagoon is a nursery for fish, such as groupers and snappers.

Because it is such a long lagoon, it is occupied by tropical species at its southern end near Fort Pierce and more temperate species at its northern end near Titusville. There are 4,315 species in the Indian River Lagoon and its uplands, including 700 salt- and freshwater fish, 2,956 animals, and 1,350 kinds of plants. About 36 are either rare or endangered, such as the manatee. For more lagoon information, contact the Indian River Lagoon Program at 321-984-4950.

trunk, because car thefts can be a problem. There is no concession, so bring whatever you need to drink and eat. During shuttle launches, access is restricted. For more information about Cape Canaveral National Seashore, call 321-267-1110 or visit <www.nbbd.com/godo/cns>. For more information about the refuge, call 321-861-0667 or visit <www.nbbd.com/godo/minwr>.

28. Kennedy Space Center

• •

A child who is captivated by stars and space should see a launch. The feel of thundering rockets, the scream of the explosion, the fireballs, and the cloud of the vapor trail create a memory to savor. If you can't coordinate your visit with a launch, this complex is still one of the most entertaining and educational stops in Florida. Plan to spend at least a half-day here. The Lunch Pad is one of several cafés onsite, so you won't need to leave for food.

Take the bus tour, narrated on tape by Apollo 11 Commander James Lovell, who was also on the Apollo 8 mission, the first flight to the moon. The bus passes security checkpoints and enters restricted areas. You drive by the shuttle landing area and the third-largest building in the world (in volume), the Vehicle Assembly Building. At the Saturn V Center, you try to take in the sight of a massive rocket, twice the size of a space shuttle. You enter the International Space Station Center, where you can watch technicians check parts for the Year 2002 launch of a space station that will be visible from Earth.

You debark back at the visitor center, where you can watch three IMAX movies: one on the Soviet space station *Mir*, one of historic footage taken by astronauts and narrated by Walter Cronkite, and one about space settlement. Visit exhibits, such as the walk-through replica of a space shuttle. You'll want to take your child's picture with an "astronaut" re-enactor or sitting in a lunar rover. Stroll among eight authentic rockets in the outdoor picnic area called the Rocket Garden.

If you are vacationing with a youth group of ten or more, you can arrange—far in advance—for a unique sleepover at the foot of the real Saturn V rocket in the Apollo Saturn V Center. Other special events for kids include two- and five-day camps, scout weekends, and more. I can't emphasize enough how stellar this destination is, so allow time and don't rush, especially if you are here during a launch, which means major crowds. The visitor center, free except for the bus tour and movie tickets, covers 70 acres of the 200-acre space center. This is one of the nation's best attractions, visited by people from all over the world.

Location: From Titusville, head east across the Indian River Lagoon via NASA Causeway to Merritt Island. The visitor center is on NASA Parkway (SR 405) about 6 miles inside the space center entrance.

"We have liftoff!"

Few words are more thrilling than those. To watch a **rocket or shuttle launch,** you just need to get within about 10 miles of Kennedy Space Center on Merritt Island. Some launches are visible from coastal beach towns north and south of Merritt Island, such as New Smyrna Beach to the north and Cape Canaveral and Cocoa Beach to the south. Or you can watch from Titusville, along the Indian River Lagoon; many waterfront cottages and motels advertise their good launch views. Another popular vantage is the State Road 402 causeway in Titusville, which leads to Canaveral National Seashore. For a closer look, you can try to get a car pass to public areas of the massive Kennedy Space Center grounds by calling 407-867-6000. For launch schedules, call 321-867-4636.

Astronauts enter a shuttle three hours before liftoff. At 9 minutes to liftoff, there's a final safety check, at 31 seconds before liftoff the computers take over, and when there are 6 seconds to go, the arms of the holding tower fall away.

Important information: Open from 9 A.M. to dusk daily except on Christmas. This is a popular destination. Expect lines for bus and movie tickets on most days but especially on weekends and holidays. The center closes during some launch events. If possible, visit on a weekday when school is in session to avoid large crowds. Arrive early in the day and buy your bus tour and IMAX theater tickets first thing. For information about special events, such as sleepovers or bus tours for student groups, call 321-449-4444. A launch schedule is available by calling a prerecorded NASA message line, 321-867-4636, and other information is available from 321-452-2121. The website is <www.KennedySpaceCenter.com>.

29. Manatee Hammock Campground

This public campground across the Indian River Lagoon from Kennedy Space Center is quite open and offers little shade. But hey, you can see the launch of your dreams from here. And it's right on the Intracoastal Waterway, with its fascinating ship traffic.

Location: In Titusville at 7275 South U.S. Highway 1.

Important information: Reservations are recommended. For more information, call 321-264-5083 or visit <www.brevardparks.com>.

30. U.S. Space Camp/Astronaut Hall of Fame

This is a five-day, overnight adventure that future mission specialists and shuttle pilots will want to experience. There's even a program that parents can attend with their children. At the Zero Gravity Wall, you can experience what it's like to construct a space station in orbit. You'll have the chance, if you have the stomach for it, to make 360-degree barrel rolls for seven minutes in an aerial simulator. You'll visit a space station module. Maneuver a robot on a Martian landscape. Try walking on the "moon" with a special harness to simulate the lunar gravitational pull. Make a moonprint in lunar dust with an astronaut boot. And there's much more.

There are also daylong events in an attraction called Astronaut Adventure. The camp and one-day events are held at the nonprofit U.S. Astronaut Hall of Fame, a heart-pumping, hands-on museum honoring the bravery and achievement of the astronauts. In the museum, you can get into a model Mercury capsule, the cabinet-sized spacecraft that once prompted John Glenn Jr., first American to orbit Earth, to quip, "You don't climb in, you put it on." If you are an educator, ask about the Academy for Educators program. The nonprofit Hall of Fame, camps, Astronaut Adventure, and Academy for Educators are overseen by astronauts and others associated with the space program.

Location: In Titusville at 6255 Vectorspace Boulevard.

Important information: The Hall of Fame museum and Astronaut Adventure are open daily from 9 A.M. to 5 P.M., extended to 6 P.M. in the summer. Children under 6 are admitted free; fees are $5.95 for children 6 to 12 and $9.95 for all others. The fee for the 5-day camp begins at $500. A good way to judge whether your child will like the rides offered at residence camp is if your child enjoys the most stomach-churning carnival rides or Disney/EPCOT rides. For more information, call 321-269-6100 or visit <www.astronaut.org>.

31. The Enchanted Forest

Fields of ferns and berry blossoms, cabbage palm trees, grapevines, moss-draped oaks, and other lush plants and trees prompted the magical name of this dense forest. There's also desertlike Florida scrub. Overall, this is a wild place for a cool walk in the winter (though quite hot in summer) at the flagship preserve in a local endangered lands program. You'll have the chance to see gopher tortoises in the wild.

Location: About 2 miles south of downtown Titusville on State Road 405, about a half-mile west of U.S. Highway 1.

Important information: Open from 8:30 A.M. to 3 P.M. Wednesdays and Saturdays, with tours offered at 9 A.M., and from 2 to 5 P.M. Sundays, with tours offered at 2:30 P.M. This is an undeveloped site. There are picnic tables, a parking lot, and portable potties. Bring water, snacks, and, in hot weather, bug spray. For more information, call a forest volunteer at 321-267-7367 or visit <www.nbbd.com/godo/ef>.

32. Jetty Park Campground

This public campground on the oceanfront is rather open, but all the better to see a rocket or shuttle launch at Kennedy Space Center. There is a beach with lifeguards, and the boating traffic on the Atlantic captivates children.

Location: In the town of Cape Canaveral next to the Port Canaveral cruise-ship headquarters, at 400 East Jetty Road.

Important information: Reservations are recommended. For more information, call 321-868-1108 or visit <www.brevardparks.com>.

33. Fort Christmas Historical Park

In the early to mid-1800s, Florida had log cabins, stagecoaches, wagon trains, and log forts. That pioneer heritage is often forgotten, except at windows into the past like this re-created village. In 1837, 70 supply wagons and 2,000 marching soldiers arrived here on December 25 to take part in the Second Seminole War. The troops decided to name their new home Fort Christmas. Today, those days are remembered with pioneer cabins and a replica of the original log fort, which looks as if it were lifted from an old episode of *Wagon Train*. The fort is what kids especially like to explore. One part of a blockhouse is devoted to the Seminole Indians and features a rare tape recording of a native medicine man telling stories and delivering a healing chant. The village includes a 1904 cottage, 1917 ranch house, and 1915 farmhouse.

This is an excellent regional park with picnic tables and a playground. It's a stop to look forward to if you are traveling between the Orlando and Cape Canaveral areas. The post office in the nearby village of Christmas is swamped every December with letters addressed to Santa, and many more people bring letters and cards here to mail so they will bear the unique postmark.

Location: From Interstate 75 at Titusville, go west about 12 miles on State Road 50, crossing the St. Johns River. At the crossroads community of Christmas, turn north onto County Road 420 and go about 2 miles to the park at 1300 Fort Christmas Road.

Important information: Open from 10 A.M. to 5 P.M. Tuesdays through Saturdays and from 1 to 5 P.M. Sundays. For more information, call 407-568-4149.

34. Lori Wilson Park

Go for a swim, dig in the sand, push the kids on the swings, have a picnic, and walk through the lush maritime forest on a boardwalk at this popular oceanfront park managed by Brevard County. There are restrooms and, in the summer, lifeguards.

Location: In Cocoa Beach at 1500 North Atlantic Avenue (State Road A1A).

Important information: Open daily from 7 A.M. to dusk. Parking is $1. For more information, call 321-455-1380 or visit <www.brevardparks.com>.

35. Brevard Museum of History and Natural Science

Three of Florida's most prominent industries—cattle, citrus growing, and fishing—are featured in exhibits here. The museum's hands-on Discovery Room is recommended by the Smithsonian Institution. One particularly amazing exhibition simulates an archaeological dig that began in 1984 in a swamp called Windover Pond, south of Titusville. Scientists uncovered a 7,000-year-old burial site and found jewelry, weapons, food, fabric, and even brain tissue that had been preserved in the muck of the ancient pond. The finds have caused anthropologists

Cocoa in the Land of Lemonade

Why, you ask, is the town of Cocoa named for a drink more associated with cold Northern climes than with the Land of Lemonade? Legend has it that when residents were considering what to name the place, a local woman got the idea from a package of Baker's Cocoa. Other folks say the name is from the cocoplum, a shrub that grows abundantly here. Either way, this is said to be the only town in the world with this name.

to revise some of their long-accepted theories of early man in North America. There are also nature trails in a 22-acre preserve setting.

Location: In Cocoa west of U.S. Highway 1 at 2201 Michigan Avenue.

Important information: Open from October through May from 10 A.M. to 4 P.M. Tuesdays through Saturdays and from 1 to 4 P.M. Sundays. Open from 10 A.M. to 4 P.M. Mondays through Saturdays the rest of the year. For more information, call 321-632-1830 or visit <www5.palmnet.net/~bre vardmuseum>.

36. Astronaut Memorial Planetarium/Observatory

This is one of the best public observatories and planetariums ever, with a 24-inch telescope, the largest public telescope in Florida. The planetarium has a three-story screen so you can see the celestial bodies as the astronauts would from space. Spend time with exhibits about space exploration and enjoy the laser light shows.

Location: On the campus of Brevard Community College, at 1519 Clearlake Road in Cocoa.

Important information: Hours and programs vary, so call ahead, 321-634-3732 or visit <www.brevard.cc.fl.us/~planet>.

37. Brevard Zoo

This relatively new zoo was actually hand-built by the community of Brevard. The elevated boardwalks lead through lush jungle and allow you to peer down upon such species as kookaburras, kangaroos, and tapirs. There's an aviary, a petting zoo with barnyard animals, and a "study zone," where you can walk into the mouth of a full-sized whale replica. With a miniature train, playground, and café, as well as side trips by kayak, this is a favorite with families.

Location: In Melbourne at 8225 North Wickham Road, just east of Interstate 95 via exit 73.

Important information: Open daily from 10 A.M. to 5 P.M.; closed on Thanksgiving and Christmas. Admission is free for children under age 2; fees are $4.50 for children 2 to 12, $5.50 for seniors, and $6.50 for all others. For animal feeding times, special events, and other information, call 321-254-3002 or visit <www.brevardzoo.org>.

38. Brevard Museum of Art and Science

Here's a rainy-day diversion with hands-on activities for young scientists who want to experiment with chemistry, physics, and mechanics. The art galleries present African and pre-Columbian collections, among others. The museum is on the Indian River Lagoon in a lush setting.

Location: In Melbourne at 1463 North Highland Avenue.

Important information: For more information, call 321-242-0737 or visit <www.artandscience.org>.

39. Wickham Park

This urban public campground has a playground, horse stables, riding trails, an archery range, a soccer field, swimming lakes, and a nature trail. The campsites are open and grassy, and rangers are in residence.

Location: In Melbourne, take exit 13 from Interstate 95 and travel about 8 miles south to Parkway Drive and the park entrance.

Important information: For more information, call 321-255-4307 or visit <www.brevardparks.com>.

40. Crane Creek Manatee Viewing Site/ Historic Downtown Melbourne

Manatees like to wander up Crane Creek, and the harbor town of Melbourne has created a way to greet them in its shady historic downtown, which is a destination in itself. There is a 10-foot-wide boardwalk from which to see these endangered marine mammals when they're here, interpretive exhibits about them, and night lighting. Nearby are several blocks of cafés, ice cream shops, antiques shops, toy stores, and historical sites in turn-of-the-20th-century buildings. The second Friday of every month, a downtown Family Fest features entertainment and other special activities.

Location: On Melbourne Avenue in Historic Downtown Melbourne, between the railroad bridge and the U.S. Highway 1 bridge.

Important information: For more information, call 321-724-1741.

41. Spessard Holland Park

With summer lifeguards, lots of parking, picnic pavilions, restrooms, and a boardwalk, this is a fine place to have a picnic and stretch your legs year-round. There's a swimming hole for the hot months.

Location: On State Road A1A about a half-mile south of Melbourne Beach. There are north and south entrances to the parking lot.

Important information: Open daily from 7:30 A.M. to dusk. Parking is $1. For more information, call 321-952-4580 or visit <www.brevardparks.com>.

42. Archie Carr National Wildlife Refuge

The refuge, which encompasses 20 miles of noncontiguous stretches of seashore between Melbourne Beach and Wabasso, is home to one of the largest nesting colonies of loggerhead sea turtles in the world. There is very limited access to the newly created refuge, and signs indicate where it is allowed. The name of the refuge honors a famed naturalist and author who spent his life unraveling the mystery of sea-turtle migration. The refuge is not yet completed and is expected to offer more public access and educational programs in the future.

Location: The refuge is along the shoreline and upland dunes of selected parcels of land between Melbourne Beach and Wabasso Beach, along State Road A1A. There is no interpretive center.

Important information: For more information, visit <www.fws.gov/r4eao> or call the refuge manager at 561-589-2089. The Archie Carr Center for Sea Turtle Research is at 352-392-5194.

43. Turkey Creek Sanctuary

Travel over 2,000-year-old sand dunes anchored with live oaks on a boardwalk that winds 4,000 feet along Turkey Creek. In some places, the sand bluffs are 20 feet tall, a fair amount of elevation for flat Florida. See alligators, river otters, and maybe even manatees. At the Margaret Hames Nature Center, enjoy exhibits about park fauna and flora. The best times to visit the 113-acre preserve are in the winter or spring, when the weather is cooler. This is a popular place for bird watchers, who might spot pileated woodpeckers, purple martins, and more.

Lights out!

With its glistening reddish brown shell, the **loggerhead** is considered by some to be the most beautiful of marine turtles. Loggerheads can stay submerged for up to three hours. They grow up to 200 pounds on a diet of blue crabs and jellyfish. The only time they come ashore—from as far as 1,500 miles away—is to lay eggs in the summer. The females are skittish when they approach shore. If a beach is lighted, the wary turtle won't leave the water. This has hatched public campaigns to require beach lights to remain off during nesting season.

If you care about saving these endangered creatures, don't flash a light at them or try to find them on your own. You can sign up to join a summertime sea-turtle watch sponsored by most federal and state coastal preserves and conservation groups.

At a dark beach, if sand hasn't been covered by jetties or pavement, turtles haul themselves out of the water awkwardly with their flippers, dig a hole, and lay eggs—an event that can take several hours. Then they lumber back to sea, leaving "tire-track" flipper gouges in the sand that beachcombers search for on summer mornings.

Archie Carr, an expert on sea turtles who founded the Caribbean Conservation Foundation, once wrote, "Everyone ought to see a sea turtle nesting. It is an impressive thing to see, the pilgrimage of a sea creature back to the land its ancestors left a hundred million years ago."

Fences and human volunteers protect the nests from raids by egg-eating animals and even poachers. When they hatch, baby loggerhead sea turtles are on their own. They run a gauntlet of dangers as they wiggle their way from nest to sea; predators such as gulls can swoop down.

The University of Florida is conducting research into the impact of sea-turtle eggs on beach health. Nutrients in the eggshells and even the fluid inside the egg replenish nutrient-deficient sand. This helps plants grow, which anchors dunes and prevents erosion. Sea turtles need the beach, but it seems the beach needs sea turtles, too.

For more information on sea turtles:

- Sea Turtle Preservation Society
  1517 Ocean Avenue
  Melbourne, FL 32951
  407-676-1701
- Sea Turtle Preservation League
  800-678-7853
  <www.cccturtle.org>
- Caribbean Conservation Foundation
  352-373-6441
  <www.cccturtle.org>

Location: In Palm Bay at 1518 Port Malabar Boulevard NE, behind the Community Center.

Important information: Trails are open from 7 A.M. to sunset daily. For more information, including hours of the nature center, call 321-952-3433 or 321-952-3400 or visit <www.iu.net/palmbay/turkeycreek.html>.

44. Long Point County Park

Here's a grassy island campground with resident rangers, playgrounds, swimming lakes, hot showers, laundry facilities, and more.

Location: About 20 miles south of Melbourne and just north of Sebastian Inlet State Recreation Area on State Road A1A.

Important information: Open daily from 5 A.M. to 10 P.M. Reservations are accepted by mail only; write 700 Long Point Road, Melbourne Beach, FL 32951.

Shipwrecked!

In August 1715, just off the Florida coast between what is now Sebastian and Fort Pierce, a storm sank a fleet of 11 **Spanish galleons**. More than 1,000 survivors struggled to shore and tended their wounds as best they could under the blazing subtropical sun. Some survived with the help of local Ais Indians. About 700 people lost their lives in the disaster.

For the next four years, the wreck site attracted hordes of Spanish salvage divers, English pirates, and other greedy brigands, because the ships had been carrying gold bars and coins made from ore extracted from the mountains of Mexico and South America. The fleet had been on its way to deliver its bounty to the Royal Spanish Treasury. Now the prize lay imbedded in sand on the ocean floor.

Tantalizing finds from the 1715 fleet have surfaced through the years, some of which is on display at the McLarty Treasure Museum. In the 1950s, a hurricane rearranged the shoreline, leading to the discovery of a Spanish salvage camp. Who knows, there could still be more treasure offshore or even under that parking lot across from the beach!

45. Sebastian Inlet State Recreation Area/ McLarty Treasure Museum

• •

This extremely popular park is located at the site of a Spanish salvage camp, set up to recover sunken treasure after a 1715 shipwreck. The site has been designated a national historic landmark. The McLarty Treasure Museum features some of the silver and gold recovered from the wreck. Other attractions at this park include some of the best surfing on the eastern coast of Florida, shady campsites that front on the Indian River Lagoon, and a ranger-led tour to Pelican Island National Wildlife Refuge, the nation's first wildlife refuge. There are also ranger-led "turtle walks" on summer nights, campfire programs, a marina, and a camp store that serves breakfast and lunch. This is one of the most historically outstanding state parks in Florida.

Many visitors to Sebastian Inlet prefer swimming in the calm lagoon waters. The surf at the inlet is dangerous; there are furious undertows and occasional sharks. This park has 3 miles of beach, so if you choose to swim in the ocean instead of the lagoon, make sure you are downshore from the inlet in lifeguarded areas. There are two park entrances, one on the north side of the inlet and one on the south side, where the campsites are located.

Location: About 15 miles south of Melbourne Beach on the north and south side of Sebastian Inlet, at 9700 South A1A.

Important information: The museum is open from 10 A.M. to 4:30 P.M. daily. The admission fee is $1. For information on the tour to Pelican Island

Hang 10

• •

Sebastian Inlet is the site of some of the best **surfing** on the east coast of Florida. If you're going to hang out with surfers, it helps to speak their lingo. VISIT Florida provides this "Surf-to-English" primer.

amped	really happy
excellent	great
gremos	someone who has no clue what they're doing out there
killa warra	an expression of intense happiness
phat waves	great waves
ride a tube	surf a wave
stick riders	surfers
stoked	happy, elated
tasty	really great

National Wildlife Refuge, call 800-952-1126. For campground reservations, call 561-589-9659. For other park information, call 321-984-4852 or visit <www.dep.state.fl.us/parks>.

46. Donald McDonald Park

Here's an Indian River County campground among scenic sandpines on the Indian River. There is a nature trail, hot showers, and boating access to the river.

Location: From the intersection of County Roads 512 and 505 in Sebastian, drive 2.5 miles north on CR 505 to the park.

Important information: For more information, call 561-589-0087.

47. Mel Fisher's Treasure Museum

If your mateys like shipwreck stories, sail into this site shimmering with real Spanish treasure—loot from Spanish galleons that were swamped by a hurricane off Key West in September 1622. In 1985, famed treasure hunter Mel Fisher brought up gold and other artifacts from the ship *Nuestra Senora de Atocha*. Don't leave without handling the real gold bar worth $250,000. Have the camera ready for this shining moment. After a visit, you're excused if you think you see a shimmering doubloon under the water as you take your ocean swims. Bumps under sand also take on a new meaning. Many confirmed Florida beachcombers got their start after visiting this museum and the McLarty Treasure Museum (see above).

Location: On North U.S. Highway 1 in Sebastian.

For more information: For more information, call 561-589-9874 or visit <www.melfisher.com>.

48. Environmental Learning Center

Learn the names of plants and birds you see in Florida, especially coastal species, at this 51-acre science center. There's a boardwalk and observation tower in a maritime forest. Saltwater touch tanks and other hands-on exhibits help tell the story of the area's endangered sea turtles, manatees, and other residents.

Location: North of Vero Beach on Wabasso Island at 255 Live Oak Drive.

Important information: For more information, call 561-589-5050.

49. Disney Vero Beach Resort

Ecotourism is emphasized at this popular oceanfront resort behind the dunes. The Audubon Society has endorsed the resort for its environmental consciousness, including its landscaping with native sand-tolerant plants, its minimal removal of trees during construction, and its replanting of removed trees at an environmental center. Even the activities here are "green": Take a cruise on the Indian River Lagoon to an ocean research center, rent a kayak for a paddle on the lagoon, learn outdoors tips from a park ranger, take a bicycle tour, have snorkel lessons, visit a treasure museum, and, in the summer, watch for endangered loggerhead sea turtles that come ashore at night to build their nests. Just offshore in 1618, the Spanish ship *San Martin* wrecked. In the summer, you may be able to see salvage boats still looking for the treasure. Off site, you can tour a 20,000-acre working cattle ranch that attracts sandhill cranes.

Location: In Vero Beach at 9250 Island Grove Terrace.

Important information: For more information, call 800-359-8000 or visit <www.dvc-resorts.com>.

50. Indian River Citrus Museum

Oranges are an enduring symbol of Florida. At this juicy rainy-day diversion, learn slices of trivia about the state's historic citrus industry, such as why growers intentionally put ice on the trees when the temperature drops.

Location: In Vero Beach at 2140 14th Avenue.

Important information: For more information, call 561-770-2263.

51. Vero Beach Center for the Book

The children's section of this expansive, two-building book emporium is a large, fun space devoted to families. Children's authors and illustrators frequently make appearances. A puppet theater, other special events, and a café help make the center a popular stop in Vero Beach.

Location: In Vero Beach at 2145 Indian River Boulevard.

Important information: Open from 9 A.M. to 9 P.M. Mondays through Saturdays and from 11 A.M. to 5 P.M. Sundays. For more information, call 561-569-6650 or visit <www.verobooks.com>.

Create crate art

The labels on Florida's wooden **citrus crates** are an artform from days past. Very vibrant colors were used not only to identify the fruit's origin, but also to attract buyers. Native deer, Seminole Indians in dugout canoes, children at the beach, circus clowns, great white herons, pink flamingos, and fanciful fruit designs were among the subjects of these drawings.

Eventually, cardboard containers and other shipping methods diminished the need for stylish crate labels. But you can always create your own citrus label. Draw a square about 8 by 8 inches. If you sold oranges, tangerines, and grapefruit, how would you want your labels to look? Don't forget to make a company name and put it prominently on the label. Several Florida museums display old citrus labels, such as the Indian River Citrus Museum in Vero Beach and the Museum of Florida History in Tallahassee.

52. Dodgertown

Florida is beloved by sports fans as the spring-training capital of baseball. But this especially popular complex deserves a special mention. Here at Holman Stadium, there's baseball almost year-round, with a local Class A team, the Vero Beach Dodgers, filling in when the Los Angeles Dodgers have finished their spring training (generally February through April). Fantasy camps where grownup boys get to pretend they're in the big league also sustain the "play ball" feeling here. For more than 50 years the L.A. Dodgers have made the annual pilgrimage to Vero Beach. Dodgertown offers the players housing, swimming pools, tennis courts, and even a citrus grove.

Location: In Vero Beach at 4101 26th Street.

Important information: Tickets to the Los Angeles Dodgers exhibition games are $10. The Vero Beach Dodgers tickets are $3 for children and $4 for adults; their season generally runs from April through September. For game times and tickets, call 561-569-6958, and for Dodgertown information, call 561-569-4900 or visit <www.vero.com/dodgers>.

Orlando Area

A family can stay happily busy in Orlando beyond visiting its famous theme park attractions. This is an exciting city set amid many lakes, with kid-friendly museums and parks. The area grew up around Fort Gatlin, which was built as a defense against Seminole Indians in 1838 and is now the site of a naval research lab. At least six historic districts with beautifully preserved homes, large shade trees, and brick streets present a side of the community that more and more visitors are discovering. The very lively Orange County Historical Museum tells about the mystery surrounding the origin of the city name and much more.

Amid sprawling development, some communities around Orlando also have attractive town centers, such as Longwood and Winter Park. You can expect lovely urban parks, some with scenic lakes. Orlando is also not far from state parks with springs, picnic spots, and campgrounds.

Since the Orlando area is so popular with families, avoid the traffic jams by taking free shuttles wherever they are offered and allow plenty of travel time to get where you are going.

53. Lake Eola Swan Boats

This beloved park in the heart of Orlando is a friendly spot. Stretch your legs by paddling a Swan Boat around Lake Eola.

Location: Between Central Boulevard and Robinson Street, near Rosalind Avenue at Lake Eola Park.

Important information: Lake Eola Café rents the boats beginning at 11:30 A.M. daily. In the summer, the hours are extended so you can enjoy the illuminated lake fountain at night. For more information, call 407-841-9856.

54. Orlando Public Library

The children's wing—new in 1999—is airy and fun, with a colorful fish mobile, a *Jack and the Beanstalk* sculpture, and the Emerald Castle of Oz in which to curl up and enjoy a book or magazine. This is a fine, free, indoor space if you need air conditioning or a place to sit and recharge, or if you simply yearn for a good story.

Location: In downtown Orlando at 101 East Central Boulevard.

Important information: Open from 9 A.M. to 9 P.M. Mondays through Thursdays, from 9 A.M. to 6 P.M. Fridays and Saturdays, and from 1 to 6 P.M. Sundays. For more information, call 407-835-7323.

55. Orlando Science Center/ John Young Planetarium

If your kids are curious about how things work, this hands-on museum will entertain them and sneak in some education, too. It's a nonprofit place to learn that's expertly disguised as a place to play. Many families make a day of it, exploring four floors of adventure and dining at the on-site cafeteria. Favorites include the BodyZone, which features a walk-through model of a human body; NatureWorks, which features a real buzzing beehive; Power Station, where you can have fun with magnets; Imaginary Landscapes, with its laser lights; and ShowBiz Science, which reveals the high-tech secrets behind some of Orlando's attractions. The planetarium is a comfortable place to watch star shows, and on weekend nights you can gaze from the observatory at the real thing. There's also an intense movie theater experience, the CineDome, which features an eight-story surround-screen. It takes you into the middle of the circulatory system, into a volcano, and underwater with a great white shark. At 42,000 square feet, this wonderful place is huge. If your time is limited, study the floor plan and decide which highlights to visit. The volunteer guides are enthusiastic, so be sure to ask questions about the exhibits and the museum.

Location: Take exit 43 (Princeton Street) from Interstate 4 and head east about a quarter-mile to the museum at 77 East Princeton Street.

Important information: Open from 9 A.M. to 5 P.M. Tuesdays through Thursdays and some summer and holiday Mondays, from 9 A.M. to 9 P.M. Fridays and Saturdays, and from noon to 5 P.M. Sundays. Children under age 3 are admitted free; fees are $6.75 for children 3 to 11, $8.50 for seniors, and $9.50 for all others. For more information, call 407-896-7151 or visit <www.osc.org>.

56. Orange County Historical Museum

Here's a local museum that sets high standards. It features a two-story, red-brick firehouse, built in 1926, that is a kid magnet with its collection of old fire engines and fire gear. Other museum highlights are Uncle Neil's General Store and a Victorian parlor. A collection of ancient arrowheads makes the point that this area of high-tech attractions was once a Native American homeland.

Location: In Loch Haven Park at 812 East Rollins Street, next door to the Orlando Science Center (see above) and near Leu Gardens (see below).

Important information: Open from 9 A.M. to 5 P.M. Mondays through Saturdays and from noon to 5 P.M. Sundays. Fees are $1 for children, $1.50 for seniors, and $2 for other adults. For more information, call 407-897-6350.

57. Turkey Lake Park

This city park boasts a super-duper wooden playground complex, a 100-year-old barn, shady picnic areas and campsites, a bicycle path, nature trails, and a fishing pier on Turkey Lake, where largemouth bass lurk. No swimming is allowed.

Location: From Interstate 4 near Universal Studios, take exit 30 to Kirkman Road North, turn left onto Conroy Road and then right onto Hiawassee Road. The park is at 3401 Hiawassee Road.

Important information: For more information, call 407-299-5594.

58. Leu Gardens

This 50-acre city park encompasses Lake Rowena, which has a resident alligator cruising in it. Among the things to see here are a 50-foot-tall, working clock made of flowers, a ravine garden, the world's largest collection of flowering camellias, a rose garden, a palm garden, and more. You can also take a lively tour of the Leu residence. When your family needs some manicured beauty, head here.

Location: In Orlando at 1920 North Forest Avenue.

Important information: Open daily from 9 A.M. to 5 P.M. Children under age 6 are admitted free; fees are $1 for ages 6 to 16 and $3 for adults. For more information, call 407-246-2620.

59. The Senator/Big Tree Park/Spring Hammock Nature Reserve

I like it when a community names its special trees. No tree in central Florida, perhaps in the entire state, is more widely known than the cypress known as the Senator. At an estimated 3,500 years old, it's reputedly the oldest cypress in the nation. The Senator is about 46 feet in diameter and 126 feet tall. Florida once had many more of these beauties, but they all fell during the early 1900s, when cypresses were being commercially logged. This last legend is in the Spring Hammock Nature Reserve, a regional park that's a fine place to have a picnic and stretch your legs. Longwood boasts a scenic historic district of shady streets and preserved Victorian buildings.

Location: Just north of Orlando in Longwood, on General Hutchinson Parkway via U.S. Highway 17/92.

Important information: Open daily from 8 A.M. to sunset.

60. Audubon's Center for Birds of Prey

If the sight of a fledgling that's fallen from its nest tugs at your heartstrings, put this Audubon site on your vacation list. The raptors here have come out on the short end of conflicts with wild animals, pets, and, sadly, people. You'll see owls, falcons, eagles, and other birds too badly injured to return to the wild. Because of the excellent work done here, many other birds not on public display will be able, after treatment, to fly the coop.

Location: North of Orlando and Winter Park in Maitland at 1101 Audubon Way.

Important information: Children under age 6 are admitted free; otherwise the fee is $2. Open from 10 A.M. to 4 P.M. Tuesdays through Sundays. You should call first for directions and to learn the schedule of guided tours, the best way to see this site. For more information, call 407-644-0190 or visit <www.adoptabird.org>.

61. Disney's Fort Wilderness Campground

Not many visitors realize that you can camp at Walt Disney World. Chip and Dale visit with young fans at the campground's nightly bonfire, where there's a sing-along and cartoons are shown outdoors after dark. Bring marshmallows to roast, as well as paper and pen so you can get the famous chipmunks' autographs. There are paddleboats, a petting farm, nature trails, the barn where the massive Disney draft horses live, a swimming beach on Bay Lake, free bus transit, and boat rides to the Magic Kingdom across the lake.

At 700 acres, this is one of the largest campgrounds you'll stay in. Reservations are a must. Most sites are shaded, but specify if you want a more secluded site. To shorten long waits at check-in, arrive early, claim a parking spot, do the preliminary paperwork, and go find something to do until check-in. The youth camping and group camping options here—popular with YMCA Guides, Girl Scouts, Boy Scouts, and others—are an inexpensive way for student groups to "do" Disney.

Location: You'll receive directions when you make a reservation, but it's located with Disney's River Country and the Hoop-De-Do Revue attractions.

Important information: Fees begin at $35 a night and reservations are a must, especially during the summer and school holidays. For more information, call 407-934-7639 or visit <www.disneyworld.com>.

62. Discovery Cove and Close-up Tours, SeaWorld

If your swimmers are comfortable having close-up encounters with sea creatures, consider the once-in-a-lifetime thrill of Discovery Cove, a new experience offered by SeaWorld. A trained specialist facilitates the meeting between your family members and dolphins in the water.

Less intensive but still rewarding, especially for budding veterinarians, is "To the Rescue," a behind-the-scenes, 60-minute look at how SeaWorld helps injured manatees, sea turtles, and birds in its rehabilitation program. The Polar Expedition tour shows you how SeaWorld has created a frozen and snowy world here in the hot Sunshine State for its penguins and its famous polar bear twins, Klondike and Snow. Bird'seye View is a very special walk around the park to learn about the 200 kinds of birds here, including the flamingos.

As for the rest of SeaWorld, everyone has their favorite places; ours is "Manatees: The Last Generation?" Some say these gentle marine mammals are on the path to extinction, like the Florida panther.

Location: About 6 miles southwest of Orlando on Interstate 4, at exit 27 if you're westbound or exit 28 eastbound. Large signs help make SeaWorld easy to find.

Important information: For more information, call 407-363-2398, 800-406-2244 (for special programs), or 800-327-2424. You can also visit <www.seaworld.com> or <www.discoverycove.com> or e-mail for information to <education@seaworld.org>.

63. Green Meadows

Meet some farm animals, even milk a cow, at this zoo designed to bring kids in touch with goats, pigs, ducks, geese, turkeys, and more. All visitors take a two-hour tour, partly via hay wagon. Shy away from a summer visit when it's just too hot and there's a bit too much *eau du farm* in the air.

Location: South of Orlando in Kissimmee at 1368 South Poinciana Boulevard.

Important information: Children under age 3 are admitted free; fees are $11 for Florida residents and $13 for everyone else. For more information, call 407-836-0770.

64. Disney Wilderness

This 11,500-acre preserve is managed by The Nature Conservancy for the Walt Disney World Company. Located within the Upper Kissimmee River Chain of Lakes, it encompasses dry and wet prairies, scrub forest, and forested wetlands—the habitat of bald eagles, sandhill cranes, scrub jays, and gopher tortoises. A former ranch site, it's being returned to its natural state in exchange for Disney's development of wetlands elsewhere. This process, called mitigation, has resulted in a new environmental education center here near the headwaters of the Everglades. The center is a state-of-the-art "green" building that gets 30 percent of its energy from solar power and features insulation made from recycled newspaper. There's a cistern to collect water for fire management and to wash equipment. Features of the preserve include interpreted nature trails, observation areas, educational exhibits, and a gift shop.

Location: In Kissimmee at 2700 Scrub Jay Trail.

Important information: Open from 9 A.M. to 5 P.M. daily except major holidays. For more information, call 407-935-0002.

65. Gatorland

This attraction—so tacky it's cute—was established in 1949 and has become a part of Florida tourist lore. It's affiliated with the University of Florida, which conducts research here, but it's truly a homegrown tourist stop and shop—one that kids enjoy. The Marsh Breeding Habitat and Bird Sanctuary shows the advantageous relationship between birds and alligators. Herons and other large birds are protected from predators as they nest in the trees above alligators. The latter deter raccoons and other egg-stealing bandits.

Gatorland alligators are fed and wrestled for your entertainment. In April and May, the reptiles' mating season, you can hear the males bellow. In June, you can see their nests of eggs. The hatchlings emerge in August and September. One part of Gatorland that I object to is the area where you can buy fish to feed the largest gators. Since feeding these creatures in the wild is a problem that can lead to dangerous attacks, I use this area to show kids what *not* to do and then visit the Gatorland education center where there are stories about alligator attacks.

There are picnic places here if you want to bring along a snack or meal, but almost everyone wants to try barbecued gator. The alligators to be slaughtered, which are isolated from the others, are fed 2,000 pounds of protein weekly. Promise you'll do everything in your power to make sure a wild gator never gets its protein from you!

Location: In Kissimmee at 14501 South Orange Blossom Trail.

Important information: Open daily from 9 A.M. to dusk. Children under age 3 are admitted free; fees are $7.50 for children ages 3 to 9, $10 for ages 10 to 12, and $17 for all others. One child aged 3 to 9 is admitted free with a paying adult. For more information, call 800-393-5297.

An alligator of a different color

You may think that Gatorland specializes in black alligators because you fail to spot a green one. The truth is that, although stuffed gators, those illustrated in children's books, the University of Florida mascot, and most toy gators are green—often lime green—real alligators aren't green at all. Nor are they brown. They have black backs and creamy white to pale yellow underbellies. Baby alligators are black with zigzaggy yellow stripes. How alligators became green in the minds of artists and toy manufacturers will probably never be known. Some old alligators have bits of green algae sticking to their backs here and there. In lakes covered with a tiny green plant called duckweed, alligators sometimes surface and become coated with the confetti-like stuff. Maybe that's the story behind the green alligator myth.

66. Lake Kissimmee State Park

Your young cowpokes will delight in meeting park rangers dressed as 19th-century cow hunters at the re-created 1876 cattle camp here. There are long-horned scrub cattle to see and tall tales to hear. This 6,000-acre park also features an isolated campground east of Lake Wales. A narrow canal leads into the lake, which is not visible from the campground or the canal boat basin. An observation tower is a good perch from which to look for soaring bald eagles. Deer are common here, and my family and I almost walked into a group of 12 beautiful, copper-feathered wild turkeys as they strutted under trees near the boat basin.

Location: From the community of Lake Wales, take State Road 60 east about 15 miles. Turn north onto Camp Mack Road and continue on it as it curves right past Old Mammoth Grove Road. The park is at 14248 Camp Mack Road.

Important information: Make sure to visit on a holiday or weekend or during a special event, when the "old" cow hunters are around. For more information, call 863-696-1112 or visit www.dep.state.fl.us/parks>.

67. Forever Florida

On a covered wagon or in an open coach, young rustlers like to roll through herds of horses and cattle on the Crescent J Ranch, part of this nonprofit ecotourism attraction called Forever Florida. Then it's on to the property's

3,200-acre wilderness preserve to see flocks of sandhill cranes, cruising alligators, palm-fringed vistas, and possibly the rare whooping crane. The 2.5-hour ride is best taken in the fall or winter, when temperatures are tolerable and wildlife sightings are more likely. A petting zoo and pony rides lure the littlest ones. Complete with hiking trails and a visitor center, Forever Florida is dedicated to the memory of Allen Broussard, a young wildlife ecologist who years ago glimpsed a Florida panther near here.

Location: From St. Cloud, take U.S. Highway 192 southeast to Holopaw and then travel south on US 441 for 7.5 miles. The site is on your left.

Important information: Call to schedule a tour at 888-957-9794 or 407-957-9794 or visit <www.foreverflorida.com>.

68. Bok Tower Gardens

Your family might welcome the manicured shade of this garden on Iron Mountain near the community of Lake Wales. You can't climb the 57-bell carillon tower, which is listed on the National Register of Historic Places, but you can enjoy its soothing melodies. Gliding swans in ponds and busy squirrels on the ground keep little ones entertained. This is a quiet, peaceful place. At 295 feet, Iron Mountain is truly considered a mountain in generally flat Florida.

Location: About 3 miles north of the community of Lake Wales, near Mountain Lake at 1151 Tower Boulevard.

Important information: Open from 8 A.M. to 5 P.M. daily. Children under age 5 are admitted free; fees are $1 for children 5 to 12 and $4 for all others. For more information, call 863-676-1408.

69. Highlands Hammock State Park

The last known ivory-billed woodpecker in Florida lived in the deep woods here. I mention this to give an idea of the lush old-growth beauty within this 5,540-acre park. Take your family to see the park's 1,000-year-old oak tree via Big Oak Trail. Measuring 37.5 feet in circumference, this grandmother oak is enormous. A boardwalk leads into a virgin hardwood forest and cypress swamp and offers probably the easiest access in the state to lush, ancient woodlands outside of the Fakahatchee Strand boardwalk, southeast of Naples. Be sure to take your children on the ranger-narrated tram tour through remote areas of the park. You can easily bicycle or drive your car along the paved, 3.1-mile loop past an old orange grove and through a hardwood hammock. Rental bikes are available. The park has eight different interpreted walks, each lasting about 25 minutes, making it ideal for families. In addition to Big Oak Trail, be sure to visit Fern Garden Trail, Young Hammock Trail, Ancient Hammock Trail, and Cypress Swamp Trail.

Most people think that Florida only has dense jungle at its southern tip, but this park will remind you that the whole state once held immense swaths of jungly growth. This remnant forest was saved from development because citizens bought it in 1931, even before the state decided to care for it. If you are traveling through the center of the state, there isn't a better park to visit and camp in than this. I think it's among the top three state parks for families who want to see a variety of wildlife, including deer, wild turkeys, otters, bald eagles, alligators, wood storks, swallow-tailed kites, and even bobcats. Ask rangers for tips on how to glimpse the latter near Tiger Branch Road. A Florida panther, an almost-extinct species, was seen here once in recent years. There's also a museum telling the story of an unsung group of early environmentalists: the Civilian Conservation Corps.

Location: About 4 miles west of Sebring on State Road 634.

Important information: You can't get a campsite in winter without a reservation. At other times, weekends are often booked, too. The park offers rental bikes. For more information or reservations, call 863-386-6094 or visit <www.dep.state.fl.us/parks>.

70. Lake Griffin State Park

This is a beautiful campground shaded by live oaks, but expect to hear traffic noise at night from nearby U.S. Highway 441/27. This very popular park is connected to Lake Griffin by a canal. Ask rangers about the chance of seeing "floating islands" in the lake. These are natural peat mats with plants and even trees on them, anchored by a tangle of roots that can break loose, allowing the "islands" to drift.

Location: From Leesburg, drive north about 2 miles on US 441/27. The park is at 3089 Highway 441/27.

Important information: For more information, call 352-360-6760 or visit <www.dep.state.fl.us/parks>.

71. West Orange Trail

This is a popular 19-mile paved path. Get rolling with rental bicycles or inline skates from the Bike and Blades concession in Winter Garden.

Location: In Winter Garden at 17914 State Road 438.

Important information: Many families just go a mile or so along the trail and then return for a short but enjoyable ride. For more information, call 407-877-0600 or visit <www.biketrail.com>.

72. Kelly Park/Rock Springs Run

Like the Ichetucknee River in the Big Bend Region, Rock Springs Run is a popular stream with inner-tube floaters. The clear water bubbles up from a rock outcropping. The regional public park is a super picnic and camping place.

Location: Near Apopka, north of Orlando, take Rock Springs Road to Kelly Park Road and turn left on Kelly Park Road into the park.

Important information: For more information, call 407-889-4179.

73. Wekiwa Springs State Park

This 6,000-acre preserve is known for its spring, a popular summer swimming hole. The campground is a beauty, and there's a snack bar by the spring. There are canoe rentals for the spring run, nature trails, occasional ranger-led events, and bicycle rentals. The park encompasses cypress swamp, longleaf pine sand hills, and prime black-bear habitat. Pocket gophers, though rarely sighted, make their presence known with their sand mounds. River otters fish here, and bobcats roam. Alligators are common. Don't approach them. It's illegal to feed them and quite dangerous. Report anyone feeding alligators to the rangers.

Location: Take State Road 436 east from Apopka and follow signs to the park.

Important information: For more information, call 407-884-2009 or visit <www.dep.state.fl.us/parks>.

74. Central Florida Zoological Park

• •

This is a well-loved regional zoo and picnic place with a reptile house, hippo, and lots of alligators and birds. A peacock strolls near the snack shop, and zoo educators offer frequent animal-encounter programs along the board-walks. There's lots of shade.

Location: Northeast of Orlando in Sanford at 3755 NW Highway 17/92.

Important information: Open from 9 A.M. to 5 P.M. daily. Admission is free for children under age 3; fees are $3 for ages 3 to 12, $4 for seniors, and $7 for all others. For more information, call 407-323-4450.

75. Katie's Wekiva River Landing

• •

This outfitter will put you on the area's crystal-clear rivers, provide fishing licenses, and steer you to a campsite, all from this shady, riverfront setting.

Location: Southwest of Sanford at 190 Katie's Cove.

Important information: For more information, call 407-628-1482 in Orlando or 407-322-4470 in Sanford, or visit <www.ktland.com>.

Pink interlopers from points south

• •

Congratulations, eagle-eyed bird watcher, if you see a **flamingo** in the wild. Al-though these pink 4-foot-tall birds with their long, slender necks and curved beaks are famous Florida symbols, they aren't true Floridians. They have never nested in the wild here. These graceful fliers were sighted in southern Florida skies in the early 1800s. But those birds were most likely visitors from islands to the south, such as Cuba. Even veteran birder John James Audubon never found flamingos in Florida, which greatly disappointed him. The birds probably stopped visiting when plume-hunters in the Everglades scared them away. To everyone's delight, an occasional Cuban interloper is blown off course by a storm and is spotted feeding on the Florida coast before flying home. Either that or a singular, stunning pink flamingo is a repeated escapee from a zoo.

WEST-CENTRAL REGION

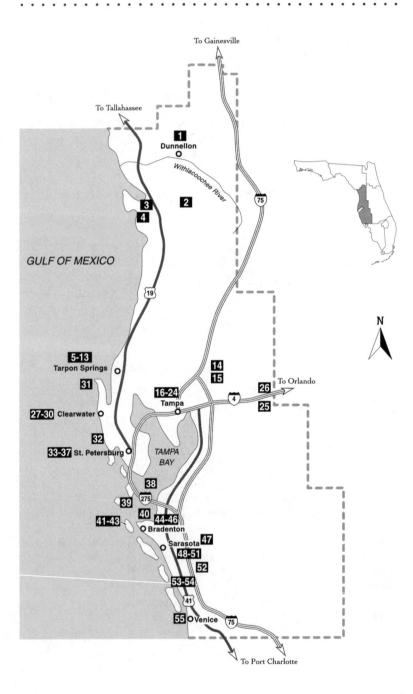

To Gainesville

To Tallahassee

1 Dunnellon

Withlacoochee River

2

3
4

GULF OF MEXICO

75

19

5-13
Tarpon Springs

31

14
15

16-24
Tampa

4 **26** To Orlando

25

27-30 Clearwater

32

33-37 St. Petersburg

TAMPA
BAY

38

275

39

41-43 **40**
44-46
 Bradenton

47

Sarasota
48-51

52

53-54

41

55 Venice

75

To Port Charlotte

N

West-Central Region

I have "sand in my shoes" for this area, because as a child, when my family moved south from New Jersey, this is the place we found paradise. Dolphins leapt in our backyard, which was the Gulf of Mexico at Siesta Key in Sarasota. The waves tossed small pink shells at my feet.

This region is still a giant, natural saltwater aquarium. Whether you introduce your children to the fishing and sponge-collecting heritage of Greek families at Tarpon Springs or hunt in the sand for sharks' teeth at Venice, you'll find the dreamy Florida of postcard views. Aqua water laps at sugar-sand beaches, and pelicans patrol clear skies. Curving bridges link barrier islands and back bayous. Thousands of canals afford boat access to a marine highway, the Intracoastal Waterway, and beyond that to the largest gulf in the world, the Gulf of Mexico.

The main cities and towns of the West-Central Region—Tarpon Springs, Clearwater, St. Petersburg, Tampa, Bradenton, and Sarasota—offer an abundance of cultural sites that children will find entertaining. Great museums, science centers, historic sites, and coastal preserves teach about Paleo-Indian, Native American, American pioneer, and immigrant periods of settlement. These sites also celebrate the fragile coastal estuaries, places where salt and freshwater mix to create natural marine nurseries for baby fish and shrimp. Gardens and zoos offer subtropical luxuriance. If you find the area's coastal zones too popular for your liking, drive east past Interstate 75 a few miles to any of the region's inland rivers, lakes, historic sites, villages, or parks, such as Myakka River State Park. You'll still find palms and sunshine, but you'll find more elbowroom, too. And of course, the inland reaches are where the alligators bellow!

You can choose from among six public park campgrounds in this region, including one at a spring-fed river, Rainbow Springs, and one near a replica of a fort built during the Seminole Indian Wars, in Hillsborough River State Park. Private campgrounds for nature lovers include Lake Rousseau Campground, Camp 'N Water Resort, Riverside Lodge, Trail's End Camp, and Chassahowitzka River Campground, all in Citrus County; Gulf Beach Campground on Siesta Key in Sarasota; and Venice Campground in Venice.

Historic lodging options include a 1920s pink palace, the Don CeSar, at St. Petersburg Beach and the 1897 Belleview Biltmore in Clearwater. The latter is reputed to be the largest occupied wooden building in the United States. Other family lodging options include Running Deer Lodge in the Withlacoochee State Forest; Port Paradise Resort and King's Bay Lodge at

Crystal River; Homosassa River Retreat, Marina Bay Inn, and MacRae's, all at Homosassa; Tarpon Turtle Inn in Tarpon Springs; Inn on the Bay in Dunedin; Palm Harbor Resort in Palm Harbor; Sea Club Rentals in Indian Shores; the Don CeSar and TradeWinds at St. Petersburg Beach; Catalina Beach Resort, Sand Pebble, Sugar Sands Apartments, Silver Surf, and Tropic Isle Inn, all on Anna Maria Island; and Azalea Gardens, Gulf Terrace Apartments, and Turtle Beach Resort, all on Siesta Key in Sarasota.

For more information about the region contact:

- Citrus County Tourism
  352-527-5233, 800-587-6667
  <www.visitcitrus.com>
- Tarpon Springs Information
  727-937-6109
  <www.tarponsprings.com>
- Greater Hernando County
  352-796-0697
  <www.hernandochamber.com>
- Gulf Beaches of Tampa Bay
  800-944-1847, 727-360-6957
  <www.gulfbeaches-tampabay.com>
- Clearwater Beach Information
  888-799-3199, 727-447-7600
  <www.beachchamber.com>
- St. Petersburg/Clearwater Visitors Bureau
  800-345-6710, 727-464-7200
  <www.stpete-clearwater.com>
- Tampa/Hillsborough Visitors Association
  800-448-2672, 813-223-1111
  <www.gotampa.com>
- Anna Maria Island Information
  <www.annamariaisland.com>
- Bradenton Area Visitors Bureau
  800-462-6283, 941-729-9177
  <www.floridaislandbeaches.org>
- Sarasota Visitors Bureau
  800-522-9799, 941-957-1877
  <www.cvb.sarasota.fl.us> or <www.sarasotaFL.org>

Citrus County

To visit the springs, rivers, lakes, ancient historic sites, and scenic parks of this rolling hills region about 90 minutes north of Tampa is like "visiting Mother Nature's theme park," as the tourism office says. Manatee-viewing is almost guaranteed here. Fishing and camping bring many vacationers to the lakes and rivers. Some historic sites commemorate human habitation that is thousands of years old. Strip shopping centers line major roadways, so at first you'll wonder how this area could be an ecotourism haven, but if you patiently make your way to the natural and historic sites a bit off the main roads, you'll be rewarded with green glens and lessons in world culture.

1. Rainbow Springs State Park

Most of Florida's springs were native campsites thousands of years ago. The area around this spring is thought to have been inhabited 10,000 years ago. The spring's basin is hundreds of feet wide and forms a beautiful pool. The name came from multicolored prisms, caused by mineral deposits, that shimmer when the sun is high. The shady park features ornamental azalea gardens that are showy with blooms in February and March. The park campground is special because it's located beside a springs river. (By contrast, there is no camping allowed in the popular Wakulla Springs State Park in the Big Bend Region.) The water is a chilly 72 degrees F year-round, so I recommend visiting in the summer to float on an inner tube on a steaming hot day. The sandy bottom of the Rainbow River near the campground has yielded mastodon and sloth bones from prehistoric times.

Location: The park day-use area is about 3 miles north of downtown Dunnellon on the eastern side of U.S. Highway 41 at 19158 SW 81st Place Road. The campground, formerly a private site, is at 18185 SW 94th Street, which you reach via County Road 484.

Important Information: For more park information or campground reservations, call 352-489-8503 or visit <www.dep.state.fl.us/parks>.

2. Fort Cooper State Park

Bring your young soldiers here to relive the time in 1836 when U.S. soldiers built a log palisade here and fought against the resident Seminole Indians. There was a Seminole stronghold in the area near the Withlacoochee River.

Each April a battle is re-enacted. A replica of the palisade, 5 miles of nature trails, swimming in spring-fed (meaning chilly) Lake Holathlikaha, and canoe rentals are among the allures of this little-known but scenic park. Your youth group can make a reservation for the tent camping area.

Location: About 2 miles southeast of Inverness off U.S. Highway 41 at 3100 Old Floral City Road.

Important information: For more information, call 352-726-0315 or visit <www.dep.state.fl.us/parks>.

3. Crystal River State Archaeological Site

● ●

Every school student eventually hears of Hernando de Soto's trek through the Florida peninsula in 1539–40. They learn about his armor-clad soldiers and the wooden sailing ships the explorers arrived in from Cuba, but often they learn little about the natives de Soto met and fought with. This site, which he probably visited, helps. Six high mounds, including temple, burial, and midden mounds, spread across 14 acres here and seem to whisper of the native grandeur that once was. Three different, evolving prehistoric cultures used this site as a highly complex ceremonial center. Think of the scene when as many as 7,500 natives walked here each year to participate in elaborate ceremonies. The natives—Indians of the Depford Culture, then the Weeden Island Culture, and finally the Safety Harbor Culture—chose this area for 1,600 years because of the abundance of fish and shellfish in nearby waters.

Museum exhibits suggest what life was like here and how burials were arranged. The site probably was also the location of an astronomical calendar. Wooden steps going up the highest temple mound allow you to walk in the path of ceremonial chiefs, who were probably arrayed in the finest feather headdresses, paints, and copper breastplates that their devoted attendants could adorn them with. At the top, turn and look out at the Gulf of Mexico, then out over an imagined mass of natives, all eyes upon you, the chief, as you. . . . That's the mystery. It will take some future anthropological or archaeological sleuth to discover exactly what took place. This site, a national historic landmark, provides an excellent opportunity to stretch your legs, picnic on a blanket, and ponder the ancients.

Location: From U.S. Highway 19 in Crystal River, take County Road 44 west for 2.5 miles to the site at 3400 North Museum Point.

Important information: For more information, call 352-795-3817 or visit <www.dep.state.fl.us/parks>.

4. Homosassa Springs State Wildlife Park

At this park, an observatory below the surface of the spring allows you to watch manatees and other marine creatures underwater. Sea catfish, sheepshead, crevalle jacks, and other saltwater fish swim up Homosassa Bay and River and collect in groups of up to 3,000 at a time. But the big winter attraction here is a herd of manatees, once considered a food source by Paleo-Indians but now designated an endangered species. The gentle mammals circle the observatory, enchanting children and adults alike. You won't want to leave. But eventually you'll want to visit the rest of the park's residents, including captive alligators, snakes, bears, bobcats, foxes, otters, and birds.

This is the state park system's wildlife rehabilitation center, so your young naturalists will have a chance to ask rangers how you get a bear to take his medicine. Injured manatees are nursed to health before being returned to the wild. Rangers also conduct boat tours on Pepper Creek. Some families, mine among them, can spend an entire day here; it's one of the most unusual parks in the United States, and I would rate it among the top three state parks in Florida for close-up wildlife observation. There is a restaurant, a snack shop, a hands-on children's center, a small museum, and plenty of photo opportunities, so bring your camera.

Location: On the west side of U.S. Highway 19 about 75 miles north of Tampa at 9225 West Fish Bowl Drive.

Important information: Open daily from 9 A.M. to 5:30 P.M., but no one is allowed to enter after 4 P.M. This park gets overcrowded, and the underwater observatory is more enjoyable without a crowd. Try to arrive on a weekday morning, near opening time. For more information, call 352-628-5343 or visit <www.dep.state.fl.us/parks>.

Tarpon Springs Area

Tarpon Springs, on the Gulf of Mexico about 30 miles north of St. Petersburg, is a cultural enclave visited by busloads of school children. The town is a port on the Anclote River, and it encompasses a lake and several bayous. The busy town dates to 1882, when it was a Victorian health resort. A mineral spring attracted visitors who hoped the waters had curative powers, which led to the construction of mansions and hotels.

In about 1905, Greek immigrants began arriving to fish, build boats, and collect sponges from the sediment at the bottom of the gulf. Sponging had existed here previously, but now it became an important commercial venture. You can learn about the risks the hardy divers took, and see some of the early underwater breathing devices that were their lifelines. The sponge industry declined in the 1940s, in part because of water pollution and the rising popularity of synthetic sponges. But thanks to rigorous enforcement of environmental controls, the sponge beds are healthy once more. Simultaneously, natural sponges are in vogue again, with demand exceeding supply.

Today, three sponge wholesalers operate from Tarpon Springs. From a tour boat, you can see their divers going about their work dressed in modern wetsuits. Many sites that showcase the Greek culture, including boat tours, are based at the Tarpon Springs Historic Sponge Docks directly off U.S. Highway 19A near Tarpon Bayou.

The origin of the town name is a source of debate. According to one legend, a woman named Mary Ormond Boyer, watching a fish jump in a bay called Spring Bayou, said, "See the tarpon spring!" There is no springs named after the fish here, but there is Lake Tarpon. Much of the town was developed by Anson P. K. Safford, a former territorial governor of Arizona.

5. Sponge Docks Welcome Center

Ask for a local map, view the pictures of divers, study the many offerings of the Sponge Docks, and pick up some brochures. The Tarpon Springs Historic Downtown Area is about a quarter-mile to the south along Tarpon Avenue. There are many restaurants and shops selling not only sponges but also imported clothes, such as Greek fishermen's caps, and gifts from Greece. Take advantage of the chance to ask questions—about Greek food, music, the sponge business—and pick up some discount coupons.

Location: In the Harbormaster's Office on the Sponge Docks at 10 Dodecanese Boulevard, west of U.S. Highway 19A in Tarpon Springs.

Important information: Open daily. For more information, call 727-937-6109 or visit <www.tarponsprings.com>. You can also contact the Sponge Docks Merchants Association at 727-942-6381.

6. Sponge-O-Rama Museum

Watch the half-hour movie about sponging, see early diving masks and breathing machines, and consider the lead weights, even iron shoes, that brave divers used to keep themselves on the gulf bottom while they collected sponges. Learn how President Calvin Coolidge rode out with sponge divers in the

1920s and then ordered the Anclote River dredged. This is the site of the original sponge exchange or sponge market.

Location: At 510 Dodecanese Boulevard in Tarpon Springs.

Important information: Free. Open daily from 11 A.M. to 6 P.M. For more information, call 727-943-9509 or visit <www.tarponsprings.com>.

7. Konger Coral Sea Aquarium

Observe the nurse and lemon sharks, stingrays, and more at this 120,000-gallon tank that has a coral reef.

Location: At 852 Dodecanese Boulevard in Tarpon Springs.

Important information: Children under age 3 are admitted free; fees are $2 for other children, $3.25 for seniors, and $4 for all others. For more information, call 727-938-5378.

The sponge sport

It's not every day that most of us think about **natural sponges,** nor do we ponder their connection with sports. But the original Greek Olympics actually featured a diving competition to collect sponges. The Aegean people valued sponges, which were used by Greek warriors to clean their shields. According to the New Testament Bible, a sponge soaked in vinegar was offered to Christ on the cross.

Sponges are saltwater animals that live in colonies much like corals in warmer waters. But sponges are soft and corals are hard. Sponges need something hard to cling to on the sea bottom, such as a rock, a coral, or even the hard shell of a crab. Meals of plankton float to the sponges on the currents. The nutrients course through a sponge colony's many chambers like pasta water through a colander.

Sponges have a dark skin covering their soft skeleton and a gray jellylike substance, called gurry, between the two. The skin and gurry are removed, and the skeleton is cleaned and sold. There are about 5,000 kinds of sponges in the world, and the Gulf of Mexico off Florida, when salty and healthy enough, grows at least 10. Florida is the only sponge-growing state in the nation.

The bath sponge that made Tarpon Springs famous is the sheeps-wool sponge, from the family Spongiidae. A processed sheeps-wool sponge is soft and pliable when wet. It's round, a tawny butterscotch color, and has a "Swiss cheese" look.

8. St. Nicholas Cathedral

A Greek Orthodox church was first built of wood on this site in 1907, reminding the immigrant worshipers of their beloved homes on the Dodecanese Islands in the Aegean Sea. As the community prospered, a larger worship center, constructed of marble, was financed with sponge and fish catches. It was built to replicate the famed Constantinople Cathedral, a world landmark of Christianity. You can visit and see the Greek marble, artwork, and ornate features.

Location: In downtown Tarpon Springs at 36 North Pinellas Avenue, about eight blocks south of the Sponge Docks and Dodecanese Boulevard.

Important information: Open from 10 A.M. to 4 P.M. daily. For more information, call 727-937-3540 or visit <www.tarponsprings.com>.

It's Greek for me!

A tasty path to cultural exchange is to sample foods from other lands. The flavors of authentic **Greek food** are too tempting to pass up in Tarpon Springs. The rich culinary tradition began here as family cooks bustled to serve the hungry appetites of sponge divers and ship builders. Today, many restaurants and cafés are still centered on the Sponge Docks and Dodecanese Boulevard.

Baklava is a nut-filled, honey-drenched pastry; one piece may be sweet enough to slice and share among two or three children. There are several other Greek pastries to sample, along with heartier fare, such as *pastitso* (a kid-pleasing Greek macaroni-and-beef dish), *kefetedes* (Greek meatballs), *moussaka* (ground meat with eggplant), *stifado* (Greek beef stew), *fela* (a cabbage dish with meat, rice, and lemon sauce), and my favorite, a flaky dough filled with feta cheese and spinach called *spanakopita*. My husband grew up enjoying his Sicilian mother's octopus and squid dishes, so he likes *calamarakia* (baby squid). Some dining establishments to try include Dino's, Mykonos, Louis Pappas, Plaka, and Parthenon Pastry Shop.

Louis Pappas, a huge restaurant that dominates the Sponge Docks, is an attraction in itself. Louis Pappamichaelopoulus arrived in Tarpon Springs from Sparta, Greece, in 1904. He shortened his name and then returned to Europe during World War I, serving as a cook for General Pershing in France. Pappas opened a restaurant in Tarpon Springs in 1925 and became an important community leader. The restaurant has remained in his family ever since.

9. Tarpon Springs Historic District/ Historical Society Museum

About a quarter-mile south of the Sponge Docks/Dodecanese Boulevard area, the downtown historic district, centered on Tarpon Avenue, reflects the era when Tarpon Springs was a winter resort. Not so long ago, many buildings were in disrepair, but restoration saved the Victorian beauties, and the district is listed on the National Register of Historic Places. Stroll on brick sidewalks under shady trees and nostalgic street lamps and sit on green benches. Visit the Tarpon Springs Historical Society Museum in the Old Atlantic Coastline Railroad Station, with its kid-pleasing HO-gauge model railroad. If you need another rainy-day diversion, the excellent new public library is here.

Location: Near Tarpon Avenue, Spring Bayou, and Craig Park in Tarpon Springs.

Important information: For detailed directions, stop at the Sponge Docks Welcome Center (see Site 5), call 727-937-6109, or visit <www. tarponsprings.com>.

10. Anclote Key State Preserve/ Anclote Lighthouse

Feel like a castaway on this island in the Gulf of Mexico, 3 miles from Tarpon Springs. The ride from Tarpon Springs and the island adventure are best for older children who like to swim and comb the beaches; there are no playgrounds or shelters there. The 4-mile-long beach, which features beautiful, high dunes, is an excellent place to go shelling. The island supports bald eagles, ospreys, and many shorebirds. The federal lighthouse there, built in 1887, once lit the night sky with a kerosene-fueled torch. President Grover Cleveland declared the island a preserve in 1886. The name Anclote probably comes from a Spanish word that means anchor.

Location: Hire a guide in Tarpon Springs to take you over. Island Wind Tours is one place that offers boat rides.

Important information: This is a wild, undeveloped beach. Take everything you need, including fresh water, sunscreen, and hats or visors. Bring all your litter back. There are no restrooms. Plan on a half-day trip. For Island Wind Tours, call 727-934-0606 and for park information, call 727-469-5942 or visit <www.dep.state.fl.us/parks>.

11. Pinellas County Recreation Trail

This 46-mile paved trail for walkers, bicyclists, and inline skaters, built on an old railroad bed, begins in Tarpon Springs and can take you all the way to St. Petersburg past some expansive Gulf of Mexico vistas that include Honeymoon Island and Crystal Beach. Rental bikes and skates are available for the glide. A 2-mile section through the Tarpon Springs Historic District is especially popular. This is part of Florida's well-known conversion of publicly owned old railroad beds into linear public parks.

Location: Parallel to U.S. Highway 19A in Tarpon Springs, connecting with Dodecanese Boulevard.

Important information: For more information and for bike and skate rentals, contact Outdoor Gear, 212 East Tarpon Avenue, Tarpon Springs 727-943-0937.

12. Fred Howard County Park

Here's a fine swimming beach on the Gulf of Mexico, accessible via a 1-mile causeway from the grassy park. The park is pretty and manicured, with playgrounds, picnic pavilions, restrooms, and showers.

Location: In Tarpon Springs at 1700 Sunset Drive. The beach is at the end of the park's causeway, Howard Drive.

Important information: Open daily from 7 A.M. to sunset. For more information, call 727-937-4938.

13. Brooker Creek Preserve

Nature trails and boardwalks take you through parts of this 8,500-acre wetland and woodland preserve. Watch for migratory birds. At the $6 million environmental education center, enjoy learning about the fragile fish nurseries called estuaries in hands-on exhibits. This new, state-of-the-art center boasts an herb garden, a large-screen theater, resident researchers, and more.

Location: In Tarpon Springs at 1001 Lora Lane, via State Road 582.

Important information: The education center, IMAX theater, and other features will open in phases. Call 727-943-4000 to find out how much of the complex is open to the public.

Tampa Area

Although not directly on the gulf shore, the Tampa region owes its existence to water. The winding Hillsborough River courses through it on a 54-mile path from the Green Swamp to Hillsborough Bay, a side bayou of the biggest bay on the Florida Gulf Coast: Tampa Bay. In addition to river-related activities, the intensely urban Tampa area offers several fun and educational attractions, and some of those reflect its history. This area was an important campsite for native peoples for thousands of years. It's almost certainly the spot where Hernando de Soto landed in 1539 to begin his expedition of conquest. Tampa was the place where Teddy Roosevelt collected his Rough Riders before leaving to fight in Cuba during the Spanish-American War. Cuban émigrés came to the area to work in cigar factories and created a village, Ybor City, which remembers their heritage in a cigar-accented historic district. The colorful Spanish influence is most often tasted at fragrant bakeries, walk-up coffee stands, and restaurants.

Tampa was once named *Tanpa*, possibly from a Calusa Indian word whose meaning is unknown. For a while, Tampa was also called Fort Brooke, for a federal fort located here in 1824. When the earlier name was restored, it was spelled with an "m."

14. Hillsborough River State Park/Fort Foster Site

There's plenty of family appeal here, including a walk through a replica of a U.S. Army fort from the Seminole Wars. Fort Foster was built in 1836 to guard a strategic bridge over the Hillsborough River, which served as a boundary between white settlers and Seminole Indians. The Seminoles were confined to land south of the river, awaiting forced emigration to the West.

Periodically, including each February, Seminole and U.S. military re-enactors set up camp and depict frontier life. The 3,738-acre park also offers a swimming lake, a suspension footbridge over the river, plenty of picnic places, nature trails through cypress swamp, freshwater marshes, and longleaf pine woods. Bobcats, foxes, otters, alligators, feral hogs, and armadillos live here, but the river is famed for flocks of white ibises that feed along its shores in the fall. Two campgrounds are shady places, with a camp store that rents canoes. The river supplies about 75 percent of Tampa's drinking water, and the park's wilderness area helps protect the watershed. It's all within 12 miles of bustling Tampa.

Location: Northeast of Tampa in Thonotosassa at 15402 U.S. Highway 301.

Important information: For more information, call 813-987-6771 or visit <www.dep.state.fl.us/parks> and <http://fortfoster.homepage.com>.

15. Canoe Escape

● ●

This outfitter knows the location of the best wildlife-watching spots along the Hillsborough River and also shares great tales of the region's lore. The guides will teach you to pronounce the Seminole name for the river, which is said to mean River Where One Crosses to Eat Acorns, and tell about the clear Crystal Springs, a prime source of river water. Ask them the ideal places for family paddling, picnics, and splashing.

Location: In Thonotosassa at 9335 East Fowler Avenue.

Important information: For detailed directions, reservations, and more information, call 813-986-2067 or visit <www.canoeescape.com>.

16. Lettuce Lake Park

● ●

Take a walk along the 3,500-foot boardwalk into a cypress swamp and climb the observation tower for a 360-degree view of a broad floodplain of the Hillsborough River. This is prime territory to spot warblers. Lettuce Lake is actually a shallow, fingerlike section of the river. This very popular park features a playground, visitor center, and bike path.

Location: In Tampa at 6920 Fletcher Avenue.

Important information: For more information, call 813-987-6204.

17. Lowry Zoological Garden and Park

● ●

The first thing to do on a hot day is to get all wet in the fountain at the entrance. Then wind your way to the fish-eye-level, manatee-viewing area in this lush and spiffy 24-acre zoo, a family favorite in the Tampa area. The rare red panda lives here, as does a Komodo dragon and almost 1,600 other wild creatures, including red wolves and panthers, both Florida natives. The free-roaming iguanas that live among the birds of the aviary are also fun for kids to spot. This is a beautiful zoo of many surprises, such as the opportunity of glass-wall close encounters with gorillas at Primate World or the chance to feed free-flying lorikeets nectar from your hands. The zoo's Discovery Center is one of the best of its kind in the state, with a walk-in globe, hundreds of touchable objects, and an unusual insect zoo. The staff presents lively and educational talks on animals. A petting zoo, restaurant, and cafés round out the offerings. The adjacent park is a great picnic place and features an amusement-park playground. This is the best zoo on Florida's Gulf Coast and among the top three in the state.

Location: In Tampa at 7530 North Boulevard.

Important information: Open from 9:30 A.M. to 5 P.M. daily except on Thanksgiving and Christmas. Children under age 3 are admitted free; fees are $4.95 for ages 3 to 11, $7.50 for seniors, and $8.50 for all others. For more information, call 813-932-0245 or visit <www.lowryparkzoo.com>.

18. Children's Museum of Tampa

Little tykes like exploring Safety Village, a mini-town where they can fight fires, keep the peace as a police officer, call for order in the court as a judge, broadcast the midday TV news, drive a car, add to their bank account, or deplete it shopping for dog food. It's located next to the Lowry Zoo and is an easy side trip.

Location: In Tampa at 7550 North Boulevard.

Important information: Open from 9 A.M. to 4 P.M. Mondays through Fridays, from 10 A.M. to 5 P.M. Saturdays, and from 1 to 5 P.M. Sundays. Children under age 2 are admitted free; fee is $4 otherwise.

19. Museum of Science and Industry

Take flights of fancy into space at the museum's own unit of the Challenger Learning Center, a 21st-century classroom that allows children to play at being astronauts and engineers. Several Challenger Centers, at sites across the nation, were created by astronauts and their families and attract young space fans from all over. Also at this three-story, 65-acre museum, you can see the effects of a gulf hurricane, walk under three-story-tall dinosaurs, turn on a light by riding a bike, check out the insect zoo, test for pH at the chemistry station, and stand still for a brush with beauty in the BioWorks Butterfly Garden. There's an IMAX dome theater, a planetarium, and an on-site restaurant. You can easily spend the day in what is possibly the largest science center in the southeastern United States. If I imagined my dream science school, it would be MOSI, a must-see place to explore space, the human body, and the environment. This is a pacesetting, county-owned venture with a Head Start Center and public library on site.

Location: In Tampa at 4801 East Fowler Avenue.

Important information: Opens daily at 9 A.M. Closing time changes seasonally. Basic admission is $5 for children ages 2 to 12, $7 for ages 13 to 18 and college students, $7 for seniors, and $8 for adults. Children under 2 are admitted free. Check in advance for information on specific Challenger Center opportunities. For specific closing times or for more information, call 813-987-6300 or visit <www.mosi.org>. For IMAX movie information, call 877-987-4629.

20. Florida Aquarium

With more than 1 million gallons of salt water and 500 native species on three floors of exhibition space, this aquarium is a Florida treasure. You'll find an oceanful to ogle, including sharks, rays, sea turtles, eels, spiny lobsters, schooling fish, jellyfish, and a coral reef and its colorful residents. You'll also meet roseate spoonbills, otters, and other Florida critters. You can touch stingrays in a touch tank. Try to time your visit to hear one of the divers' talks, at 11 A.M., 1 P.M., and 3 P.M. The youngest children will want to get all wet at Explore a Shore, the aquarium's innovative version of a petting zoo. They can dig in the sand, climb among mangrove roots, safely touch creatures in a tidal pool, and crawl through a marine cave. Young scientists will want to visit the aquarium's real laboratory. Free behind-the-scenes tours are offered three times a day. Call ahead for tour times and for information on special kids' events such as Deep Sea Slime Time and a storytime called Fish Tales.

Location: In Tampa at the Port Authority's Garrrison Seaport at 701 Channelside Drive.

Important information: Open from 9 A.M. to 6 P.M. daily, but tickets are not sold past 4 P.M. Tickets are $5.95 for children to age 13 and $10.95 for all others. The parking fee is $3. For more information, call 813-273-4020 or 800-353-4741 or visit <www.flaquarium.org>.

21. Seminole Indian Reservation, Tampa

Not far from the Florida State Fairgrounds, a re-burial ground for Seminole Indian graves dug up during regional development led to the formation of this reservation. A cultural center provides a glimpse into Seminole Indian heritage, including a replica village where crafts are demonstrated. The tribe operates a bingo hall and casino in a separate building.

Location: In Tampa just west of Interstate 4 at 5221 Orient Road.

Important information: For more information, call 800-282-7016 or 813-620-3077 or visit <www.seminoletribe.com>.

22. Castillo's Café

You won't want to leave the Tampa area without tasting some local specialties. At the very least, sample warm Cuban bread, flan (a custard dessert), and black beans and rice. All are available in many area restaurants that don't necessarily specialize in Cuban fare. If you want to sample some in a kid-easy setting that's not as pricey and elegant as some Cuban restaurants, try this popular family cafeteria with local flavor.

Location: In Tampa at 1832 East Seventh Avenue.

Important information: Opens at 7:30 A.M. for breakfast. There is usually a pause in service between breakfast, lunch, and dinner offerings, so call ahead, 813-248-1306, to be sure of hours.

23. Mel's Hot Dogs

To me, you can't have kids and a real Florida vacation without also piling on the hot dogs. This longtime local eatery is a popular family hangout. It serves kosher hot dogs, Polish sausage, and tons of toppers served in that favorite of the 1950s, the red plastic basket. If meat is not your thing, there is also a veggie burger.

Location: In Tampa at 4216 East Busch Boulevard.

Important information: For more information, call 813-985-8000.

24. Big Bend Manatee Viewing Center

This place is out of your way if you're traveling in the Tampa/St. Petersburg area using the Sunshine Skyway Bridge. But if you're taking Interstate 75 or U.S. Highway 41, it's worth a detour to see the winter herd of manatees. (The site is closed from mid-April to mid-November.) Warm water from a nearby power plant attracts the marine mammals, which need warmer water for good health. As many as 120 have been seen crowded into the canal during the coldest weather. A platform over the water offers excellent views of the herd if it is in residence.

In addition to manatees, look for catfish, mullet, snook, and even tarpon. A boardwalk through the mangrove trees offers a chance to look for fiddler crabs among the mangrove roots. An environmental education center shares the story of the giant but delicate manatee, an endangered species that could become extinct without human help.

Location: From I-75 in Tampa, take exit 47 and travel west on Big Bend Road, crossing US 41 at the traffic light. Continue on Big Bend Road to the park entrance at the intersection of Big Bend Road and Dickman Road.

Important information: The site is generally open from about November 18 through April 6. For more information, call 813-228-4289.

25. Polk Museum of Art/Lake Morton Park

If you're heading east from Tampa to the Orlando area, this free museum is an inspiring stop for your young artists. Its main mission is education, and unlike some exclusive art museums, children and families are made to feel very welcome here. There are workshops and classes for all ages, and exhibitions are presented so that they appeal to all ages. The collection includes Florida artists, Georgian silver, Asian art, and pre-Columbian artifacts, such as sculpted ceremonial drinking cups. The patio sculpture garden with its waterfall wall is an eye-catching place. From the art museum, it's an easy stroll next door to the public library on Lake Morton. The lake is the centerpiece of a lovely city park and home to a flock of swans that nests on the shore every spring. Bring bread to feed the swans and ducks.

Location: In Lakeland at 800 East Palmetto Street, just east of Lake Morton.

Important information: Admission to the art museum is free. Open Tuesdays through Fridays from 9 A.M. to 5 P.M., Saturdays and Mondays from 10 A.M. to 5 P.M., and Sundays from 1 to 5 P.M. For more information, call 863-688-7743 or visit <www.polkmuseumofart.org>.

26. Fantasy of Flight

Older children can climb behind the controls of a flight simulator here and soar into battle with the best of them. Adults appreciate the way this private collection honors the freedom fighters of World War II. This is a fine place for grandparents and children to have fun together, since there is something to appeal to each end of the age spectrum. Replicas of the Wright Brothers' 1903 flyer and Charles Lindbergh's *Spirit of St. Louis* are poised to take off.

There is a four-passenger flying boat, but the car-plane is what children really remember. All movie fantasies aside, a flying automobile, the Roadair, was actually built in 1959. No, it didn't take wing, and you can try to guess why as you look at it here. The on-site restaurant serves breakfast and lunch, making this a convenient stop on the east-west ride between Tampa and Orlando.

Location: From Interstate 4 in Polk City, take exit 21. The museum is at 1400 Broadway.

Important information: Open daily from 9 A.M. to 5 P.M.; the restaurant is open from 8 A.M. to 4 P.M. Children ages 4 and under are admitted free; fees are $13.95 for ages 5 to 12 and $24.95 for all others. For more information, call 863-984-3500 or visit <www.fantasyofflight.com>.

Clearwater/St. Petersburg Area

A Russian exile of noble birth built a railroad from Lake Monroe near Sanford westward to this area in 1888. According to local legend, he won a coin toss to name the area after his hometown. Sunshine and the railroads soon brought winter visitors, who liked to sail on Tampa Bay and visit islands in the Gulf of Mexico. Fishing is big business today, as is catering to vacationers who like the beaches and retirees who seek shade in the parks.

This area on the sandy Pinellas Peninsula, across Tampa Bay from Tampa, supports about 15 waterfront communities that meld into one another south of Tarpon Springs. The busy region, dominated by St. Petersburg and Clearwater, attracts beach-goers from the greater Tampa area. There are several important children's sites to see, including outstanding aquariums and an expansive science center.

27. Clearwater Marine Aquarium

For months after my family visited this aquarium, my daughter still talked about Sunset, the resident 5,000-pound porpoise. Sunset stranded herself not far from the aquarium and, because of her injuries, couldn't return to life in the wild. So she represents her species here with educational demonstrations that are different from typical dolphin "shows." This small, nonprofit, waterfront science center—with its own dock and boat for field trips—occupied us for half a day, marine fans that we are. Your family or kids' group can arrange a private water safari in nearby shallows. Older students and adults may qualify to spend the day as a dolphin trainer; plan ahead.

Among the several tanks, expect to connect with a flurry of undersea residents. The rarely seen Florida lobster seems to be all spiny skeleton. Sea turtles, sharks, and groupers cruise slowly in tanks you can view from varying perspectives. Our favorite part was Stingray Beach, an indoor tank gussied up to look like a beach with a boardwalk, where guides encourage you to gently touch small rays the size of pancake griddles. (Their barbs are clipped; no danger here.) The critters are captivating, the way they roll their small wings at the surface of clear salt water, seemingly begging to be touched. Then they flip a tiny splash of water as they scoot off to settle in the sand. While most Florida aquariums have touch tanks these days, this site is generally less crowded, so you have plenty of breathing room around the animals.

Location: In Clearwater, take State Road 60 (Gulf-to-Bay Boulevard) west to Memorial Causeway, toward Clearwater Beach. From Memorial Causeway, look for the aquarium sign and turn right onto Island Way and then left onto Windward Passage. The aquarium is at 249 Windward Passage.

Important information: For more information, call 888-941-9414 or 727-441-1790 or visit <www.cmaquarium.org>.

28. It's Our Nature

This outfitter based in Clearwater specializes in kayaking and nature walks and caters especially to women and girls. Special activities include wildflower hikes, journal writing, and seaside shell collecting. Ask about the Child Exploration event.

Location: In Clearwater at 929 Bay Esplanade.

Important information: For more information, call 727-441-2599 or visit <www.itsournature.com>.

29. Moccasin Lake Nature Park

Here's an urban opportunity to watch wildlife and learn about energy alternatives. Take the cool 1-mile hike to 5-acre Moccasin Lake. From its observation pier, you're likely to see cruising alligators, soaring bald eagles, and snapping turtles. At the interpretive center, brush up on your fish identification. You can also learn how the park supplies some of its own energy needs, and check out how the building conserves energy.

Location: In Clearwater at 2750 Park Trail Lane.

Important information: Open from 9 A.M. to 5 P.M. Tuesdays through Fridays and from 10 A.M. to 6 P.M. Saturdays and Sundays. Children under age 3 are admitted free; fees are $1 for ages 3 to 13 and $2 for all others. For more information, call 727-462-6024 or visit <www.clearwater-fl.com/parksrec>.

30. Heritage Village

• •

At selected times of day, people in pioneer costumes walk you through the log house, general store, and 1920s auto garage of this intriguing nonprofit history park. The shady, 21-acre park features 27 old buildings, including a small museum. Be sure to visit the old railroad depot and the one-room school. Call ahead for a schedule of special events, because you don't want to miss the re-enactment festivals.

Location: In Largo, south of Clearwater, at 11909 125th Street North.

Important information: Open from 10 A.M. to 4 P.M. Tuesdays through Saturdays and from 1 to 4 P.M. Sundays. For more information, call 727-582-2123 or visit <www.FloridaFrontier.com>.

Wagon, ho!

• •

It's so hard to look at the urban neighborhoods and shopping centers near Florida's gulf shore and remember that covered wagons and ox-drawn carts rumbled here. But settlers first came to this region, as well as other parts of Florida, in the 1700s and 1800s. Here's some of what one girl, Morning Elizabeth Curry McDaniel, once wrote about Florida travel in the late 1890s: "Some of the trip required four oxen which is called a two yoke outfit. Mother usually did the driving of the team while daddy rode horseback with his gun. As the country was sparsely settled and there were many wild animals as well as cattle in those days, daddy would ride along with the team. It was a long slow trip, as oxen are slow travelers, but that was the way almost everyone traveled. Sometimes we used horses for our travels. This was the only way of transportation through that part of Florida at the time; no trains, buses or trucks; there were only country roads, cow and deer trails." It's something to ponder as you wait for the traffic light to turn green. Source: Tampa Bay History

31. Honeymoon Island State Recreation Area

No, this popular island on the Gulf of Mexico isn't just for couples. The name is said to be a promotional gimmick dating to the 1930s, when the island was touted as a paradise for newlyweds. It was previously called Sand Island and then Hog Island, because of a hog farm located there, so Honeymoon was a sweet improvement. The park features showers, restrooms, picnic tables, nature paths, and a fine swimming beach.

Location: From Dunedin, take State Road 586 west across St. Joseph Sound. The road ends in the park.

Important information: For more information, call 727-469-5942 or visit <www.dep.state.fl.us/parks>.

32. Suncoast Seabird Sanctuary

This may be the largest wild-bird rescue operation in the nation. Each day the sanctuary takes in about 20 injured newcomers—birds hooked by fishing lures, tangled in nets and fishing lines, made sick from swallowing plastic, or

When you've hooked a feathery fish

If you fish—or spend a lot of time around people who do—you or a co-traveler may accidentally hook a pelican or other bird. Here are some tips on what to do, offered by Suncoast Seabird Sanctuary near St. Petersburg.

- Don't cut the line. This is actually a certain death sentence for the bird.
- Slowly reel the bird to you.
- Put a towel or other cloth over the bird's head, because darkness can calm it.
- Let the bird keep its beak open. This is how it breathes.
- If you can, push the hook through the skin until you see the barb.
- Cut the barb with wire cutters, which you can pick up at many bait shops.
- Remove the cut hook and the line before letting the bird go.
- If you can't deal with the hook after putting a towel over the bird's head, ask the nearest bait shop where to find the nearest wildlife rescue center and take the bird there immediately.

in other ways needing care. Take a tour and visit the 500 or so "patients." Junior veterinarians, as well as anyone who fishes, ought to visit one of Florida's wildlife rescue operations, such as this premier one, if only to learn how to handle a hooked bird. You *don't* cut the line. See "When You've Hooked a Feathery Fish" to learn the proper procedure.

Location: Just north of St. Petersburg Beach in Indian Shores Beach at 18328 Gulf Boulevard.

Important information: Tours are offered at 2 P.M. Wednesdays and Sundays. A donation is requested. For more information, call 727-391-6211

33. Native American Cultural Center

This region has been appreciated for thousands of years for its abundance of seafood and its sheltered location. At this new hands-on, state-of-the-art museum, created with the assistance of the Smithsonian's Museum of the American Indian, learn about the people who fished, hunted, and built mounds here 11,000 years ago.

Location: On Weedon Island in St. Petersburg at 1500 Weedon Drive.

Important information: The center was scheduled to open in late 2000 or early 2001, so call 727-217-7208 for up-to-date information and specific directions.

34. Great Explorations/The Pier

Great Explorations is an incredible hands-on science museum on the third floor of The Pier, in St. Petersburg. Tackle the sensory-deprivation Touch Tunnel if you dare. Test your muscles at the Body Shop. Wee folks may want to try Explore Galore.

The Pier itself is a unique piece of Florida architecture. Ask your kids what the five-story building reminds them of. Most say an upside-down pyramid. An aquarium occupies its second floor, while the top floor features a unit of the famed Florida restaurant, the Columbia, where you can't possibly pass up the Cuban bread, black bean soup, or flan. Downstairs you can try a mango milkshake or coconut ice-cream cone, rent bicycles or skates, or cruise through the many shops and restaurants.

Location: From Interstate 275 in St. Petersburg, take exit 10 to Beach Drive. Turn south onto Second Avenue NE, a street that extends into the bay as a drive-on causeway-pier. Park in the designated lot and take a free tram ride to the building entrance at 800 Second Avenue NE.

Important information: Great Explorations is open from 10 A.M. to 5 P.M. Mondays through Saturdays and from noon to 5 P.M. Sundays. For information, call 717-821-8992 or visit <www.greatexplorations.org>. For other pier information, call 727-821-6164 or visit <www.stpete-pier.com>. For information about the Columbia Restaurant, call 727-822-8000.

35. St. Petersburg Museum of History

Walk through time at this museum dedicated to the way things were. Located next to The Pier (see above), the museum makes a good rainy-day destination. Visit the re-created 1870 country store and see the 3,000-year-old mummy.

Location: At the foot of The Pier in St. Petersburg, at 335 Second Avenue NE.

Important information: Children under 6 are admitted free; fees are $1.50 for children 6 to 17, and $4 for adults. For more information, call 727-894-2123.

36. Don CeSar Beach Resort

The towering and turreted Don CeSar, which glistens like a wedding cake iced in pink, supplies heritage and charm for Florida's Gulf Coast. Its terraces, garden patios, shell-strewn beach, restaurants, and public areas once welcomed Clarence Darrow and F. Scott Fitzgerald. Stroll the grounds and sample the marble-accented public areas of this treasure, which is listed on the National Register of Historic Places. Perhaps you will glimpse Lucinda or Thomas, two ghosts said to visit this castle by the sea. This late-1920s building on the gulf inspired its own history book, *The Don CeSar Story*, by Jane Hurly Young. It also hosts history tours, garden tours, and children's events. At the edge of the hotel parking lot, a small boat-launching park, an access to Boca Ciega Bay, offers a place to look for manatees.

Location: In St. Petersburg Beach at 3400 Gulf Boulevard.

Important information: For more information, call 800-282-1116 or visit <www.doncesar.com>.

When beaches were mountains

The sand under your feet probably started out as part of the mountains of the Carolinas or Georgia, but the rock gradually eroded and went for a ride. Rain and rivers, and then currents of the ocean or gulf moved the sand underwater. Finally, more water or wind brought it from the sea to the beach. Wind-blown sand is rounder than waterborne. Sand moves almost constantly, usually but not always to be replaced by other sand. Florida's sand varies in color and texture from baby-powder white to pink, from coarse orange to brown. The color often is caused by the addition of finely ground shells. Can a grain of sand disappear the same way rock slowly is ground into sand? Most likely not. Wet sand holds a bit of water about itself, and this prevents any further erosion.

Florida is a peninsula surrounded by barrier islands made of sand. Once, the islands were all towering sand dunes, taller than the tallest storm waves. The job of the barrier islands is to bear the brunt of hurricanes and lesser storms and keep the mainland from washing away. If people would only confine their building to the mainland, the barrier islands would provide them with free flood and storm insurance, but they don't.

A poet who must have vacationed in Florida once wrote, "Sand on the beaches, sand at the door, sand that screeches on the new-swept floor. In the shower, sand for the foot to crunch on; sand in the sandwiches spread for luncheon...."

37. Boyd Hill Nature Park

This is a locally popular picnic place at the south end of Lake Maggiore in south St. Petersburg. There are 3 miles of trails and boardwalks, including the Willow Marsh Trail, from which you can spot alligators. There's a nature center with aquariums, an observation beehive, and displays of local flora and fauna.

Location: From Interstate 275 in St. Petersburg, take exit 4 and head east on 54th Avenue South to Ninth Street. Turn left (north) onto Ninth Street and go to Country Club Way. The park is at 1101 Country Club Way South.

Important information: Open from 9 A.M. to 5 P.M. daily; hours are extended to 8 P.M. on Tuesdays and Thursdays from April to October only. Admission is 50 cents for children and $1 for adults. Call for a schedule of popular guided night walks, when you might be able to see a flying squirrel. For more information, call 727-893-7326.

38. Skyway State Fishing Pier

Take a walk on what used to be the longest fishing pier in the world: the original Sunshine Skyway Bridge, which carried many a vacationing family from St. Petersburg across Tampa Bay to the south shore and Bradenton. The old bridge is now closed to automobile traffic, but its north and south sections are ideal scenic spots from which to fish and view the bay. Fishing from here requires special equipment, such as heavy-duty tackle, because fish tend to get hung up under the bridge on barnacle-encrusted pilings. Concessions sell bait and snacks.

Location: The pier can be reached from pull-over rest areas on either end of the newer Sunshine Skyway Bridge, which connects St. Petersburg and Bradenton via Interstate 275 and U.S. Highway 19.

Important information: Free. For more information, call 727-865-0668 or 727-893-2627, or visit <www.dep.state.fl.us/parks>.

39. Fort De Soto County Park

This 900-acre park encompasses a group of five islands at the mouth of Tampa Bay, south of St. Petersburg Beach. But unlike other Florida islands that you must boat to, you can drive to these. Plan on a day of picnicking, wading, and beachcombing. Or you can camp overnight in one of the most scenic onshore campgrounds in the state. The campground is locally popular but not widely known outside the region because it's not part of the state park system. Young explorers enjoy the part of the park on Mullet Key, where you can take a nature path to Fort De Soto, which was built during the Spanish-American War and is now listed on the National Register of Historic Places. Bird watchers flock here to see the spring migratory birds, including a raft of shorebirds, warblers, and other songbirds. Try the woods near the Arrowhead Family Picnic Area for bird watching. Sea turtles lay eggs on the park's beaches in the summer. Other features of the park include a café, playgrounds, covered shelters, showers, restrooms, a fishing pier (where you can rent rods), and 7 miles of glistening beach.

Location: From St. Petersburg, head west on the Pinellas Bayway (State Road 682). Turn south onto SR 679 and follow it over a causeway straight into the park.

Important information: Swimming is risky here because of swift currents in some areas; consult with seasonal lifeguards about the safest swimming areas, and be alert. You'll pay 85 cents in tolls to reach the park, but otherwise it's free. To reserve a fishing rod, call 727-864-3345. For campground reservations, call 727-582-2267. For other park information, call 727-866-2484.

Bradenton Area

• •

Once a pioneer town named for 19th-century settler Dr. Joseph Braden, Bradenton and its busy environs comprise a booming community along the Manatee River at its confluence with the Gulf of Mexico. The area's gulfshore villages are low-key, family-friendly resorts that try very diligently to remain attractive and resist the sprawl of condominium towers.

40. De Soto National Memorial

• •

Hernando de Soto, a Spanish conquistador in South America, ended his rough career with a long march into the interior of North America. He hoped to find gold, explore and colonize "La Florida," and pacify the natives. De Soto reached the Florida Gulf Coast on May 30, 1539, though where he made landfall is unknown. Historians theorize that it was in the Tampa Bay area, possibly near this spot at the mouth of the Manatee River.

Ask your family to imagine the dramatic scene. Visualize nine 16th-century, wooden sailing ships with tall masts. Men are unloading squealing pigs, horses, and mules. As many as 600 sturdy conquistadors splash ashore, some wearing heavy metal armor that glints in the harsh Florida sun. There are also some black slaves, a few determined women secretly dressed as men, and 12 priests. They carry Spanish flags of red, white, and yellow bearing the royal emblem of lions. They also carry wooden casks of food, tools, and medical supplies, and they are accompanied by ferocious war dogs, such as greyhounds and mastifs.

From here, de Soto led a cruel march of conquest, torturing or killing any natives who resisted his advance. He tromped through Florida wetlands and dry scrub. He didn't like the place. After a two-month rest in Tallahassee, where he took over the bountiful agricultural capital, he pressed on through much of what came to be the southeastern United States. Inhabitants who didn't have time to flee and who weren't killed in battle or during torture contracted diseases from the Europeans. De Soto himself died in 1542 of fever near the Mississippi River.

Visitors sometimes confuse this site with Fort De Soto, a ruins from the Spanish-American war, and Fort De Soto Park, a county campground in St. Petersburg.

Location: From Interstate 75 near Bradenton, take exit 42 and follow State Road 64 west for about 12 miles to 75th Street NW. Turn right (north) onto 75th Street NW and go 2.5 miles to the park. From exit 1 of I-75, follow U.S. Highway 19 into Bradenton. Turn west onto SR 64 and go about 5 miles to 75th Street NW. Turn right (north) onto 75th Street NW and go 2.5 miles to the park.

Important information: There is a small admission fee. For more information, call 813-792-0458 or visit <www.nps.gov/deso/>. From December through April, park rangers dress in period costumes. In late March and early April, de Soto's landing is commemorated with a community history festival. Although history rules here, don't miss the half-mile nature walk along the shore. Look for tropical mangroves, whose odd roots curving into the water trap debris and build Florida islands.

41. Anna Maria Island

This 7.5-mile-long gulfshore island with plenty of parks and playgrounds is a low-key family vacation resort. For nearly 30 years, the islanders have worked hard to preserve the look of an old-fashioned beach town, despite persistent attempts to expand development. The reward is a lovely island with many small charms. It holds steady in a coastal zone of tall condominium towers (the island has a three-story height limit) and does its best to preserve its natural features, such as sand dunes. There are many apartments to rent, lots of screened porches on which to string a hammock, and a family-friendly feel.

Try several picnic places, including Bayfront Park at the northern end of the island and Coquina Beach Park at the southern end; both are places to spot manatees in the winter. You might also see manatees at the Kingfish Boat Ramp just as you enter the island via State Road 64. In one island village, Holmes Beach, walk or bike around and see if you can spot the free-roaming peacocks. Everywhere, look for hand-painted murals on buildings and for vest-pocket parks. You can try your fishing luck at public piers. The historic fishing community of Cortez, which you pass through on the southern access road to the island, looks like a miniature version of Key West. It has artists' studios, boat builders, and more. It puts on an environmental and seafood party the third Saturday in February. From Cortez, you can take a boat to Egmont Key State Park, a shorebird preserve on an isolated island about 3 miles from Anna Maria Island.

Location: Anna Maria Island is west of Bradenton in the Gulf of Mexico. You reach it via SR 64 (Palma Sola Causeway) or SR 684 (Cortez Boulevard).

Important information: For more information, call 941-729-9177, 941-778-1541, or 800-462-6283, or visit <www.floridaislandbeaches.org>.

42. Café on the Beach/Manatee Beach

Bring the kids here for the all-you-can-eat pancake breakfast or for tasty lunches and dinners, too. This much-loved local concession is located at Manatee Beach, one of several public beaches on Anna Maria Island. The beach has lifeguards, restrooms, and showers.

Location: In Holmes Beach on Gulf Drive, at the beach end of State Road 64.

Important information: For beach information, call 941-742-5923; for café information, call 941-778-9784.

43. Leffis Key Preserve/Coquina Baywalk

The 30-acre Leffis Key Preserve is a haven of tropical mangroves on the southern end of Anna Maria Island facing Sarasota Bay. The Coquina Baywalk leads through the preserve via boardwalks and footpaths and allows you to get a close-up view of the estuary. Wade in the clear lagoon waters near blue crabs, marine snails (such as whelks and conchs), fiddler crabs, and white ibises, among many abundant species. You don't need to go far from your car to enjoy this great picnic spot and nature retreat.

Location: About 3.5 miles south of Manatee Beach on Gulf Drive, at Coquina Beach on Anna Maria Island. The preserve is marked with a sign.

Important information: For more information, call 941-749-3070, extension 6823.

44. South Florida Museum/Bishop Planetarium

Although history from prehistoric times to the Space Age is thoughtfully presented here, I also like to catch the planetarium events, including Friday and Saturday night laser light shows, Saturday morning children's shows, afternoon star shows, and weekend evening stargazing in the observatory. I also like to visit with an old friend, Snooty, the captive manatee. Snooty was born in the 1940s and is the oldest manatee born in captivity.

Location: In downtown Bradenton at 201 Tenth Street West, at the intersection of Tenth Street and the Tamiami Trail (U.S. Highway 41), one block south of the Manatee River.

Important information: The museum and the planetarium each charges an admission fee. Planetarium star shows and laser light shows are at specific times, so call ahead to arrive on time. You can pick up a schedule at area lodging locations, restaurants, and information centers. For more information, call 941-746-4131.

45. Gulf Coast Railroad Ride and Museum

Hop aboard and choo-choo on down the line for a sunny 70-minute ride on 1950s railroad cars on the Manatee Route. It's a hoot, and you can visit the museum and circus railroad car, to boot. Ask about special theme rides.

Location: Just south of Bradenton in Parrish, at the intersection of 83rd Street East and U.S. Highway 301.

Important information: From January through April, rides are offered at 11 A.M., 1 P.M., and 3 P.M. Saturdays and at 1 and 3 P.M. Sundays. From May through December, the 11 A.M. ride isn't offered. Children under age 3 can ride free; fees are $5 for ages 3 to 11 and $8 for all others. For more information, call 941-722-4272.

46. Manatee Historical Village

Walk into Florida's past among old boat works, a 1903 store, an 1860 courthouse, and an old outhouse, barn, and church.

Location: In Bradenton, at the intersection of 15th Street and Manatee Avenue.

Important information: Open from 9 A.M. to 4:30 P.M. weekdays and from 2 to 5 P.M. Sundays. For more information, including a schedule of special events held in March, call 941-749-7165.

47. Hermann's Lipizzan Ranch

You can bring your family to see the famous white Lipizzan stallions at their training camp, about 30 miles east of Bradenton.

Location: Off State Road 70 near Myakka City. Ask for directions when you call for show times.

Important information: Performances are held from January through March on Thursday and Friday afternoons and Sunday mornings. Be sure to call ahead for specific times, 941-322-1501.

Sarasota Area

The bayside city of Sarasota is one of Florida's premier cultural centers, with an impressive art museum and a community tradition of sponsoring the arts. The area's gulfshore islands, especially Siesta Key and Casey Key, are lush family resorts. On City Island, an internationally known marine-science center is a popular and educational destination for families. Parakeets fly free near creeks in the area. In the countryside east of the city, an expansive state-park campground is a bird watcher's paradise and a year-round place to see alligators. The beaches at Venice attract beachcombers, who are likely to find sharks' teeth.

Like most coastal areas in Florida with island-sheltered bayous, Sarasota Bay was a prized village site of early Indians, such as the Calusa, who harvested shellfish and left piles of shells to prove it. Modern Sarasota was founded at the end of the Seminole Wars. The Whitaker family moved to the waterfront in 1845, and others later followed. In the late 1890s, a Scottish family bought land for development. The name Sara Sota was already informally attached to another tiny settlement, but in 1902 the larger community of 52 voters appropriated it. A social leader and holder of a French Legion of Honor medal, Bertha Honore Potter Palmer, came to the area from Chicago to live part-time and bought extensive holdings. This spurred wealthy friends to join her.

48. Ringling Museum of Art

A visit to this public art shrine is like experiencing Europe's grand galleries and palaces. Stroll through columned halls around a sunny Italian piazza on Sarasota Bay. With its outdoor sculptures, rose gardens, vast lawn, picnic spaces, 30-room Venetian palace, zany circus collection, and frequent outdoor festivals, this museum has a lot to offer.

In the museum proper, there are Baroque and Flemish Renaissance treasures, 17th-century tapestries, and Old Masters that attract art connoisseurs from all over. The palace tour is especially good for children in second grade or older. A 19th-century theater, imported from Asolo, Italy, features a nationally known repertory company. Check to see which plays on the schedule appeal to children.

Location: In Sarasota at the intersection of U.S. Highway 41 and University Parkway, just south of Sarasota-Bradenton International Airport.

Important information: Open from 10 A.M. to 5:30 P.M. daily except New Year's, Christmas, and Thanksgiving Days. Children 12 and younger, as well as Florida students and teachers, are admitted free; fees are $9 for adults and $8 for seniors. On Saturdays, admittance to the art galleries only is free. An on-site café, the Banyan, is located next to a huge specimen of this odd African tree. A medieval fair is held here every February. For more information, call 941-359-5700 or visit <www.ringling.org> or <www.sarasotafl.org>.

49. Sarasota Jungle Gardens

This 10-acre jungle is like a visit to the tame tropics, with close-up encounters with flamingos, alligators, and snakes. Multicolored macaws may perch on your shoulder during a bird show that explains why and how we need to protect these threatened South American natives. You'll want to spend time at the petting zoo, shell museum, and kiddie playground. Bring the camera.

Location: In Sarasota at 3701 Bay Shore Road, about 1 mile south of the Ringling Art Museum (see above).

Important information: For more information, call 941-355-5305.

50. Pelican Man's Bird Sanctuary

Native birds of a feather flock together here, under the gentle care of the sanctuary staff. Learn how castoff fishing line, old fish hooks, pesticides, other pollutants, and speeding boats injure sea birds. This center releases back into the wild about 60 percent of the 7,000 birds it treats each year. Junior vets in your family will want to visit with the temporary and permanent bird residents and learn how volunteers conduct emergency rescues of vulnerable pelicans and other shorebirds.

Location: On City Island in Sarasota at 1708 Ken Thompson Parkway. From U.S. Highway 41 (Tamiami Trail), take the John Ringling Causeway west to St. Armands Circle and exit from the circle toward Longboat Key and City Island via State Road 789. When the road takes a left to Longboat Key, continue straight onto City Island via Ken Thompson Parkway.

Important information: Admission is free, but almost everyone leaves a generous donation behind to help continue the year-round work of licensed wildlife rehabilitator and sanctuary founder Dale Shields. For more information, call 941-388-4444.

51. Mote Marine Laboratory and Aquarium

Ever been tickled by a starfish? You can feel what that's like here, at a shallow 30-foot-long touch tank. Gently handle some Gulf of Mexico residents, such as starfish and the marine snails called whelks. Sleek sharks, eels, giant sea turtles, and other species swim out of reach in other aquariums. This internationally known research center made its reputation years ago defending the value of all sharks. Today, it teaches the importance of keeping the seas clean. You can also take a boat tour of Sarasota Bay from here. This is an excellent marine-science center, with working scientists sharing their findings.

Location: On City Island in Sarasota at 1600 Ken Thompson Parkway. From U.S. Highway 41 (Tamiami Trail), take the John Ringling Causeway west to St. Armands Circle and exit from the circle toward Longboat Key and City Island via State Road 789. When the road takes a left to Longboat Key, continue straight onto City Island via Ken Thompson Parkway.

Important information: Mote Café offers cold drinks, bagels, and sandwiches. For more information, call 941-388-2451.

52. Myakka River State Park

Boat rides on Lake Myakka and tram tours of this lush bird watcher's marsh are kids' favorites here. Easy sightings of alligators in the wild are almost guaranteed. (Don't forget, it's illegal to bother or feed alligators—and stupid, too. Alligators that are taught to associate humans with food may lunge at people and injure them, or worse. If you see visitors feeding gators, please let a ranger know.) This is Florida's only state park with cabins made from palm-tree logs. If you camp here, you're almost sure to see deer in the evening. Reserve a spot and plan an overnight stay.

Location: From Interstate 75 in south Sarasota, follow State Road 72 east about 9 miles to the park at 13207 SR 72. The park entrance is on the left side of the road and is well marked.

Important information: For more information, call 941-361-6511 or visit <www.dep.state.fl.us/parks>.

53. Oscar Scherer State Recreation Area

• •

This recreation area features a scenic pinewoods campground and an unusual fishing hole for both freshwater and saltwater anglers. Look for bald eagles, which nest here from October through May, and for threatened Florida scrub jays, a unique Florida species that raises its young communally. Although the jays seem almost tame here, enjoy them without feeding them.

Location: About 2 miles south of Osprey on U.S. Highway 41 (the Tamiami Trail). Look for the sign and entrance on the east side of US 41.

Important information: You can rent canoes and buy snacks and supplies here. For more information, call 941-483-5956.

54. Historic Spanish Point

• •

Calusa Indians lived here at Little Sarasota Bay for at least 3,000 years, piling up discarded shellfish, broken pottery, and other trash into large middens, or mounds. They also left sacred burial mounds. At the visitor center, learn about the long-gone native, Spanish, pioneer, and other residents of this area—including wolves and bears. Explore a 15-foot-high midden. In January, attend a prehistoric art presentation here.

Location: In Osprey at 500 North Tamiami Trail (U.S. Highway 41).

Important information: For more information, call 941-966-5214.

55. Venice Beaches

• •

Fossil hunters know that the Venice beaches are among the best places in North America to seek 50-million-year-old sharks' teeth. My father dug a 3-inch specimen of a giant, prehistoric shark called a carcharadon from the sands at Venice in the late 1960s, when our family lived in nearby Sarasota. Large teeth aren't often found today, but diligent seekers usually can find a handful of tiny, ancient teeth to take home. Fossil teeth are black; they are relatively abundant because sharks generally have several layers of teeth that are easily shed. One shark may lose 25,000 teeth in 10 years of life.

An especially productive area in Venice is Caspersen Beach. It's also scenic, with abundant beach plants, such as sea grapes. It has a 750-foot-long fishing pier with a restaurant and snack bar. Beach concessionaires also rent sand shifters, to help you in your fossil search. A park playground, restrooms, nature trails, and picnic areas help make this an ideal stop.

Location: Caspersen Beach is south of Venice Beach at 1600 Harbor Drive South, the south end of Harbor Drive.

Important information: Every August, Venice hosts the Sharks' Tooth and Seafood Festival, with teeth displays, a sharks' tooth scramble, and more. For information, call 941-488-2236. Venice Campground is an unusually nice private campground, located in an old-growth oak tree hammock on the Myakka River. To contact the campground, call 941-488-0850. If you don't find any sharks' teeth, the Venice Chamber of Commerce often will give your kids a small free sample, so call ahead and check to see whether they've got some ready, 941-488-2236.

Sharks!

I have been swimming in Florida waters for years, and I've never, ever been bitten by a fish. But I have had some nasty scrapes on my feet from stepping on oyster bars. Submerged oysters scare me. **Sharks** don't.

Sharks are perhaps Florida's most notorious fish, but they aren't the only biters. Barracuda can also inflict a painful chomp. To avoid places where sharks may be feeding, don't swim in waters near inlets, which is where the majority of shark-bite incidents seem to occur. Sharks use the inlets for two reasons. They want to get from ocean and gulf waters into bays. So an inlet is a marine highway, just as it is for boats. Lots of other fish and marine mammals use inlets for travel, too. So there is lots of potential food in inlets, and sharks do some of their most successful hunting there.

When a shark bites someone, it's frequently a surfer whose foot or leg is dangling from a surfboard near an inlet, where surfers find the bigger waves. If you want to avoid sharks, try swimming only in water that is clear, and avoid swimming at night, which is when some sharks are more active. Another way to avoid sharks is to get out of the water immediately if you realize you are bleeding. And, if you are fishing, don't stay in the water with a netted or hooked fish or other sea creature.

If you do come face to face with a shark, it will most likely be small; I've never hooked one over 3 feet long. The larger ones you occasionally see at boat marinas were captured in deep water. Calmly but quickly make your way to shore; thrash the water as little as possible. If you see a fin in the water, don't assume it's a shark. Porpoises and dolphins have curved dorsal fins—shark fins have a straight edge—and these mammals usually show some of their humped back and airhole as they hunt for food inshore. If you feel something brush against you, it could be seaweed, litter, driftwood, a sea slug, a submerged pal, or your imagination.

SOUTHEAST REGION

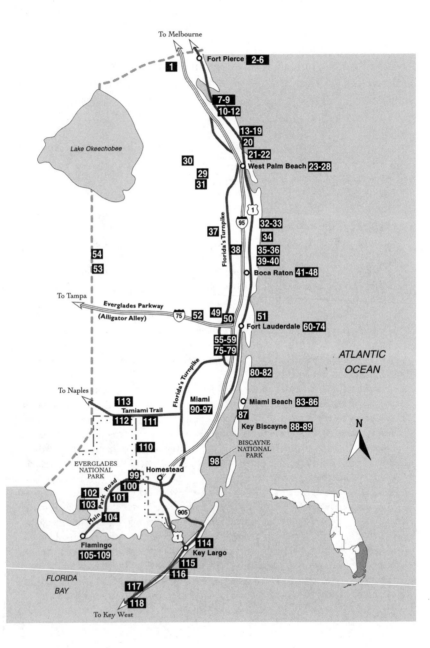

To Melbourne

Fort Pierce **2-6**

1

7-9
10-12

13-19
20
21-22
West Palm Beach **23-28**

Lake Okeechobee

30
29
31

1

95

32-33
34

Florida's Turnpike

37

38
35-36
39-40

54
53

Boca Raton **41-48**

To Tampa

Everglades Parkway
(Alligator Alley)   **75**   **52**   **49**
50   **51**
Fort Lauderdale **60-74**

ATLANTIC
OCEAN

55-59
75-79

Florida's Turnpike

80-82

To Naples

113
Tamiami Trail
112   **111**

Miami
90-97

Miami Beach **83-86**
87
Key Biscayne **88-89**

N

110

BISCAYNE
NATIONAL
PARK

98

EVERGLADES
NATIONAL
PARK

99
Homestead

102   **100**
103   **101**

Main Park Road

104

905

Flamingo
105-109

1

114
Key Largo

FLORIDA
BAY

115
116

117

118
To Key West

SOUTHEAST Region

This region supplies what many families envision when they dream of a balmy Florida vacation. The weather is always warm, and so much that is exotic exists within sight of aqua waters and tropical garden parks. Here you find the wild Everglades, with its alligators, crocodiles, and manatees. The Seminole and Miccosukee tribes share their traditions with visitors here. In Miami, expect international music and delicious Cuban and Caribbean cuisine. The mood is often jovial. You'll see people strolling around public parks and plazas with monkeys, iguanas, or cockatoos perched on their shoulders. Pet parrots dwell on family porches.

Worried about bundling up against the cold? Here that means grabbing a sweater. In this hothouse region, bamboo, mahogany and banyan trees, as well as native mangroves and orchids, grow. You can pick oranges and mangos right from the trees. Along the shore, the majestic Atlantic Ocean frequently takes on the aqua color of the tropical sea, and it often laps at the shore with gentle waves. At Fort Lauderdale, the warm Gulf Stream flows so near the shore that you can actually see it from hotel rooftop gardens.

Many families return to their favorite destinations in southeastern Florida with the intention of visiting the rest of the state this time, too. But instead they always find one more intriguing park, historic site, museum, zoo, garden, resort, beach, or boat ride to try in the Southeast.

There are few state park campgrounds in this region. One that's very popular with families is Jonathan Dickinson State Park, which also has cabins. There are also three campgrounds in the part of Everglades National Park that lies within this region. Private campgrounds to sample in the northern part of the region are Nettles Island, Jensen Beach, and Lion Country Safari, west of West Palm Beach at Loxahatchee. For other family lodging, you might try Islander Inn at Vero Beach; Harbor Light Inn Resort in Fort Pierce; Cove Resort and Marina and Indian River Plantation, both in Stuart; the Breakers in Palm Beach; Tahiti on the Ocean on Singer Island; Boca Raton Resort and Club in Boca Raton; Martindale at the Beach and Ocean Hacienda Inn in Fort Lauderdale; Royal Flamingo Villas at Hillsboro Beach; A Little Inn by the Sea, Breakaway Inn Guest House Motel, Ocean Hacienda, and Villas by the Sea, all in Lauderdale-by-the-Sea; and Rettger Resorts Beach Club at Deerfield Beach.

See the Miami section for Miami-area lodging and for Miami/Everglades tourism information sources.

For information about the rest of the region, contact:

- Fort Pierce/St. Lucie County Tourism
  561-462-1535, 800-344-8443
  <www.stlucieco.gov>
- Greater Delray Beach Chamber of Commerce
  561-278-0424
  <www.delraybeach.com>
- Greater Fort Lauderdale Visitors Bureau
  954-539-3000, 800-227-8669
  <www.sunny.org> or <www.co.broward.fl.us/sunny>
- Greater Pompano Beach Chamber of Commerce
  954-941-2940, 800-746-5708
  <www.pompanobeachchamber.com>
- Hutchinson Island Tourism
  561-225-3000
- Jensen Beach Chamber of Commerce
  561-334-3444
  <www.metrolink.net/jensen>
- Lauderdale-by-the-Sea Chamber of Commerce
  954-776-1000, 800-699-6764
  <www.lbts.com>
- Palm Beach Visitors Bureau
  561-471-3995, 800-554-7256
  <www.palmbeachfl.com>
- Stuart/Martin County Chamber of Commerce
  561-287-1088
  <www.goodnature.org>

Fort Pierce Area

Fort Pierce is among the legion of Florida towns born as a strategic head-quarters for U.S. soldiers trying to drive the Seminole Indians from the peninsula in the 1830s. The fort, under the command of a brother of President Franklin Pierce, was built of sabal palm logs and is long gone. Today, coastal development is interspersed with dune-filled park beaches pounded by waves that delight surfers and toss up "keeper" shells for young beachcombers. Fishing, surfing, and pleasure boating are popular. In contrast, the Fort Pierce area evolves a few miles farther west into vast agricultural lands of cattle and famed Indian River citrus groves.

1. Florida Ranch Tours

You can explore a little-known aspect of Florida heritage on a group tour of this working ranch, founded in 1937 by a retired Florida Supreme Court justice. The Adams family developed a hardy breed of cattle, and their ranch later became the first in Florida to receive a state environmental leadership award for wildlife protection. The 55,000-acre ranch encompasses citrus groves, cypress swamps, and wet and dry prairie. A family member will take you on a guided tour of 18,000 acres of this ranching empire. You are likely to see not only cattle, but also deer, alligators, flocks of sandhill cranes, and other bird species, such as the crested caracara, a strong raptor that John James Audubon noted would occasionally walk in the water and seize a young alligator with its claws. At a natural spring, the tour stops for country cooking. Children also can climb into the homegrown tree house.

Location: In western St. Lucie County, west of Fort Pierce on County Road 68 (the Florida Cracker Trail).

Important information: You will get specific directions when you make your reservation for a tour. Call 561-467-2001 or visit <www.flranchtours. com>.

2. Harbor Branch Oceanographic Institution

Future aquanauts will want to plumb the depths of this nonprofit center where undersea vessels and ocean-floor robots are developed, the raising of clams and ornamental fish is researched, marine creatures are studied for medicinal therapeutic components, and other salty topics are explored. You'll learn the amazing story of the four-person Sea-Link Submersible, a roving underwater laboratory that can dive to 3,000 feet and that has been used in archaeological work. Volunteers lead tours of the center via open-air tram in mild weather or air-conditioned bus. You can also take a boat tour to watch for wildlife. If your family is intrigued by the possibilities of oceanographic work, make sure to berth your crew here for an informative docking.

Location: In Fort Pierce at 5600 U.S. Highway 1.

Important information: Tours leave the visitor center promptly at 10 A.M., noon, and 2 P.M. Mondays through Saturdays except on Thanksgiving and Christmas. The visitor center is free. Tours are free for children under age 6; fees are $6 for ages 6 to 18 and $10 for adults. Reservations aren't required, but seating is limited, so there may be a wait for the next tour time. For more information, call 561-465-2400, extension 688 or 689, or 800-333-4264, extension 517, or visit <www.hboi.edu>.

3. Pepper Park/Navy SEALS and Underwater Demolition Team Museum

Get in the swim at this ocean-to-lagoon public park with plenty of picnic space and a small museum, too. The U.S. Navy's excellent underwater swimmers, the Frogmen and SEALS units, are honored here with stories of their renowned exploits. In 1943, the U.S. Navy brought 140,000 soldiers here for amphibious training and began the Frogman program on the local beaches.

Location: In Fort Pierce on North Hutchinson Island at 3300 North State Road A1A.

Important information: For more museum or park information, call 561-595-5845. The museum is open from 10 A.M. to 4 P.M. Tuesdays through Saturdays and from noon to 4 P.M. Sundays.

4. Fort Pierce Inlet State Recreation Area/ Jack Island Preserve

Even small stretches of wild beach help soothe the spirit when urban development is all around you. This state beach combines with nearby Pepper

Trees that grow oysters

Mangroves are trees that grow oysters. They also "walk," and in so doing they build land. The roots of these evergreens look like legs because they grow from the thin tree branches and arch into salt water. These curved roots, which provide much of the tangled "jungle" look of subtropical coastal areas, are more than dramatic window dressing. They trap leaf litter, sand, and soil, gradually building land around a mangrove's base. Entire islands are built this way over time, if the mangroves are allowed to do their job.

Mangroves are crucial to the healthy life of the coastal zone, especially in land preservation. All species of mangrove—including red mangrove, the most prevalent—are officially protected. A kind of oyster, the small coon oyster, grows on the mangrove roots. The sight of dozens of oysters clinging to the trees is a hallmark of South Florida coastal mangrove forests.

Park (see above) to make a fine corridor of natural seashore. There are sand dunes, a youth camp, great picnic spots, and a nearby island with nature trails amid the mangroves, Jack Island Preserve. (If anyone in your family is named Jack, be sure to take a picture of him next to the preserve sign!)

Location: In Fort Pierce on North Hutchinson Island at 907 Shorewinds Drive. Jack Island Preserve is about 1.5 miles north, off State Road A1A.

Important information: The youth camp is available for groups by reservation only. For more information, call 561-468-3985 or visit <www. dep.state.fl.us/parks>.

5. A. E. "Bean" Backus Gallery/Manatee Observation and Education Center

These twin sites in a waterfront park make for an intriguing stop. The gallery features scenic Florida paintings by a longtime, popular Florida artist, the late Bean Backus. The education center next door on Moore's Creek is perched over a winter waterland for manatees. As many as 30 of these slow, endangered marine mammals collect here in the warm water discharged by a power plant into the Indian River Lagoon.

Location: In Fort Pierce at 480 North Indian River Drive, about a half-mile south of the South A1A Bridge and opposite the H. D. King Power Plant.

Important information: Both sites are open only in season. The Manatee Center is open from November 1 to April 15 from 10 A.M. to 5 P.M. Tuesdays through Sundays. For Manatee Center information, call 561-466-1600, extension 3333. For more gallery information, call 561-465-0630.

6. South Beach Boardwalk/ Kimberly Bergalis Memorial Park

These two beach beauties feature swimming spots with lifeguards, as well as good beachcombing and picnic places. The memorial park is named for a courageous young woman who spent her time educating the world about the AIDS disease after she contracted it.

Location: In Fort Pierce on Hutchinson Island, about 1 mile south of Fort Pierce Inlet on State Road A1A.

Important Information: For park information, call 561-462-1521.

7. Bathtub Reef Park

Wouldn't you like your kids to splash in a shallow natural pool, sheltered from the ocean by a protective reef? They can take that sort of plunge at Bathtub, an enormously popular family park on Hutchinson Island. An off-shore coral reef creates a saltwater cove, a clear-water "bathtub" for splashing, swimming, and snorkeling. There are lifeguards, showers, restrooms, and picnic shelters.

Location: In Stuart, at the southern end of Hutchinson Island on State Road A1A.

Important information: For more information, call 561-287-1088.

8. Elliott Museum/Stuart Beach/ Coastal Science Center

Your budding inventors can step back in time at the Elliott Museum, an eclectic oceanfront collection that is dedicated to the man who invented an unusual four-wheeled bicycle. That and other old bikes are on display here, along with more curious inventions by Sterling Elliott. You can also enjoy old automobiles, Victorian-era village dioramas, a watch and clock collection, a blacksmith forge, old dolls, and a replica of an open-air Seminole Indian house called a *chickee*. This is a popular family stop. It's set in a seaside park with plenty of amenities, such as a beach boardwalk, a café, restrooms, picnic tables, showers, lots of parking, a grassy lawn, and lifeguards. The latter are important for families of young ones. The steep slope of the beach into the water and submerged coral outcroppings make this a less-than-ideal swimming beach for children. You'll see lots of surfers, though. The Coastal Science Center has a visitor center just across State Road A1A from the museum and beach. Explore the saltwater touch tanks and take a nature trail through the mangroves.

Location: The Elliott Museum is in Stuart at 825 NE Ocean Boulevard (SR A1A), at the southern end of Hutchinson Island. Stuart Beach shares the same entrance. The Coastal Science Center is across the street at 890 NE Ocean Boulevard.

Important information: For more information, call the Elliott Museum at 561-225-1961. For Stuart Beach information, call the Martin County Parks Department at 561-221-1418. The Coastal Science Center is at 561-225-0505.

9. Gilbert's Bar House of Refuge

Just 1.5 miles south of the Elliott Museum (see above) is another unusual museum on the southern end of Hutchinson Island. Despite the name, you can't order a brewski here. Gilbert's Bar is an offshore sandbar. The 1875 building is the last of a series of shelters built along the Atlantic coast by the U.S. government for shipwreck survivors. It's now full of rescue-related lore, early life-saving equipment, and model ships.

Location: In Stuart at 301 SE MacArthur Boulevard, on the southern tip of Hutchinson Island.

Important information: For more information, call 561-225-1875.

10. Hobe Sound National Wildlife Refuge

This refuge has a unit on the mainland and one on Jupiter Island. On the 232-acre mainland parcel, the Elizabeth W. Kirby Interpretive Center depicts the importance of Hobe Sound as a marine nursery. A quarter-mile path through Florida scrub gives you the chance to look for the rare scrub jay, a blue bird of uncommon beauty that lives in large family groups. White-tailed deer and bobcats also live here. At the 735-acre seashore unit on Jupiter Island, volunteers and staff answer questions about the stunted scrub trees and the summer nesting cycle for sea turtles. Picnicking isn't allowed here, and there are only portable restrooms, so the mainland unit is the best place to visit with children. In the summer, refuge rangers lead popular nighttime walks to glimpse mother sea turtles laying their eggs.

Location: The refuge headquarters is about 2 miles south of the community of Hobe Sound on U.S. Highway 1.

Important information: For refuge information, call 561-546-6141; for interpretive center information, call 561-546-2067 or visit <www.fws.gov/r4eao>.

11. Blowing Rocks Preserve

This postage-stamp-sized preserve, where sea-turtle mothers nest in summer, is stunning on windy days when the rough surf makes the most of holes in the beachfront cliffs, which are composed of sedimentary layers of age-old coquina shell. On such days, the Atlantic Ocean roars in like thunder, sending saltwater plumes as high as 50 feet into the sky. The sight is sure to make an impression on young salts. This preserve is the property of The Nature Conservancy, which welcomes visitors. Dedicated volunteers will patiently answer your questions about everything from pelicans to sea oats, from jellyfish to mangroves. It's a small place and one of the most unusual coastal sites in Florida.

Location: On Jupiter Island in the community of Hobe Sound at 574 South Beach Road.

Important information: Open daily from 9 A.M. to 5 P.M.; a $3 donation is requested. No food or drinks are allowed at the preserve, so don't plan a picnic here. For more information, call 561-744-6668.

12. Jonathan Dickinson State Park

This 11,500-acre park on the Loxahatchee River encompasses acres of woodland and wetland in which to roam. The park is outstanding in several ways. You can take a short hike to Hobe Mountain, a 200-foot-tall sand dune with a 22-foot-tail observatory tower on it that offers a view of Hobe Sound. Children will especially enjoy a boat ride upriver to the exotic Trapper Nelson cabin, to see how a Florida eccentric who ran an island zoo lived in the 1930s. The Loxahatchee is the only river in Florida designated a national wild and scenic river. You can rent canoes here to paddle on it. In early morning or before dusk, you might see otters frolicking in it. Manatees also seek shelter in its waters. The park is home to 140 kinds of birds, including the rare Florida scrub jay, found only in Florida and only in the sandy, parched habitat called scrub, which this park shelters. There are several footpaths here, including a 9.3-mile portion of the Florida National Scenic Trail. This is an exceptionally popular state park, with two shady campgrounds and simple cottages for overnight stays.

Location: About 12 miles south of Stuart in Hobe Sound at 16450 SE Federal Highway.

Important information: For cottage and canoe reservations, call 561-746-1466. For other park information, call 561-546-2771 or visit <www.dep.state.fl.us/parks>.

Palm Beach Area

. . . .

Palm Beach is an exclusive winter home for the wealthy, so it figures that you'll find polo fields here. In winter, well-tended hooves thunder back and forth in weekly polo matches that are open to the public. And leave it to Palm Beach to sink a Rolls-Royce to create an artificial reef. But there are also familiar family diversions in this well-manicured region. In 1878, Spanish Main sailors unloaded a shipload of about 20,000 coconuts here. Quicker than you can say sprout, the nuts rooted. So the beach got coconut palms; these non-native tropical palm trees aren't found everywhere in Florida. Besides finding coconuts on the ground (don't eat them, they may have an antibiotic in them to prevent a deadly tree blight), children will enjoy a drive-through animal safari, a small garden zoo, a science museum, nature centers, boat rides, citrus-grove tram tours, a marina where it's easy to feed fish, and a serene but very family-friendly Japanese museum and gardens.

The area lures lots of scuba divers; many guideboats to reefs are based at area marinas. Parking at Palm Beach beaches is usually metered or restricted to residents, and the beaches themselves are sometimes badly eroded. Conditions are not ideal for families and swimming. But some beaches are good access points for snorkeling.

You won't find wild public park campgrounds here, but a developed county park campground is steadily booked. Or you can stay overnight at the Lion Country Safari, a unique private campout that's a real roar. (The nearest state park campground is north of here at Jonathan Dickinson State Park.) Resorts in the area are predictably high-priced; two that woo families are also beautifully historic: The Breakers in Palm Beach and the Boca Raton Resort and Club in Boca Raton.

13. Jupiter Inlet Lighthouse/ Florida History Center and Museum

. . . .

Children over 4 feet tall are allowed to climb the 105 steps to the top of this isolated federal lighthouse and pretend to be members of the pioneer family that tended it in the 1860s. Every year, a boat arrived with a 12-month supply of flour, lamp oil, and other necessities. The pet dogs and family sewing machine were salvaged from shipwrecks. The lighthouse is Palm Beach County's oldest structure and is listed on the National Register of Historic Places. It's maintained by the Florida History Center and Museum in cooperation with the U.S. Coast Guard.

Location: From U.S. Highway 1 in Jupiter, on the north side of the Jupiter Inlet, take State Road 707 east over the bridge and immediately take the first right into Lighthouse Park.

Important information: The lighthouse is open from 10 A.M. to 4 P.M. Sundays, Mondays, and Fridays, and from 10:30 A.M. to 4 P.M. Tuesdays, but the last tour is at 3:15 P.M. Fee is $5. For more lighthouse information, call 561-747-8380. The museum is open Tuesdays through Fridays from 10 A.M. to 5 P.M. and weekends from 1 to 5 P.M. For more information, call 561-747-6639.

14. Canoe Outfitters

It's a good idea to make reservations for this outfitter's guided canoe and kayak tours on the Loxahatchee River, Florida's only federally designated Wild and Scenic River. This jungle land is home to otters, deer, and manatees.

Location: In Jupiter at 8900 West Indiantown Road.

Important information: Open Wednesdays through Saturdays from 8 A.M. to 5 P.M. Call 561-746-7053 or visit <www.canoes-kayaks-florida.com>.

15. Coral Cove County Park

Try this oceanside picnic place in the small, exclusive community of Tequesta, which was named for an early Native American tribe. It features lifeguards on duty daily, showers, a playground, and free parking. The eroded beach isn't well suited for swimming, but the setup is a delight for snorkeling families.

Location: On Jupiter Island north of Jupiter Inlet and the town of Jupiter, on the eastern side of State Road A1A.

Important information: For recorded beach conditions (updated daily at 9 A.M.), call 561-624-0065.

16. Burt Reynolds Park/ Florida History Center and Museum

Burt Reynolds, movie star and former Florida State University student, grew up in this area; his dad was a police chief. This picnic place straddling U.S. Highway 1 celebrates one of Reynolds's interests: Florida heritage. At the park's Florida History Center and Museum, on the eastern side of US 1, walk through a re-created Seminole village and see exhibits in the Florida Cracker-style building. On the western side of US 1, the park has an information-packed Chamber of Commerce.

Location: In Jupiter at 805 North U.S. Highway 1.

Important information: For more information, call 561-747-6639.

17. Dubois Park/Dubois House Museum

This park on the southern side of Jupiter Inlet sports a scenic view of the fire-engine red Jupiter Inlet Lighthouse (see above) on the northern side. A developed beach with lifeguards, a small fishing pier, shaded picnic tables, and the Dubois House Museum (a restored 1898 pioneer home) help to make this park a magnet for children.

Location: In Jupiter at 19075 Dubois Road.

Important information: Free parking. For more information, call the Dubois Park and Museum office at 561-747-6639.

18. RJ Gator

Do you really want to leave Florida without offering your kids a sample of fried alligator nuggets? This local bar is equally fun for kids and grownups.

Location: In Jupiter at Chasewood Plaza, 6390 Indiantown Road.

Important information: Call 561-746-9660.

19. Jupiter Outdoor Center

This outfitter is an excellent source of information about outdoor-recreation possibilities and a good place to rent bicycles, kayaks, and electric paddleboats.

Location: In Jupiter at 18095 State Road A1A.

Important information: For more information, call 561-747-9666.

20. Loggerhead Park/
Marinelife Center of Juno Beach

Climb the observation tower for coastal views at this family park, which straddles U.S. Highway 1 in Juno Beach. The play area, bike path, and free parking are a plus. At the Marinelife Center, an excellent, nonprofit operation run by volunteers, kids reach into saltwater touch tanks and meet offshore creatures. The beach is patrolled by lifeguards, but it disappears at high tide. Loggerhead also has a cool treat some beaches don't: showers. It's named, of course, for the sea turtle that nests here in the summer but only comes ashore if lights are out.

Location: In Juno Beach, just north of the intersection of U.S. Highway 1 and Donald Ross Road.

Important information: Open daily from sunrise to sunset. The Marinelife Center is open from 10 A.M. to 3 P.M. Tuesdays through Saturdays and from noon to 3 P.M. Sundays. For center information, call 561-627-8280 or visit <www.marinelife.org>; for park information, call 561-966-6600.

21. John D. MacArthur Beach State Park/
William T. Kirby Nature Center

Wild dunes are protected from development at this 225-acre refuge on Singer Island. You tromp to the beach via a 1,600-foot-long boardwalk across Lake Worth Cove, through a mangrove-fringed estuary where you'll spy armies of tiny, reddish fiddler crabs. If you don't want to hike, a handy shuttle scoots the family from the parking lot to the dunes at the ocean's edge. The park is extremely bug-infested in the summer.

The William T. Kirby Nature Center here is tops; it interprets the barrier island's plant and animal communities, including the endangered loggerhead, green, and leatherback sea turtles that clamber ashore on summer nights to lay their eggs. Within this refuge, they may make as many as 1,000 nests every summer. While that sounds like a lot, very few hatchlings survive to adulthood. They have to navigate from their nests high on the beach past predators on sand and in water to the relative safety of floating seaweed. If you have older children who can keep quiet and stay up late, make a reservation for a memorable, nighttime "turtle walk" (with no guarantee of seeing turtles), led by rangers in June and July.

Shelling along nearly 2 miles of beach here is often good. The narrow beach, which is not patrolled by lifeguards, also sports a warning about submerged rocks, but splashing at the water's edge will cool off everyone. This is an ideal destination for school groups.

Location: At the northern end of Singer Island in North Palm Beach, 2.8 miles south of the intersection of U.S. Highway 1 and PGA Boulevard on State Road A1A.

Important information: State park fees apply. The nature center is closed on Tuesdays but otherwise is open daily from 9 A.M. to 5 P.M. The park is open daily from sunrise to sunset. For more information, call 561-624-6950 or visit <www.dep.state.fl.us/parks>.

22. Riviera Beach Municipal Park

The kids can splash along 1,000 feet of nice, sandy beach, with lifeguards watching and showers handy.

Location: On Singer Island in Riviera Beach, at the intersection of Blue Heron Boulevard and State Road A1A (Ocean Boulevard).

Important information: Metered parking. For details, call 561-624-0065.

23. Henry M. Flagler Museum

Henry Flagler, who founded Standard Oil in 1870 with John D. Rockefeller, built the Beaux-Arts–style mansion known as Whitehall here in 1902. Today, it houses the Flagler Museum and is on the National Register of Historic Places. Your budding interior decorator or museum curator might want to walk through this opulent estate full of swell furnishings, which has been described as the "Taj Mahal of North America." It is full of Florida history and lore. Children like the Rambler, Flagler's private railroad car, which has been restored to its original appearance and is on display on the museum lawn.

Location: In Palm Beach at 1 Whitehall Way.

Important information: An admission fee is charged. Open from 10 A.M. to 5 P.M. Tuesdays through Saturdays and from noon to 5 P.M. Sundays. Call 561-655-2833 for information or visit <www.flagler.org>.

24. The Breakers

This site across from Whitehall (see Henry M. Flagler Museum, above) is a palace by the sea. It opened in 1896 as the Palm Beach Inn but was renamed in 1901. It is now listed on the National Register of Historic Places. Visiting The Breakers is like spending an afternoon in Italy; it was modeled after the Villa Medici in Florence. You stroll among classical fountains, arches, and statuary, down tapestry-hung hallways, and past 20-foot-high windows overlooking courtyard gardens. If your room is on the ocean side, you'll feel like you are at sea; the waves break right upon the hotel seawall. Despite its posh style, the hotel courts conventions and vacationing families. It offers nature programs for kids, a miniature railroad station, a beach playground, and sleeping bags for young children who want to snooze on the floor of their room.

Location: In Palm Beach at 1 South County Road. From Interstate 95, take the West Palm Beach/Okeechobee exit. Drive east to South County Road and then north to The Breakers.

Important information: For more information, call 561-655-6611 or visit <www.thebreakers.com>.

25. Palm Beach Polo

From January through April, young horse lovers will want to visit the impeccable Bermuda-grass polo grounds and stables and watch a match from the 1,600-seat grandstand. Prince Charles plays here. The wealthy live here and ride their horses through the Big Blue Cypress Preserve next door. It's a splurge, but your young rider can also stay overnight. Reserve your room near the equestrian facilities and make her dream come true.

Location: Easy to find behind the tall hedges at 13420 South Shore Boulevard in West Palm Beach.

Important information: Call 561-930-7656 or 561-793-1440 for up-to-date seasonal hours, match times, and tour information. Matches are usually held on Sundays at 3 P.M. in season.

26. Sailfish Marina and Resort

Steer over to Sailfish Marina and Resort to hop aboard the Palm Beach Water Taxi, a jaunty, 20-person launch. The captain narrates your cruise to Peanut Island, a scenic park accessible only by boat. You can camp, fish, picnic, and bicycle or skate around the island's perimeter path. Visit President John F. Kennedy's bomb shelter, an old Coast Guard station/boathouse that was transformed into a presidential refuge from atomic bombs during the Cold War of the 1960s. You can learn how the leader of the free world (who had a home in nearby Palm Beach) would have commanded troops from underground. It's an unusual site, now called the Palm Beach Maritime Museum.

Upon your return, let the fish eat free; buy a bag of fish food and gaze at the subtropical species that throng in the marina waters. Dine on their ultra-fresh relatives in the newly remodeled Sailfish Marina Restaurant.

Location: On Singer Island in Palm Beach Shores at 98 Lake Drive.

Important information: Reach the water-taxi concession at 561-930-8294. The marina is at 800-446-4577 or 561-844-1724 or via <www.sailfish marina.com>, and the restaurant is at 561-842-8449.

27. Palm Beach Zoo at Dreher Park

The Komodo dragon and exotic Bengal tiger are among the worldwide creatures bred here with a goal of species preservation. Native animals on display in this 23-acre garden include the nearly extinct Florida panther. Children especially enjoy the regularly scheduled animal encounters and feeding demonstrations.

Location: In West Palm Beach at 1301 Summit Boulevard.

Important information: Children under 3 are admitted free; fees are $4 for children 3 to 12, $5 for seniors, and $6 for all others. Open from 9 A.M. to 5 P.M. daily except Thanksgiving. For more information, call 561-533-0887 or visit <www.palmbeachzoo.org>.

28. South Florida Science Museum/ Aldrin Planetarium

In addition to dozens of pull-'em-and-push-'em exhibits and super saltwater aquariums, you can sit down here in the cool of the Aldrin Planetarium for laser light concerts and planetarium shows. An excellent rainy-day, post-sunburn, or after-the-zoo diversion.

Location: In West Palm Beach at 4801 Dreher Trail North, just behind the Palm Beach Zoo at Dreher Park (see above).

Important information: Open from 10 A.M. to 5 P.M. Saturdays through Thursdays and from 10 A.M. to 10 P.M. Fridays. Children under age 4 are admitted free; fees are $2 for ages 4 to 12, $4.50 for seniors, and $5 for all others. Call 561-832-1988 or visit <www.sfsm.org>.

29. Loxahatchee Preserve Nature Center

This 12,160-acre inland preserve is a good place to stretch your legs. Try the half-mile Eagle Trail or the 1,500-foot boardwalk, which leads through sawgrass prairie and cypress swamp. Kids are likely to see alligators, wading birds, turkey vultures, and red-shouldered hawks. *Hatchee* means river or creek in a Seminole Indian language. The meaning of the rest of the name is debated. The *Seminole News* reported in the 1960s that *loxa* meant "a lie" and that the river represented the boundary of an area in which the Seminoles were supposed to be able to live free in the 1830s. According to the report, the U.S. government lied and didn't honor the boundary.

Location: From Interstate 95 in West Palm Beach, take the Northlake Boulevard exit and drive west on Northlake Boulevard (County Road 809A) for about 4 miles to the preserve entrance, about 1 mile west of the intersection of Northlake Boulevard and Bee Line Expressway.

Important information: For more information, call 561-627-8831. This preserve is often confused with the Arthur R. Marshall Loxahatchee National Wildlife Refuge, farther south off U.S. Highway 441 (see Site 37).

30. Lion Country Safari

In 1967, this became one of the country's first cageless zoos. Take the 4-mile, self-guided drive through exotic-animal territory. Giraffes, elephants, ostriches, zebras, rhinos, and lions get up close and personal—if they choose. It's a thrill for kids, grandparents, and everyone in between. Bring lots of film and observe rules about keeping windows rolled up, pulling over, and speed. The complex also offers a jungle boat ride, carousel, reptile park, bird display, picnic area, paddleboats, and a petting zoo. There's even a KOA campground next door, so you can lie in your tents and listen to the lions roar.

Location: In Loxahatchee at 2003 Lion Country Safari Road. From Interstate 95 in West Palm Beach, take exit 50 and drive west about 18 miles on U.S. Highway 441/98 (Southern Boulevard). Turn north to reach the zoo. The KOA campground is at 2000 Lion Country Safari Road.

Important information: Opens at 9:30 A.M.; last ticket sold at 4:30 P.M. For best value, arrive early, because the ticket allows unlimited safari trips and on-site rides. Children under 3 are admitted free; fees are $9.95 for ages 3 to 9 and seniors, and $14.95 for all others. For more information, call 561-793-1084 or visit <www.lioncountrysafari.com>. To find out more about the KOA campground, call 800-562-9115 or 561-793-9797 or visit <www.lioncountrysafari.com>. Reservations are advised.

31. Okeeheelee Nature Center

One of several nature centers in this region, this one sits in the corner of a 1,000-acre park that has ballfields, tennis courts, and a 170-acre lake for boating, waterskiing, and fishing. The park is a reclamation project, created out of a former shell-rock mine. In winter, birds flock to the East Marsh Trail area.

Location: From Interstate 95 in West Palm Beach, take Forest Hill Boulevard west for about 5 miles and look for the park entrance at 7715 Forest Hill Boulevard, about 1 mile beyond Jog Road. The nature center is about 1 mile inside the park. Although the park borders Florida's Turnpike, there is no access directly to or from the turnpike.

Important information: For hours and program information, call 561-233-1400.

32. John Prince Park

With miniature golf, a swimming pool, tennis courts, batting cages, a wheelchair course, lake fishing, and the self-guided Custard Apple Nature Trail, this highly developed but scenic inland public park and campground on Lake Osborne is an urban gem for families.

Location: In the community of Lake Worth, about 1 mile south of the intersection of State Road 807 (Congress Avenue) and Sixth Avenue.

Important information: Reservations are required; no drop-ins accepted. For more information, call Palm Beach County Parks and Recreation at 561-966-6600 or visit <www.palmbeachfl.com>.

33. Lake Worth Municipal Pier

The warm Gulf Stream flows within 5 miles of the Atlantic coast here, allowing anglers to sometimes hook into ocean sportfish from this pier. It's a 1,000-foot-long public fishing perch with a tackle shop and restaurant. In the summer, expect to catch mangrove snapper and permit fish.

Location: From U.S. Highway 1 in the community of Lake Worth, take State Road 802 (Lake Worth Road) east almost one mile to SR A1A and the pier.

Important information: For general information, call 561-533-7367. The pier tackle shop can be reached at 561-582-9002.

34. Lantana Municipal Beach

A public park with a restaurant rates high on my list of family destinations, and this oceanside mini-retreat in Lantana also offers an inshore reef, dunes, a playground, and showers.

Location: In Lantana at the intersection of State Road 12 and SR A1A (Ocean Boulevard).

Important information: Metered parking. For more information, call 561-540-5731.

35. Knollwood Groves

Take a 1.5-hour tour by tram through 30 acres of orange groves and jungle hammock at this commercial site planted in the 1930s. The tour includes a replica of a Seminole Indian village. There are also alligator-wrestling demonstrations, and you can watch the citrus being transformed into fresh juice, one of Florida's famous symbols.

Orange you glad you like juice?

Everyone samples the many varieties of **fresh citrus** in Florida, but sooner or later most appetites settle on one favorite fruit. It might be sweet, easy-to-peel Dancy tangerines, key limes for pie, lemons for lemonade, ruby red grapefruits, or navel oranges.

Citrus fruits aren't native to Florida; they're from the Orient. The first trees in the Sunshine State were planted by the Spanish in 1570 at St. Augustine. Despite freeze cycles that kill some trees, the Florida citrus industry today is the world's leading grapefruit producer, and the state supplies as much as 79 percent of the U.S. orange crop. St. Lucie County in Florida's East-Central Region contains more citrus-producing acreage than any other Florida county. No citrus is commercially grown north of Putnam County, which is just north of Ocala National Forest.

One of the least-known citrus products is citrus molasses. You can't buy it in the stores. It's made from byproducts of citrus processing and used as an ingredient in animal feed, so even farm critters enjoy Florida citrus.

Location: In Boynton Beach at 8053 Lawrence Road.

Important information: Closed Sundays and major holidays. For more information, call 561-734-4800 or visit <www.knollwoodgroves.com>. The tram ride costs $1.

36. Palm Beach Groves

This grove is open every day, but there's no alligator wrestling. Plenty of citrus and citrus products, though.

Location: In Boynton Beach at 7149 Lawrence Road.

Important information: For more information, call 561-955-6699 or visit <www.pbgroves.com>.

37. Arthur R. Marshall Loxahatchee National Wildlife Refuge

This 146,000-acre inland preserve protects a portion of the northern Everglades; it's a hangout for bird watchers and an easy place to see alligators. It has a visitor center, the 0.4-mile Cypress Swamp Boardwalk that leads through ferns and air plants, and a 0.8-mile pond trail with an observation tower. You may be able to spot egrets, ibises, herons, and, if you're lucky, pink-tinged roseate spoonbills.

Location: From Interstate 95 in Boynton Beach, take exit 44 and go 7 miles west on State Road 804 to the intersection with U.S. Highway 441. Turn south onto US 441 and go 2 miles to the refuge headquarters entrance on the western side of the road.

Important information: Mosquitoes are bad here in warm weather. For more information, call 561-734-8303.

38. Morikami Museum and Japanese Gardens

A group of Japanese pioneers who sailed to Florida in 1904 is honored in this unique public park that stages many family events. Step into the replica of a Japanese villa, with its pebble garden and ancestral photographs of the Yamato farming colony. The Seishin-An Tea House, fishponds, bonsai trees, paper lanterns, Japanese calligraphy, and origami toys help transport you in your imaginations to a foreign land. Enjoy your picnic in pavilions near gentle waterfalls, or sample tasty offerings in the tiny open-air Japanese café. If your family isn't ready for the excellent ginger-marinated tofu, they'll likely enjoy pork dumplings, egg rolls, teriyaki chicken, or sesame noodles with peanut sauce. Morikami is the most unusual county-operated public park that my family enjoys in Florida.

Location: From Interstate 95 in Delray Beach, just north of Boca Raton, exit onto Linton Boulevard and head west for about 4 miles to Jog Road. Turn left (south) onto Jog Road and continue 0.75 mile to Morikami Park Road. Turn right (west) and drive to the park at 4000 Morikami Park Road.

Important information: A Japanese tea ceremony, complete with a sip of tea and a sweet treat, is staged on the third Saturday of every month at 1, 2, and 3 P.M. Annual festivals include a New Year celebration with family games in January and a children's holiday festival in April. In August, the Obon Festival honoring ancestors features fireworks and floating lanterns on the pond at night. The park grounds are open daily, including holidays, from sunrise to sunset. The museum hours are 10 A.M. to 5 P.M. daily except Mondays and major holidays. Park admission is free. Children under age 6 are admitted free to the museum; fees are $2 for ages 6 to 18, $3.75 for seniors, and $4.25 for other adults. For more information, call 561-495-0233.

39. Old School Square

• •

Restored buildings create a fine cultural district. Visit an art gallery—the Cornell Museum—housed in a 1913 school. Walk to the Old School Bread Company, a mouth-watering bakery known for its kid-pleasing "muffin heads," and to Doc's All American, an ice-cream parlor and award-winning hot-dog stand/diner extraordinaire, overlooking Old School Square.

Location: From Interstate 95 in Delray Beach, take exit 42 onto Atlantic Avenue and travel east to its intersection with Swinton Avenue. Turn left onto Swinton and the square is on the right.

Important information: For more information, call the Cornell Museum at 561-243-7922, the Old School Bread Company at 561-276-0013, Doc's All American at 561-278-3627, or visit <www.oldschool.org>.

40. Colony Hotel

Grandparents nostalgic for the 1930s and 1940s, and well-behaved grandkids who love the attention of their elders go well together at this thoroughly charming, rattan-filled, three-story guesthouse built in 1929. The room rates include breakfast, dinner, and endless shuffleboard. A sweet resort reminiscent of a different era.

Location: In Delray Beach at 525 East Atlantic Avenue.

Important information: Open from November 1 to April 30. For more information, call 800-552-2363 or 561-276-4123 or visit <www.thecolonyhotel.com>.

Boca Raton Area

You'll feel "in the pink" in this stylish town filled with flamingo-hued buildings. Boca Raton is a swell retirement mecca for sophisticates. It especially attracts New Yorkers, who love to indulge their grandchildren in all the best ways. There are loads of kid-pleasing places to explore and plenty of scenic Spanish-style buildings, plazas, and fountains for tossing pennies into and making wishes.

41. Spanish River Park

Kids think it's fun to walk under busy State Road A1A through the tunnel that connects the seaside part of this park with the riverfront part. This small but lush family park boasts an observation tower and a small lawn that's soft and cool on infant feet.

Location: In Boca Raton on SR A1A, about 2 miles north of Palmetto Park Road.

Important information: There is an $8 parking fee for nonresidents. Spaces fill fast, especially on weekends, so arrive early or try visiting during the early evening or late afternoon, when most folks head home to clean up for dinner. The park is open from 8 A.M. to sunset. For more information, call 561-393-7811.

42. Red Reef Park/Gumbo Limbo Complex

This small, oceanfront park is worth a detour. A pleasant place to swim and picnic, it's also an exceptional snorkeling area; there are rocks and a reef near the beach in just 2 to 6 feet of water. Lifeguards, a 40-foot-tall observation tower, a boardwalk through mangroves, and one of the best oceanfront nature centers in Florida, the Gumbo Limbo Complex, make this a destination in itself. The gumbo limbo tree, South Florida's "tourist tree," is known for its bark, which turns red and peels just like the skin of an imprudent tourist. See the snake display and enjoy the large saltwater tanks, where baby sea turtles and fish swim. There's a shell collection and a beehive to observe. It's easy to see land crabs in the wild here.

Location: From U.S. Highway 1 in Boca Raton, head east on Palmetto Park Road (County Road 798). Cross the Intracoastal Waterway and, at the intersection of Palmetto Park Road with State Road A1A, turn north onto SR A1A. Red Reef Park is about a half-mile north at 1400 North Florida A1A.

Important information: If you aren't snorkeling, be sure to swim in the designated area, away from the snorkelers. There is an $8 parking fee for nonresidents. The park is open from 8 A.M. to 10 P.M. daily; Gumbo Limbo is open from 9 A.M. to 4 P.M. For more information, call 561-338-1473.

43. Sports Immortals Museum

Your sluggers and slam-dunkers will ogle what the Smithsonian Institution has called "absolutely the most outstanding" single collection of sports memorabilia.

Location: In Boca Raton at 6830 North Federal Highway.

Important information: Open from 10 A.M. to 6 P.M. Mondays through Saturdays and select hours on Sundays. Admission to the first floor is free; fees for the rest of the site are $3 for children to age 12 and $5 for everyone older. Wallet warning: The gift shop sells 10,000 sports items. Call 561-997-2575 for more information or visit <www.sportsimmortals.com>.

44. Boca Raton Resort and Club

Even if you don't splurge on a room, this landmark hotel on the National Register of Historic Places welcomes quiet visitors. The famous pink palace

Chrissie's charity

At age 15, Fort Lauderdale resident Chris Evert defeated the top-seeded player in an exhibition tennis match and was propelled to stardom. For the next 18 years, she dominated world tennis, winning three times at Wimbledon, seven times at the French Open, and 18 Grand Slams. She was eventually inducted into the International Tennis Hall of Fame. Chrissie retired from professional sports in 1989. Today, she lives part of the year in Boca Raton, where she is a tireless fundraiser for the fight against child neglect. Every October, she hosts the **Chris Evert/Ellesse Pro-Celebrity Tennis Classic,** a charity event held at the Boca Raton Resort and Club. For more information, call Chris Evert Charities at 561-394-2400.

features fountains, a plaza, statuary, red-tile roofs, arched open-air walkways, a family restaurant with a tropical theme, a garden with a giant kapok tree, birds-of-paradise and other hat-sized flowers, and caged tropical birds. A kids' program keeps young ones busy; magicians entertain nightly in Malone's Magic Bar. The elegant main resort, named the Cloister, dates to 1925, but many families prefer the newer oceanfront digs. Don't miss a spin on the yacht that ferries guests between the mainland and beach areas.

Location: In Boca Raton at 500 East Camino Real.

Important information: For more information, call 800-327-0101 or 561-447-3000 or visit <www.bocaresort.com>.

45. Children's Museum of Boca Raton

This small, rainy-day diversion not far from the Boca Raton Resort is ideal for well-behaved children ages 7 and younger. They will delight in the kid-sized bank and grocery store, pioneer kitchen, and back-porch archaeological digs. Special events include a KidFest in April and tons of snow delivered to the lawn every December.

Location: In Boca Raton, take Palmetto Park Road west to Northwest Second Avenue at City Hall. Take the next right turn after City Hall on Crawford Boulevard. The museum is at 498 Crawford Boulevard.

Important Information: For more information, call 561-368-6875.

46. International Museum of Cartoon Art

Kids who dig in their heels when it's time to visit a museum will be animated by the thought of this one. Mort Walker of Beetle Bailey fame began this shrine to cartoonists—both those featured on the funny pages and the editorial pages. The collection includes a create-a-cartoon center. A great rainy-day diversion to "make your mind smile."

Location: From Interstate 95 in Boca Raton, take the Palmetto Park Road exit and head east to its intersection with Plaza Real. The museum is at 201 Plaza Real at Mizner Park.

Important information: Open from 10 A.M. to 6 P.M. Saturdays and Tuesdays through Thursdays and from 10 A.M. to 9 P.M. Fridays. Admission is free to children under 6, $3 for ages 6 to 12, $4 for students with school ID, $5 for senior citizens, and $6 for all others. For more information, call 561-391-2200.

47. Little Palm Family Theater

If you want a creative change of pace some Saturday morning or Sunday afternoon, bring your troupe to see the likes of *The Velveteen Rabbit* or some other equally family-pleasing production under the special spotlights of the Little Palm.

Location: In downtown Boca Raton at the Royal Palm Dinner Theater, in the open-air Royal Palm Plaza at 300 South Federal Highway.

Important information: Shows are usually at 9:15 A.M. Saturdays and 1 P.M. Sundays. For current listings and more information, call 561-394-0206.

48. Sugar Sand Park Science Playground/ Children's Science Explorium

Can you imagine a three-story playground where you can crawl through an amazing wooden head and also play with a giant Florida mastodon? This playground set is the best in Florida. And guess why. School kids helped design it. What they wanted, and got, includes a magic-eye camera that triggers spouts of water, light sensors that help compare a child's speed with that of a cheetah, and a walk-through space shuttle. There's also an area just for tiny tots. It's too wonderful. Next door, the Children's Science Explorium has hands-on exhibits on dinosaurs, weather, space, and the human body.

You can take these seashells to the bank

What's brown and hairy and white and smooth? **Sand dollars** are shells that live in beds on the sandy bottom of the sea. They don't move about. Instead, these brown discs are covered with hundreds, maybe thousands, of tiny hairs, top and bottom. The minuscule hairs comb plankton and other organic matter from the water and move it along to the shell's mouth.

We call these creatures dollars, but there's no evidence that people ever used them for money the way natives used cowry shells. When you see a smooth, white sand dollar on the beach, it's okay to take it home as a souvenir. It's been dead some time and bleached by the sun. Always leave living shells alive, so they can reproduce.

Location: In Boca Raton south of Palmetto Park Road at 200 South Military Trail.

Important information: For more playground information, call 561-417-4559.

Fort Lauderdale Area

Bustling Fort Lauderdale is a mecca for snorkelers and divers who gravitate to the area's three-tiered natural reef hoping to encounter angelfish and other subtropical species. With 300 miles of navigable inland waterways and canals, the city also bills itself as the "Venice of America." Other aquatic attributes include 23 miles of sandy oceanfront, 81 artificial reefs, 18 major shipwreck sites, a jaunty water taxi, a winding riverwalk, a sunny beach boardwalk, a port for 35 oceangoing cruise ships, a swimmers' museum and hall of fame, a sportsfishing information center, berths for 42,000 yachts, boat parades, and a natural aquarium. Scuba divers rate the area as one of North America's best diving destinations.

Greater Fort Lauderdale, about 30 miles north of Miami, is intensely urban and traffic-intensive. About 1.5 million people inhabit the area. Yet Fort Lauderdale has a family-friendly historic district downtown along the scenic New River. In 1996, *Money* magazine named Fort Lauderdale the best big city in America in which to live. The entire region, Florida's Broward County, has 29 different towns. This guide will steer you away from commercial strip malls along U.S. Highway 1. Ask your campground or resort staff for the best local routes to travel.

If and when you tire of water sports, there are many other regional diversions, including an enchanting butterfly park, nine museums, and two children's theaters. The Seminole tribe operates a replica thatched-hut village nearby and offers a side trip into Big Cypress Swamp to visit a larger Seminole museum and wildlife park. If you try to see all the main family sights in this area, your visit can easily occupy a long weekend.

Public campsites are urban and very limited. For camping options, try several private campgrounds in western Broward County, which is where the Everglades begin. Farther west, a real camping adventure awaits in the middle of Big Cypress Swamp at the Seminole tribe's Billie Swamp Safari, a wildlife attraction with rustic cabins.

For other lodging information, contact the Greater Fort Lauderdale Convention and Visitors Bureau at 954-765-4466; listen to recorded information at 800-227-8669, extension 771; or visit <www.sunny.org>.

49. Butterfly World/Tradewinds Park

Flit through the public gardens here among 5,000 butterflies. Stand like a statue to allow a "fluttering flower," as part-time Florida resident Robert Frost called them, to settle on your shoulder. About three times a day, watch as new butterflies emerge from cocoons in the glassed-in butterfly nursery. Giant moths and zippy hummingbirds also fill the air. This 3-acre garden is tucked into a superb Broward County park and picnic place called Tradewinds. Butterfly World is lush, with a secret garden maze abloom with unusual

A butterfly of a different stripe

For ages, Florida had no official state butterfly. Yet, with its abundance of sunny days and balmy breezes, the state shelters hundreds of species. So the solar-powered insects that so delight children got a lift from a popular children's advocate, Florida First Lady Rhea Chiles. In 1996, she led a successful campaign by Florida children to lift the yellow-and-black-striped **zebra longwing** above other species and name it the state butterfly.

The zebra longwing searches out an especially exotic-looking native plant, the purple passionvine. The vines are prolific in wild areas such as undisturbed fields. The flowers are lilac-colored, saucer-sized, and fringed with black. As you travel around the peninsula, you'll see that many Florida parks, schools, historic sites, and even vest-pocket patches of greenery are abloom with butterfly gardens.

flowers. If time limits forced me to choose only one site in this area to visit with young children, I'd fly directly here.

Location: About ten minutes north of Fort Lauderdale in Coconut Creek, at 3600 West Sample Road. Take the Sample Road exit off Interstate 95 and head west beneath Florida's Turnpike past the Festival Flea Market. Butterfly World is on the south side of Sample Road.

Important information: Open from 9 A.M. to 4 P.M. Mondays through Saturdays and from 1 to 4 P.M. Sundays. Closed on Thanksgiving and Christmas. Although Butterfly World is enclosed and the butterflies can't fly away, they take cover amid the plants and trees during rainstorms, so you may get wet. If it storms during your stay, rainchecks are given. Children 4 and under are admitted free; fees are $6.95 for ages 4 to 12 and $11.95 for all others. For more information, call 954-977-4400 or visit <www.co.broward.fl.us/parks>.

50. Fern Forest Nature Center

Let the little ones work off some energy along several nature trails and boardwalks and then visit the native-plant arboretum. The habitats to explore include open prairie, cypress swamp, and a tropical hardwood thicket called a hardwood hammock. The 254 acres encompassed by this urban park hide bobcats and gray foxes. About 30 species of ferns give the park its name. Spread a blanket and enjoy a picnic.

Location: From Interstate 95 in Pompano Beach, take exit 34 and head west along Atlantic Boulevard for almost 3 miles to its intersection with Lyons

Road South. Turn left and watch for park signs and the entrance on the right at 201 Lyons Road South. I recommend avoiding Atlantic Boulevard between I-95 and U.S. Highway 1, because it leads through a garish district of strip joints and X-rated stores, centered on US 1.

Important information: For more information, contact 954-971-0150.

51. Anglin's Fishing Pier

If your children are young salts, this 875-foot pier in the low-key, old-style beach town of Lauderdale-by-the-Sea will allow them to walk out over the depths. Below swim crevalle jacks, barracuda, and Spanish mackerel, year-round. In the spring and fall, anglers haul in tasty pompano. Summer brings blue runner, jack, and barracuda in the day and mangrove snapper and sil-ver-scaled tarpon at night. The pier was built by the U.S. government during World War II as part of a string of East Coast lookout towers intended to guard against attack from German U-boats that lurked offshore. The 30-year-old, down-home Pier Coffee Shop offers indoor and outdoor seating and an ocean view.

Location: From the intersection of U.S. Highway 1 and NE 50th Street (State Road 870) in Lauderdale-by-the-Sea, take NE 50th Street east across the Intracoastal Waterway to the coastal highway, State Road A1A. The pier is straight ahead.

Important information: Fees are $1 for children, $3 for adults. For more information, call 954-491-9403.

Blame it on the barracuda

One of Florida's top 25 game fish, these sleek and silvery creatures usually hover motionless near reefs or submerged structures, such as bridge pilings and chunks of concrete block. But they can strike like a torpedo. Smart divers avoid **barracuda** because they have a mouth full of razor-sharp teeth and can inflict a bad bite. They are attracted by shiny jewelry and are known to slash at any object. A large one—they can grow to 5 feet—might attack a swimmer on rare occasions. Folks who reel in their line to find their catch half-chewed should think twice before blaming a shark. It could have been a 'cuda.

A river of sawgrass

Sawgrass, the plentiful plant of the Everglades, can grow to be 8 feet tall. It's not really a grass but a wetland sedge with tiny saw-toothed edges that can cut your skin. Sawgrass is as crucial as rainwater to life in the Everglades. When it ages and dies, it decays and becomes a rich peat that supports other plant life, such as willows and cypresses.

Around the underwater stems of sawgrass and neighboring plants, an unseen universe exists. This is the world of **periphyton,** a living yellowish green mass that floats in the water. It's made up of algae, zooplankton, and other organisms. Periphyton is the very beginning of the food chain in the Everglades, so it's the most important life form in a habitat full of wildlife. And tough sawgrass is periphyton's guardian in the famed River of Grass.

52. Sawgrass Recreation Park

At this private park, you can get your Everglades experience off to a touristy splash. You can visit a re-created Seminole Indian village, take a boat tour through the famous sharp-toothed sawgrass, try your luck fishing for freshwater species, or see displays of alligators and birds of prey.

Location: About 15 minutes west of Fort Lauderdale at 5400 North U.S. Highway 27.

Important information: Open daily from 6 A.M. to 6 P.M., with boat tours offered from 9 A.M. to 5 P.M. Fees are $7.15 for children and $14.68 for adults. For more information, including campground rates (RVs only), call 800-457-0788 or visit <www.evergladestours.com>.

53. Ah-Tah-Thi-Ki Museum

A member of the Seminole tribe may greet you with *che-hun-ta-mo,* which means hello, when you visit the Ah-Tah-Thi-Ki Museum. The museum is operated by the tribe deep within the Big Cypress Reservation, about one hour west of Fort Lauderdale. The name Ah-Tah-Thi-Ki means "a place to learn." And this small museum, which opened in 1997, is an outstanding educational center affiliated with the Smithsonian Institution's Museum of the American Indian. The introduction to the museum is a fast-paced, poignant film titled "We Seminoles." Well-crafted walk-through exhibits present the story of Seminole economy, culture, and traditional spiritual

How can this be "the Everglades"?

All of the Everglades isn't contained within Everglades National Park. About a half-million acres of it stretch north into the region west of Palm Beach. While visitors are surprised to find the Everglades this far north, experts on this slow-flowing river understand that it originates in the Lake Okeechobee area. Its movement south toward Florida Bay is almost imperceptible and is helped by a slight drop in elevation.

Fort Lauderdale suburbs have sprawled into the Everglades wetlands, which makes Everglades specialists angry. The Everglades is a vital wetland. An expensive federal program is attempting to fix years of mistakes made in trying to rearrange the natural flow of Everglades water.

beliefs. Rare artifacts here include war rifles, beaded bags, palmetto splint baskets, and tools. Outdoors, a 2-mile boardwalk leads into the dense Big Cypress Swamp for a close-up look at orchids and other air plants, ferns, strangler figs, and cypress trees. The path takes you past a re-created ceremonial grounds and palm-thatched huts called *chickees*, where crafts are demonstrated. After a visit to this 60-acre site, you may feel so fully informed that you'll want to say *sho-na-bish*, which means thanks, to your guides.

Location: From Fort Lauderdale, travel west via Interstates 595 and 75 (Everglades Parkway) to exit 14, which is labeled Indian Reservation. Head north on County Road 833 (Snake Road) through wet and dry prairie and scattered grazing land, past the Miccosukee Plaza gas station. On the left is Big Cypress National Preserve, on the right is the Miccosukee Indian Reservation, and ahead on both sides of Snake Road is the Big Cypress Seminole Indian Reservation. About 17 miles after leaving I-75, Snake Road intersects on the left with West Boundary Road. On the left at this intersection is the well-marked museum; parking is on the right.

Important information: Open from 9 A.M. to 5 P.M. Tuesdays through Sundays; closed many holidays. Since the museum is in an extremely rural and isolated area, check your gas gauge before setting out. It's worth planning this visit so you have enough time to see the nearby tribal wildlife park and campground (see below). The museum is air-conditioned, but expect outdoor summer temperatures of 95 degrees F or more, biting bugs, and frequent afternoon thunder and lightning storms. From fall through spring is the best time to visit. Fees are $4 for students and seniors and $6 for all others. For more information, contact 941-902-1113 or 800-617-7516 or visit <www.seminoletribe.com>.

54. Billie Swamp Safari Wildlife Park/ Big Cypress Cabin Campground

Just a couple of miles north of the Ah-Tah-Thi-Ki Museum (see above) along West Boundary Road in the Big Cypress Seminole Indian Reservation sits the tribe's wetland adventure, Billie Swamp Safari Wildlife Park. Children delight in climbing into the park's swamp buggies, which are elevated touring platforms atop tires as tall as small cars; they bounce through mudholes with ease. You can also take the family canoeing here, on other boat tours, for a walk, or to look at reptile, alligator, and exotic-animal exhibits. For a treat in the fall through spring, book a night here in a rustic, palm-thatched screened-in cabin and be treated to special events, such as campfire storytelling. A café offers customary camp fare and also regional specialties, such as alligator nuggets, frog legs, and pumpkin fry bread.

Location: Follow the directions for the Ah-Tah-Thi-Ki Museum (see above) and then continue west for a couple of miles along West Boundary Road, following safari signs. The wildlife park is on the right.

Important information: Open from 8:30 A.M. to 5 P.M. daily. The tribal café is open from 7 A.M. to 8 P.M. daily. Since the emphasis here is almost entirely on the outdoors, I strongly recommend a visit in late fall, winter, or spring. In the summer, biting bugs and temperatures of 95 degrees F and higher are unpleasant. Most cabins are not air-conditioned. Entrance fee is $6. For general safari information and overnight accommodations, call 800-949-6101 or 941-983-6101 or visit <www.seminoletribe.com>.

55. Everglades Holiday Park

This private park at the edge of the Everglades offers camping, fishing, boat rentals, boat tours, and a replica of a Seminole Indian village.

Location: About ten minutes west of Fort Lauderdale. From Interstate 95, exit at Griffin Road and head west to the park at 21940 Griffin Road.

Important information: Open from 9 A.M. to 5 P.M. daily. Airboat tours are $6 for children and $12.50 for adults. For more information, call 800-226-2244 or 954-434-8111 or visit <www.introweb.com/everglades>.

56. Flamingo Gardens

This 60-acre site features a significant botanical collection, a pioneer home, and a wildlife encounter. Make sure to see the whopper fig tree and other Florida Champions, the largest of their species in the state. Some tree oddities include the exotic sausage tree and the native "sunburn" tree, the gumbo limbo, which has peeling red skin. If you're curious about the source of your breakfast drink, take the narrated tram tour of the gardens' real citrus grove. And yes, there are flocks of flamingos. This stop is fun and scenic.

Location: In Davie at 3750 Flamingo Road. From Interstate 95 in downtown Fort Lauderdale, exit onto Griffin Road and drive west for about seven minutes to the community of Davie. Turn right at the intersection of Griffin Road and Flamingo Road and follow the signs to Flamingo Gardens.

Important information: Open from 9:30 A.M. to 5:30 P.M. daily, except closed Mondays June through September. The wildlife encounter is offered at 12:30, 1:30, and 2:30 P.M. For more information, contact 954-473-2955.

Who likes hurricanes?

You might think no one would like a hurricane, but treasure hunters don't mind them a bit. After any storm, but especially a hurricane, a special breed of dedicated beachcombers seriously searches the rearranged coast in hopes of finding ancient Spanish artifacts from the mid-1500s to 1700s—those left behind by explorers and those washed up from shipwrecks.

57. Buehler Planetarium

You'll be star-struck at this state-of-the-art astronomy center. Midnight laser shows, special children's star shows, evening stargazing events, and events such as telescope-building with scientists light up the planetarium schedule.

Location: In Davie at 3501 SW Davie Road on the campus of Broward Community College.

Important information: Because the planetarium is affiliated with the college, its hours may vary from semester to semester. Shows are generally held Saturday and Sunday afternoons. For a schedule and other information, call 954-476-6880 or 954-476-6682.

58. Young at Art Children's Museum

This is a colorful detour if you want a creative indoor setting for an hour or two. The hands-on projects and fun demonstrations let kids roll up their sleeves and become artists.

Location: In Davie, just west of Fort Lauderdale, at 11584 State Road 84.

Important information: Open from 10 A.M. to 5 P.M. Mondays through Saturdays and from noon to 5 P.M. Sundays. Children 2 and under are admitted free; fee is $4 for all others. For more information, call 954-424-0085.

59. Davie

To sample Florida's little-known but colorful cracker/cow-hunter heritage, ride the urban range west of the Greater Fort Lauderdale area to the town of Davie. While other Florida places with cattle ranching roots hung up their spurs long ago, small parts of Davie still harken back to the time when cattle rustling and intrigue flavored the state. Frederick Remington traveled with some of Florida's cowhands, who were known as cow hunters. He thought their life was rougher than those of cowboys in the Old West. Florida cowhands had to hunt for cattle that often wandered into and got stuck in swamps. They also had to maneuver their steeds past hissing alligators, a skill not needed in the West. In Davie, you can see a rodeo each Thursday night and a professional rodeo the last weekend of every month. Some new buildings look cowpunching (don't say Western!) in keeping with the spirit of the open-range days. Expect some fast-food restaurants with hitching posts and salt licks for the horses. Among states that still round up cattle, Florida is third in the number of bovines it produces. As any roper knows, you can't run cattle without horses. That's why you'll see a few shops selling saddles.

Location: Davie is about five minutes west of Greater Fort Lauderdale/Hollywood International Airport via Orange Drive. The Davie Pro Rodeo grounds is at the corner of Orange Avenue and 66th Way just west of Davie Road.

Important information: Each Thursday night, the Davie–Cooper City Rodeo attracts local residents. The professional rodeo is held at 8 P.M. on the fourth Friday and Saturday of every month. Fees are $5 for children and $10 for adults. For more information, contact 954-384-7075.

60. Seminole Okalee Indian Village and Museum

The Seminole tribe of Florida incorporated in 1957 and established a showcase village here three years later. The village re-opened in 1998 following a $2 million remodeling. Palm-thatched, open-air homes on stilts, called *chickees*, evoke the camp-style flavor of life in the Everglades in the 1920s and 1930s. Learn about Seminole crafts, such as the tribe's renowned, machine-stitched, patchwork clothing. Expect alligator and snake shows, and spend time in an art gallery that showcases many talented tribal artists and Seminole-related themes. A small but significant museum exhibiting artifacts is also here.

Location: In Fort Lauderdale, drive south via U.S. Highway 441/State Road 7. The village is at the intersection with Stirling Road at 5845 SR 7.

Important information: Open from 9 A.M. to 5 P.M. Tuesdays through Saturdays and noon to 5 P.M. Sundays. Children under age 5 are admitted free; fees are $7 for other children and seniors, and $10 for all others. For more information, call 954-966-6300 or visit <www.seminoletribe.com>.

61. Old Dillard Art and Cultural Museum

Explore the history of black peoples from around the world, see several galleries of distinctive art, and learn about a pioneer African-American schoolhouse at this downtown Fort Lauderdale historic site, listed on the National Register of Historic Places. The site is also on Florida's Black Heritage Trail.

Location: From Interstate 95 in Fort Lauderdale, take the Sunrise Boulevard exit and drive east to NW Ninth Avenue. Follow NW Ninth Avenue south to its intersection with Fourth Street. The Old Dillard Museum is at the intersection, at 1009 Fourth Street.

Important information: Open from noon to 4 P.M. Tuesdays through Saturdays and from noon to 8 P.M. Wednesdays. Free admission. For more information, contact 954-765-6952.

62. Museum of Discovery and Science

The youngest kids will bubble with excitement at the gigantic bubble-making machine, and they'll also delight in a discovery center for toddlers and preschoolers. Then zoom over to the Space Station, stop for a breather at the

Health Encounter, listen up with Sound Sensations, and meet some of Florida's critics, including bees, bats, alligators, and snakes. You can also visit a living coral-reef aquarium and a five-story IMAX theater. This jazzy hands-on science center redefines the term museum. While some museums are best visited during bad weather, this one's worth visiting anytime.

Location: In Fort Lauderdale, take Interstate 95 to the Broward Boulevard exit. Head east to Second Street. The towering theater is hard to miss at 401 SW Second Street.

Important information: Open from 10 A.M. to 5 P.M. Mondays through Saturdays and from noon to 6 P.M. Sundays. Museum fees are $5 for children and seniors, and $6 for adults. Children under age 3 can get into the IMAX theater free; tickets are $7 for other children, $8 for seniors, and $9 for all others. Combination museum/theater admission is $10.50 for all children, $11.50 for seniors, and $12.50 for all others. For more information, call 954-467-6637 or 954-467-4629 or visit <www.mods.org>.

63. Fort Lauderdale Museum of Art

This modern, 30,000-square-foot gallery is for well-behaved little art lovers. Take them through the state's largest collection of Oceanic, West African, pre-Columbian, and Native American art and they might get some ideas for back-seat sculpting and scribbling on the ride home.

Location: In Fort Lauderdale's downtown historic and cultural district at 1 East Las Olas Boulevard.

Important information: Open Tuesdays through Saturdays from 10 A.M. to 5 P.M., and Sundays from noon to 5 P.M. Children ages 4 and under are admitted free; fees are $2 for ages 5 to 18, $7 for college students with ID, $8 for seniors, and $10 for other adults. For more information, contact 954-525-5500 or visit <www.museumofart.org>.

64. Fort Lauderdale Museum of History

A replica of the fort for which the city was named is one of several big draws for children at this museum, a super salute to colorful frontier history. Major William Lauderdale and his battalion came here in March 1838 during the Second Seminole War and hastily built a stockade to defend area settlers from the Indians. Soldiers later built a second temporary fort and, later still, a third one, this time on the beach at the site of the Bahia Mar Hotel and Yacht Center on Seabreeze Boulevard.

The three Seminole wars

From about 1763 to 1783, when Britain controlled the Florida peninsula, it often tried to thwart settlement by southward-migrating Americans by inciting the Seminoles against them. After Britain ceded Florida to Spain, American settlers as well as Spanish colonists poured into the area. But animosity between the Seminoles and the Americans continued. It escalated when Seminoles harbored black slaves who had escaped from plantations in the Southern states. The U.S. Army attacked the Indians in 1818 in what became known as the First Seminole War. Forces under General Andrew Jackson quickly defeated the Indians.

In 1821, the United States acquired Florida from Spain and immediately began enticing and then requiring the Seminoles to relocate to Indian Territory, in present-day Oklahoma. Some agreed, but others refused to leave their homeland and fled into the Everglades to hide. The United States began seriously enforcing its Indian removal policy in 1835, which led to the Second Seminole War (1835–1842). This is considered the fiercest war waged by the federal government against an Indian people.

The Third Seminole War broke out in 1855, when conflicts—mostly over land—erupted between white settlers and some Seminoles who had remained in Florida. It ended in 1858, after war and relocation had reduced the Seminole population to only about 200 people.

Location: In the Fort Lauderdale historic district at 231 SW Second Avenue.

Important information: Open Tuesdays through Fridays from noon to 5 P.M., Saturdays and Sundays from 10 A.M. to 5 P.M. Children under age 6 are admitted free; fees are $2 for ages 6 to 16 and $4 for all others. For more information, call 954-463-4431.

65. Story Theater Productions at Parker Playhouse

Lucky you, if your visit coincides with a run of a major production, such as *The Frog Prince,* creatively staged for fledgling theater fans. This is an ideal indoor diversion.

Location: In Fort Lauderdale at 707 NE Eighth Street.

Important information: Make sure a production is scheduled before you visit by calling 954-763-8813.

66. Stranahan House

To see how much things have changed, visit Fort Lauderdale's old Seminole Indian trading post, post office, and town hall, preserved as a two-story, Victorian-era house of antiques.

Location: On the northern side of the New River in downtown Fort Lauderdale at 325 East Las Olas Boulevard. Stranahan House is right next to the U.S. Highway 1 (Federal Highway) tunnel under the New River.

Important information: Open from 10 A.M. to 4 P.M. Wednesdays through Saturdays and from 1 to 4 P.M. Sundays. For more information, call 954-524-4736.

67. Big Pink

Home-style cookin', large portions, a big kids' menu, and a stylish dining room decorated with pink plexiglass make this eatery a good place to plant your brood when they need to renew their energy.

Location: In downtown Fort Lauderdale on the Las Olas Boulevard Riverfront at 300 SW First Avenue.

Important information: For more information, call 954-463-7465.

68. Shirttail Charlie's

This is a boat ride, a place to swim, and a local seafood restaurant all in one. The swimming pool, interactive fishing machine for kids, and after-dinner boat ride are part of the meal deal.

Location: In Fort Lauderdale at 400 SW Third Avenue.

Important information: Open for lunch and dinner; prices are a bit cheaper on the docks than in the dining room. This place is so popular with families that it's best to reserve a table on weekends and holidays. Call 954-463-3474.

69. Fort Lauderdale City Beach

The public beach here is no longer a haven for rowdy spring-breakers. Today, it attracts cosmopolitan international travelers, some of whom, families should note, are wearing skimpy bikinis. Visitors like the cafés and shops just steps away from the sand. Families appreciate the manicured lawn, wide expanse of sand, and open ocean views, the latter thanks to Fort Lauderdale's refusal to sell its beach to condominium developers. With lifeguards and showers, this is a fine place to spend an hour, although parking is hard to find unless you arrive early. If you drive by at night, look for the neon sculpture tube that pulses in sherbet colors.

Location: In Fort Lauderdale, take Las Olas Boulevard east across the Intracoastal Waterway to State Road A1A (Ocean Boulevard). The public beach spreads out to the left and right along SR A1A.

Important information: There is free street parking in the central area, metered street parking in the northern area, and a large beach parking lot where you can park for $6 a day in the southern area. Restrooms and picnic tables are only available at the southern beach area.

70. Hugh Taylor Birch State Recreation Area

This 180-acre urban park is part beach and part mangrove forest. Not only is it a good place to picnic or swim in the ocean, but it also has a visitor center in a historical pioneer home, bike trails, lovely walking paths, and a group campground. The park is named for the pioneer who owned this property for close to 50 years. Wishing to preserve his subtropical paradise from development, he donated it for use as a public park in the 1940s.

Location: From Interstate 95 in Fort Lauderdale, take the exit for Sunrise Boulevard East (State Road 838) and drive east across the Intercoastal Waterway to the intersection of SR 838 and SR A1A, where the park sits.

Important information: Open from sunrise to sunset daily. Your group can make advance reservations to use the campground and six cabins; there is no individual family camping allowed. The park is on the western side of SR A1A, so an underground walkway takes you under the highway to the beach. State park fees apply. For more information, contact 954-564-4521 or visit <www.dep.state.fl.us/parks>.

71. Bonnet House

Children often don't take to historic home tours the way parents do, but this oceanfront museum is a kid-pleaser. Once owned by two unconventional artists, Frederick and Evelyn Bartlett, Bonnet House nestles on 35 exclusive acres and 700 feet of oceanfront. It has its own swimming swans and is named for a native lily found in wild places like the Everglades. The art studio and the shell room, with a sandy collection worth emulating, will inspire budding collectors and artists.

Location: From Interstate 95 in Fort Lauderdale, exit onto Sunrise Boulevard East (State Road 838) and head east across the Intracoastal Waterway. Turn right onto North Birch Road just one block before you reach SR A1A and follow the signs to Bonnet House at 900 North Birch Road, one block south of Sunrise Boulevard.

Important information: Tours are $7 for children and $9 for adults and are conducted at 10 A.M. and 1:30 P.M. Wednesdays through Fridays and at noon and 2:30 P.M. weekends. For more information, contact 954-563-5393.

72. International Swimming Hall of Fame

In the 1930s, college swim coaches discovered that Fort Lauderdale was an ideal place for summer workouts. Super swimmers have stroked the waters ever since. Future Olympic swimmers will want to look for future and past Olympians splashing at the pool, which is open to anyone for lap swimming or scheduled water aerobics. Woolly swimsuits of more modest days and Olympic mementos are displayed high and dry in the 10,000-square-foot museum. Also, enjoy the country's only gallery dedicated to swimming art.

Location: In downtown Fort Lauderdale, take Las Olas Boulevard east across the Intracoastal Waterway to State Road A1A. The hall of fame is directly ahead at the end of Las Olas Boulevard.

Important information: Fees are $1 for students, seniors, and members of the military, $3 for adults, and $5 per family. For more information, call the hall of fame at 954-462-6536 or the pool at 954-468-1580. *Las olas* means waves in Spanish. The hall of fame is part of a spiffy beachfront complex that includes a pretty promenade.

73. *Jungle Queen* Cruises

This triple-decker has plied Fort Lauderdale waterways for 50 years. During the day, you can take a three-hour float to see exotic animals at an island. The night cruise is a boisterous, four-hour floating festival of sing-alongs, alligator-wrestling at the island, and an all-you-can-eat barbecue, riverboat style.

Location: In downtown Fort Lauderdale, take Las Olas Boulevard east across the Intracoastal Waterway to State Road A1A. Take SR A1A south to Bahia Mar Yachting Center, the *Jungle Queen*'s home port. It's just south of the International Swimming Hall of Fame (see above).

Important information: Day cruises begin at 10 A.M. and 2 P.M. The night cruise shoves off at 7 P.M. and lasts four hours, so bring blankets for the youngest, who may get some shut-eye by trip's end. You can get tickets in advance; cost is $11.50 for the day cruise and $24.50 for the dinner trip. For more information, contact 954-462-5596 or visit <www.junglequeen.com>.

74. 15th Street Marina and Restaurant

This pricey but friendly seafood house is a good catch, because the seafood is succulent, the views and presentation are super, and you can take a dockside stroll before or after your meal. Try specialties such as Flying Fish appetizers, entertainingly prepared in an instant at your table. Also consider Smoking Florida Stew, stocked with fresh fish and scallops.

Location: At the 15th Street Marina in Fort Lauderdale, 1900 SE 15th Street.

Important information: Call 954-763-2777 for more information or visit <www.15streetfisheries.com>.

75. John U. Lloyd State Recreation Area

Splash into the surf at this popular beach with more than 2 miles of sandy shoreline. You can also rent a canoe for an exploratory trip up mangrove-lined Whiskey Creek. Fishing for snapper and grouper is often good at the ocean jetties at the northern end of the park on the inlet, opposite the cruise-ship berth of Port Everglades. Rangers lead guided tours and tell about Florida's famous barefoot mailmen of the 1880s, who delivered mail on the beach in the days before roads and bridges. There are canoe and kayak rentals, life-guards, a snack shop, Coco's Café, picnic tables, restrooms, and showers.

Location: From U.S. Highway 1 in Dania, take Dania Beach Boulevard (State Road A1A) east across the Intracoastal Waterway to the peninsula, where it intersects with Ocean Drive. Follow the signs to the park at 6503 North Ocean Drive.

Important information: Open daily from 8 A.M. to sunset. Plan a weekday visit if you are vacationing during the summer season, March through

September. The park reaches capacity on summer weekends and closes to new arrivals; surprisingly, that can happen at 10 A.M. or even earlier, especially on holidays. For information, contact 954-923-2833.

76. Dania Pier

Take a 922-foot walk out into the ocean on this pier, either to take in the view or to fish, especially for yellowtail and mutton snapper.

Location: From U.S. Highway 1 in Dania, take Dania Beach Boulevard (State Road A1A) east across the Intracoastal Waterway. The pier is directly ahead on the beach.

Important information: Open 24 hours a day. For more information, call 954-927-0640.

77. Graves Museum of Archaeology and Natural History

Dig into days gone by at this spirited, homegrown place designed for inquisitive kids. Highlights include a complete *Tyrannosaurus rex* skeleton, fossilized dinosaur eggs, a dazzling 3.5-ton quartz crystal, a replica of the King Tut mummy, and a glimpse at the lives of native South Florida families who staged beachfront seafood bakes in the 1500s. This museum is a little-known gem.

Location: In Dania, about 1 mile south of the Fort Lauderdale airport, at 481 South Federal Highway (U.S. Highway 1).

Important information: Open from 10 A.M. to 4 P.M. Tuesdays through Fridays, from 10 A.M. to 6 P.M. Saturdays, and from noon to 6 P.M. Sundays. Children ages 3 and under are admitted free; fees are $6 for ages 4 to 12, $7 for senior citizens and students with a school ID, and $9.95 for everyone else. According to a museum sign, "Dinosaurs Admitted Free!" For more information, call 954-925-7770 or visit <www.gravesmuseum.org>.

78. International Game Fish Association World Fishing Center

Kids will delight in learning to cast with special rods, and they can also sit in a boat with a simulated motor to learn about water safety at this 60,000-square-foot museum that is the headquarters for a game fish association.

Displays of prize catches, the history of fishing gear, a hands-on discovery center for young children, conservation exhibits, and a marina provide lots of fishy experiences. The center sits within the 51-acre Sportsman's Park on Tigertail Lake.

Location: From Interstate 95 in Dania, exit onto Griffin Road and travel west to Anglers Avenue. Head south on Anglers Avenue and turn into the center at 300 Gulf Stream Way.

Important information: Open from 9:30 A.M. to 5 P.M. daily. On Wednesdays, hours are extended to 8 P.M. Children under age 3 are admitted free; fees are $5 for ages 3 to 12 and $9 for everyone else. For more information, contact 954-922-4212 or visit <www.igfa.org>.

79. Anne Kolb Nature Center/West Lake Park

All of coastal South Florida once shimmered with natural mangroves such as those preserved at this sanctuary and picnic place in West Lake Park. The 1,500-acre park shelters wading birds, such as white ibises and herons, which feed on the mud flats. Eagle-eyed visitors might spot roseate spoonbills. Nature trails wind through the site. A fishing pier, bicycle trails, a five-story observation tower, a backcountry boat tour, and four canoe trails all invite exploration. Complete with an exhibit hall, a 4,000-gallon saltwater aquarium, floor puzzles, birdcall stations, tidewater boat tours, and canoe, kayak, and johnboat rentals, this is an excellent environmental stop and a great place to picnic. It's named for a civic leader whose dedication saved this stunning stand of coastal mangroves.

Location: About five minutes south of Fort Lauderdale in Hollywood, on the Intracoastal Waterway. From Interstate 95 in Hollywood, exit onto Sheridan Street (exit 24) and travel east about 2.5 miles to the park entrance. A second entrance farther east on Sheridan Street, just after the Sheridan Street Bridge over the Intracoastal Waterway, leads to the exhibit hall, tour-boat dock, and fishing pier.

Important information: Free on weekdays; fee is $1 for people 5 and older on weekends. Entrance to the exhibit hall is $1.50 for children and $3 for adults. Tidewater Tours are $4 for children and $8 for adults. For more information, call 954-926-2410 or visit <www.broward.org/parks>.

Fluttery "flowers" under the sea

Among the prettiest creatures on an underwater reef, **anemones** look like fluttery undersea flowers. They attach themselves to a hard surface, such as a pier piling or reef rock. Then they stay put, waiting for currents to bring food along. The fringed, flowery part that seems to wave in the water is actually the creature's tentacles. Don't touch, because they can sting. That's how anemones stun and capture their food, which they pass along to their central digestive cavity. Anemones range in color from pale white to vibrant orange and in size from just a portion of an inch to several feet across. If they are poked, they contract their tentacles and try to appear as still and invisible as possible.

Miami Area

Miami is an international city. It's not only the business capital of the Caribbean Islands, but also a playground for wealthy European, Central American, and South American travelers. Miami attracts more foreign visitors than any other U.S. city, so spending a vacation here is like arriving in a far-off port without ever leaving the states.

Spanish is the primary language here. You can also expect to hear English, French, Yiddish, Portuguese, German, and Italian. The eclectic Miami menu will offer you a chance to sip mango *batidos* (fruit milkshakes), munch salted plantain chips, or enjoy a big bowl of matzoh-ball soup. It's heartening that a Jewish community of rugged Holocaust survivors and their descendants, a successful Cuban community, an African-American community, and immigrants from Central and South America and a range of Caribbean Islands, such as the Bahamas and Haiti, are all blended here in a galaxy of art, food, music, sports, and other pastimes.

This is the only subtropical part of the United States other than Hawaii, and the roadside floral displays prove it. Expect to see exotic plants, such as the orange and purple blooms of birds of paradise and the tangled roots of giant banyan trees. You'll see tiny green tree frogs with suction-cup feet hopping among the plants and meet chameleons doing tiny pushups on your resort patio.

This river port has attracted people for thousands of years. In downtown Miami, on the Miami River, archaeologists discovered a site occupied by humans 2,000 years ago. They also found a curious stone circle up to 700 years old, providing graduate students with a new focus of study. Miami has a great story of modern development, too. It also has infamous high-crime areas and, because of that, exclusive, gated communities that protect families of great wealth. If you fly in, don't be surprised if some airport workers are unfriendly or even rude.

As in any metropolis, some sections of the city are just not suitable for families. One such locale is Miami Beach's throbbing nightclub zone, South Beach, at the south end of Miami Beach. You may encounter topless sunbathers or openly gay couples there.

It's worth keeping safety in mind when you visit the Miami area. Use parking garages when possible and lock valuables in your car trunk. Beware of conmen who approach you to chat while their partner picks your pocket. Avoid downtown Miami at night and stick to the major attractions during the day. It's easy to get lost and wind up in an unsavory area.

Many savvy visitors base themselves farther north, such as in Fort Lauderdale, which also has an international airport, and then drive down for the sights. Others fly into the Naples/Fort Myers area on the Florida Gulf Coast, stay there, and scoot over to the Miami area for day visits. If you want to stay closer by, I recommend Key Biscayne, which is expensive but not as busy. It's also closer to family attractions in South Miami/South Dade County. On Miami Beach, as a rule, the farther north you go from South Beach, the more likely your family is to feel comfortable.

Other popular Miami-area lodging options for families are at the villages of Surfside, Bal Harbour, and Sunny Isles Beach, all north of Miami Beach proper. But you may have your heart set on the lavender, yellow, and flamingo pink colors of Miami Beach buildings. The city is famous for having the largest group of Art Deco–style buildings in the world.

For a more rustic camping experience, try Everglades National Park, about 45 miles to the southwest. See the Everglades section of this book for specific recommendations.

For more Miami-area information contact:

- Art Deco Welcome Center
  305-531-3484
  <www.southbeach.org>
- Coral Gables Development Department
  305-460-5311
- Greater Miami Convention and Visitors Bureau
  305-539-3000, 800-283-2707
  <www.miamiandbeaches.com>
- Miami Beach Latin Chamber of Commerce
  305-674-1414
- Miami Beach Visitor Information Center
  305-672-1270
- Sunny Isles Beach Resort Association
  305-947-5826

80. Newport Fishing Pier

Public fishing piers are rare in the Miami area. This one's a 918-foot walk out over the ocean. It's open 24 hours a day and crawling with anglers all year. It adjoins the Newport Beachside Crowne Plaza Resort, where you can find a deli and restaurants.

Location: About 10 miles north of Miami Beach in Sunny Isles Beach, at the point where Sunny Isles Boulevard (State Road 826) dead-ends into SR A1A.

Important information: For more information, call 305-949-1300.

81. Haulover Park/Skyward Kites

This public swimming beach and shady picnic spot, where an early 19th-century sponge fisherman hauled his boat across the dunes from Biscayne Bay to the Atlantic Ocean, is a mixed bag. At the beach there are lifeguards, showers, and concessions. The northern end of the beach is reserved for nude sunbathing and swimming. The southern end is where families congregate, and a rocky ocean jetty there attracts fish and hopeful surf-casters.

Cross State Road A1A via an underground path to visit Haulover Park Marina, which rents boats for exploring the Intracoastal Waterway. From afar, you probably noticed the vibrant windsocks and fancifully shaped kites fluttering in the air. Now, up close, you find them tethered to Earth and available for sale here at Skyward Kites.

Location: Just north of Bal Harbour in Sunny Isles Beach at 10800 Collins Avenue (State Road A1A).

Important information: The park is open daily from sunrise to sunset. Fee is $3.50 per car. For more information, call 305-947-3525. For marina information, call 305-947-3912, and to contact Skyward Kites, call 305-945-1681.

82. Oleta River State Recreation Area

In the midst of condos, this 850-acre bayside park offers picnicking, swimming, canoeing, and fishing off a pier. In the winter its calm waters might even reveal an endangered manatee. Ask park rangers about recent sightings. Concessionaires rent pedal boats, kayaks, and canoes. Groups can reserve the primitive youth camp and cabins.

Dolphins and Marlins and Panthers, oh my!

From beach volleyball to major-league sports, Miami is known as **Sports City.** In 1972, only six years after their inaugural season, the Miami Dolphins had the only perfect professional football season in history. Their preseason camp is held in July and August in Davie, about 20 miles north of Miami, at 7500 SW 30th Court. To find out when young fans can watch their practices for free, call 954-452-7000. Regular games are at Joe Robbie/Pro Player Stadium, 2269 NW 199th Street, Miami. For ticket information, call 305-620-2578; for other information, call 954-452-7000.

The Florida Marlins put Miami on the major-league baseball map beginning in 1993. They are also based at Joe Robbie/Pro Player Stadium, where there's an adventure playground. Call 305-626-7400 for Marlins information or write 2267 NW 199th Street. Billy the Marlin, based on a Florida deep-sea sportsfish, is the team mascot.

The Florida Panthers are hockey players who can hit a mean puck. Their escapades on ice began at the Miami Arena but moved to a new place near Sawgrass Mills in Broward County. For information, call 954-835-7000. Stanley C. Panther is the team mascot. He represents a dwindling species, the endangered Florida panther, which haunts the nearby Everglades.

Since 1988, the Miami Heat have been providing professional hoop action. They have a new stadium near Biscayne Bay and Bayside Marketplace. Call 305-577-4328 for a schedule and ticket information.

Location: On the northern end of Biscayne Bay on the Intracoastal Waterway. From U.S. Highway 1 in North Miami, take Sunny Isles Boulevard (State Road 826) east about 1 mile to the entrance at 3400 NE 163rd Street.

Important information: Open daily from sunrise to sunset. State park fees apply. For more information and group camping reservations, call 305-919-1846 or 305-947-6357 or visit <www.dep.state.fl.us/parks>.

83. North Shore Open Space Park

Park here for a good, shady, seaside picnic spot. The park has boardwalks over the dunes to the beach, lifeguards, showers, and a bike path. At 40 acres, it's a huge expanse of undeveloped beach, in contrast to the surrounding apartment condos and resorts.

Location: In Miami Beach along Collins Avenue (State Road A1A), between 87th and 79th Streets.

Important information: Open daily from 7 A.M. to 8 P.M. There is on-street parking, and admission is $1 per person. For more information, call 305-993-2032.

84. Wolfie Cohen's Rascal House

A visit to this family emporium is like going home for comfort food, complete with the agreeably nagging aunt (here, your waitress) who may wisecrack about any uneaten blueberry blintzes. The chicken soup and potato pancakes are even better than the ones my father made. Kids have their own menu and can win a free dessert—make it cheesecake! Wolfie's has been a reliable beach fixture for more than 40 years.

Location: In Miami Beach at 2038 Collins Avenue.

Important information: Like any Florida eatery that caters to grandparents, there's an early-bird special. For more information, call 305-947-4581.

85. Holocaust Memorial

This poignant outdoor sculpture in Miami Beach deserves a meditative pause. Tell your family about the Holocaust, its survivors, and, most important, its victims. They are the ones to whom this outstretched, beseeching hand is dedicated. South Florida is home to the third-largest Jewish community in the nation, and some Holocaust survivors live in Miami Beach today.

Location: In Miami Beach at 1933-45 Meridian Avenue.

Important information: For more information, call 305-538-1663.

86. Sanford L. Ziff Jewish Museum of Florida

A former synagogue is now a busy cultural center with an outstanding permanent Florida-history exhibit. The Ziff features citrus labels in Yiddish and more, including special events that don't necessarily focus exclusively on the Jewish experience, such as a living-history presentation about fascinating Florida women.

Location: In Miami Beach at 301 Washington Avenue.

Important information: Open from 10 A.M. to 5 P.M. Tuesdays through Sundays. Free on Saturdays. For more information, call 305-672-5044.

Dawdling in the Deco district

You'll know you've reached the stylish **Miami Beach Art Deco district**—about Fifth Street to Dade Boulevard, radiating from Ocean Avenue—when it seems like you're moving through a stage set. You'll see street after street of lavender, flamingo pink, and lemon yellow buildings, frosted-glass windows etched with flamingo and palm-tree designs, ornately decorated screen doors, and lush courtyards. Many of the hotels and shops cater to supermodels and other bar-hopping sleepyheads. Since these folks might dine at 10 P.M. and sleep late after a long night of promenading, rollerblading, and dancing, morning is a good time to take the family on tour. You can arrange a self-guided, audio walking tour at the Art Deco Welcome Center at Tenth Street and Ocean Avenue, 305-531-3484 or 305-674-0150. It's a beaut of a building itself, with a shape that suggests an ocean liner. It's also a fun backdrop for vacation photos with its outdoor calendar clock that proclaims the balmy temperature.

Two Deco district resorts that are family friendly are the beachfront Bel-Air Hotel at 6515 Collins Avenue, 305-866-6511, and the Alexander at 5225 Collins Avenue, 305-865-6500, <www.goflorida.com/alexander/>. Farther north, in Bal Harbour, families who want to splurge can check out the Sheraton, which has its own aquatic playground that rivals the best water park.

87. Seaquarium

This newly renovated aquarium on a small patch of land called Virginia Key (on the way out to Key Biscayne) presents marine shows, such as a magnificent killer whale that splashes the audience on cue. If captive choreography is to your liking, you'll also want to see the dolphins and sea lions put through their paces. There are sea turtles, manatees, and crocodiles to watch, along with a coral-reef aquarium presentation. You can even reserve a two-hour opportunity to "Swim with Flipper." Behind the scenes, the aquarium offers a therapy program for handicapped children that involves swimming with dolphins. It's available by reservation only and has a long waiting list.

Location: From Miami, head east over the Rickenbacker Causeway—a $1 toll ride—to Virginia Key, a small island in Biscayne Bay. Seaquarium is at 4400 Rickenbacker Causeway, on the southern side of the island.

Important information: Open daily from 9:30 A.M. to 6 P.M., but the last tickets are sold at 4:30 P.M. Admission is free for kids under 3, $16.95 for ages 3 to 9, and $21.95 for all others. The price includes seven shows, so plan your time accordingly. For more information, call 305-361-5705 or visit <www.miamiseaquarium.com>.

88. Crandon Park/Marjory Stoneman Douglas Biscayne Nature Center

Look for this landscaped, 3-mile-long beach park near the northern end of Key Biscayne. It features lifeguards, an old-fashioned carousel, lots of parking, and a convenient snack bar. The shrubs with almost perfectly round leaves the size of dessert plates are seagrapes. A popular place for picnicking and swimming, the park is also home to the Marjory Stoneman Douglas Biscayne Nature Center, which offers guided field trips. Expect huge beach crowds on weekends and holidays.

Location: From Miami, take the Rickenbacker Causeway east across Biscayne Bay and Virginia Key to Key Biscayne. The park is at 4000 Crandon Boulevard, at the northern end of the island.

Important information: Open daily from 8 A.M. to 7 P.M. Admission is $3.50 per car. Be sure to leave valuables locked in your car trunk. For more park information, call 305-361-5421; for nature center information, call 305-361-8097.

89. Bill Baggs Cape Florida State Recreation Area

This 400-acre park comes with an 1825 lighthouse, one of the earliest still standing in Florida. It and the lightkeeper's home are on the National Register of Historic Places. Twice a day enthusiastic rangers take the first ten people who sign up on tours. They'll regale you with the horrific tale of a deputy lightkeeper who was left for dead by attacking Seminole Indians during the Second Seminole War. In addition to the lighthouse, this bay-to-ocean park is often ranked as one of the best beaches in the country. With lifeguards, fishing platforms, a lighthouse café, a boater's café with a bait and tackle shop, bike paths, and a host of rentals, from umbrellas to inline skates, this is a full-service recreation park. It is extremely popular with families.

Location: At the southern tip of Key Biscayne at 1200 South Crandon Boulevard.

Important information: Open daily from 8 A.M. to sunset. Fee is $4 per car. For more information, call 305-361-5811 or visit <www.dep.state.fl.us/parks>.

The curious circle at the center of the city

Surrounded by high-rise buildings along the Miami River in downtown Miami is an empty lot that has yielded evidence of 2,000 years of habitation. Starting in 1998, archaeologists have uncovered beads, pottery, and stone tools that are hundreds of years old. The biggest find to date is a large 500- to 700-year-old chunk of limestone with a circle of holes carved into it. It is called **the Miami Circle.**

What is it? Who built it? What did they call it? It could be the calendar of an ancient tribe, the Tequesta Indians of South Florida. The town of Tequesta north of West Palm Beach is named for these prehistoric natives. The stone, which would just fit into a garage, has one carved hole that faces directly east toward Miami's Biscayne Bay. The hole is shaped like a human eye with a stone pupil. Whoever carved the hole would have been able to peer through it at the sun rising over the bay.

Some theorize that the circle represents a link between Florida's prehistoric people and the Mayan civilization of Mexico. Ocean-going canoes may have allowed the two cultures to interact. Some of the stone tools found at the Miami site are made of volcanic rock and aren't from Florida. They could have been given or traded to the early Miami people by tool makers in the Georgia region.

Another big find at the Miami Circle was the remains of a shark buried with teeth and vertebrae intact. It may have been a religious offering. The site's economic, ceremonial, and religious significance will be studied for years to come. Because of it, archaeologists are reconsidering their theories about early human habitation in Florida.

90. The Barnacle

Future ship captains and boat designers will want to tinker around this state historical site. It's the real 1891 bayfront home of Commodore Ralph Munroe, a Massachusetts transplant whose inventions are delightful. Check out the yellow workshop with its hurricane-proof walls, the unusual air-conditioning system, and the commodore's stylish shallow-draft sailboat. The home is set amid a lush portion of the remaining Miami Hammock, a dense tropical hardwood forest. A footpath that served long ago as a regional highway still meanders through the yard.

Location: In downtown Coconut Grove at 3485 Main Highway.

Important information: Open from 9 A.M. to 4 P.M. Fridays through Sundays, with tours at 10 A.M., 11:30 A.M., 1 P.M., and 2:30 P.M. If the gate is locked, the ranger is on tour. Fee is $1. For more information, call 305-448-9445 or visit <www.dep.state.fl.us/parks>.

91. Villa Vizcaya Museum and Gardens

Walk through the ultimate fantasy palace, built by a Chicago industrialist between 1900 and 1916 to look like a 400-year-old Italian estate. The 34-room mansion overflows with ornate treasures, such as large wall tapestries and Roman sculptures. On the 35-acre grounds, secret paths lead through elegant fountain gardens. What usually intrigues kids is the bathroom sink with three faucets: for hot, cold, and salt water. Their interest is also piqued by the fact that the main kitchen is on the upper floor, where the view is better, and that the house has hidden elevator, vacuum, telephone, and re-frigeration systems. Legend has it that Christopher Columbus once stood on one of the carpets that now hangs on the museum walls; that seems unlikely, but it does make you look at the tapestry twice. *Vizcaya* is a Spanish word for a high place, and this villa is named for a province in Spain.

Location: In Coral Gables at 3521 South Miami Avenue, on Biscayne Bay.

Important information: Open daily from 9:30 A.M. to 5 P.M., but the ticket office closes at 4:30 P.M. Children under 6 are admitted free; fees are $5 for ages 6 to 12 and $10 for all others. For more information, call 305-250-9133. To contact the café/gift shop, call 305-856-8189.

92. Miami Museum of Science

This popular science center is right across the street from Villa Vizcaya (see above), allowing families with split loyalties between art and science to con-veniently divide and conquer according to individual preferences. The site features a small birds-of-prey center, a hands-on insect display, and a fossil exhibit. Often, this site is more popular with younger kids, while Vizcaya across the street holds the attention of older students who are developing expensive taste in grand things. A planetarium here offers special star shows and laser light shows on its 65-foot-high dome. You can also get a guided tour of the night sky in the Southern Cross Observatory.

Location: In Coral Gables at 3280 South Miami Avenue.

Important information: Open daily from 10 A.M. to 6 P.M. Children under age 3 are admitted free; fees are $5.50 for ages 3 to 12, $7 for students and

The city of Coral Gables

This architecturally scenic community stretches from Biscayne Bay west to Red Road and from Eighth Street south to Sunset Boulevard. It is a jewel known for its public Venetian pool, abundant small parks, fountains, wide streets, tennis courts, cafés, stylish and landscaped homes and office buildings, art galleries, international bank offices, and the campus of the University of Miami. It was created as a model, The City Beautiful, beginning in 1925. The developer was a man who arrived in Florida as a child and sold the family's produce in Miami. His model works because this neighborhood is one of the most desirable in the region. Most of the architecture is in the Mediterranean style, and local laws ensure that the city remains lovely, banning billboards, highway overpasses, and fortresslike or garish construction.

senior citizens, and $9 for all others. Admission to the observatory is free on Thursday nights. For more information, call 305-854-4247 or 305-854-4242 or visit <www.miamisci.org>.

93. Venetian Pool

This park in the heart of Coral Gables encompasses the only public swimming pool listed on the National Register of Historic Places. The Venetian Pool was created in 1923 on the quarry site where coral rock was extracted to build Coral Gables. A fresh spring provides the 820,000-gallon pool with crystal water. The grottoes, waterfalls, Venetian lampposts, coral caves, bridge, lookout tower, and tiny sand beach add to the magic of this, one of the most famous pools in the United States.

Location: In Coral Gables at 2701 De Soto Boulevard.

Important information: Open Tuesdays through Sundays. For more information, call 305-460-5356.

94. Fairchild Tropical Gardens

You'll walk through the world's largest collection of palm trees here in the largest tropical botanical garden in the nation. In the exuberant spirit of David Fairchild, this is a hands-on garden and an excellent site to stretch your legs. Fairchild believed that people should touch nature, so enthusiastic guides ask you to crush and smell lemon grass and to sample other elements in the 5,000-species collection. An unusual element is the hurricane garden, a swath left unchanged since Hurricane Andrew hit the region in 1992, in order to demonstrate the natural inclination of plants and trees to take root. Elsewhere amid the 83 acres, there's a miniature rain forest, a mangrove forest, 11 little lakes, hidden trails, vines, orchids, a tram through a sunken garden, and a café. Plus, there's a public beach next door!

Location: In Coral Gables at 10901 Old Cutler Road.

Important information: Open from 9:30 A.M. to 4:30 P.M. daily except Christmas. Free for children under age 13, $8 for all others. For more information, call 305-667-1651 or visit <www.ftg.org>.

95. Matheson Hammock County Park

Next door to Fairchild Tropical Gardens (see above), this popular, 600-acre local park offers a sheltered bayfront beach that's a waveless, natural lagoon. There are large trees for young adventurers to climb, bike paths, jogging paths, picnic areas, a mangrove forest, and more. Add lifeguards, showers, and a café—the Redfish Grill—and no wonder this is one of the best urban parks in all of Florida. The term hammock refers here to an elevated area of dense trees and plants near lower-lying wetlands.

Location: In Coral Gables at 9610 Old Cutler Road.

Important information: Open daily from 6 A.M. to sunset. Fee is $3.50 per car. For more information, call 305-666-6979.

96. Parrot Jungle

Many people expect to see parrots flying freely in subtropical South Florida. You may see a back porch escapee or occasional flocks of lorikeets or parakeets, especially in Fort Lauderdale, Miami, and Sarasota. But the native Florida parrot, a large beauty called the Carolina parakeet, which John Audubon painted, was hunted to extinction. You can learn all about Central and South American natives at Parrot Jungle. They fly free here. Also visit with alligators, orangutans, and chimpanzees, and make new friends at the petting zoo. The backdrop is a pleasing tropical garden with orchids and palms. Bold children can let brilliantly colored macaws nibble sunflower seeds from their hands; it makes a fun vacation photo. There's also a café and children's playground on the lush acres of this destination, which dates to 1936.

Location: Just west of Coral Gables at 11000 SW 57th Avenue. (Parrot Jungle was considering a move in 2000, so check before you visit.)

Important information: Open daily from 9:30 A.M. to 6 P.M. Because it's out-of-doors, this isn't a good site to visit in the rain. For more information, call 305-666-7834 or visit <www.parrotjungle.com>.

97. Miami MetroZoo

This zoo wins accolades for allowing animals to roam freely on "islands" surrounded by moats. You can get startlingly up-close views by walking into dark caves where only a glass wall separates you from the animals. The layout of this vast park, home to 260 different species, is easy to understand if you take the monorail first for an orientation. At the end of the ride, get off and take the long walk back to the entrance, enjoying the exhibits on the way. Allow several hours to visit.

Location: In South Dade just west of Interstate 95 at 12400 SW 52nd Street.

Important information: Open daily from 9:30 A.M. to 5:30 P.M.; ticket sales end at 4 P.M., but it's best to arrive in the morning, when the animals are more likely to be stirring and temperatures are cooler. The monorail is air-conditioned. In the summer, the park is extremely hot and has little shade. Children under age 3 are admitted free; fees are $4 for ages 3 to 12 and $8 for adults. For more information, call 305-251-0400 or 305-251-0401 or visit <www.metro-dade.com/parks/metrozoo>.

Questing after the Tequesta

Tequesta might sound like a Spanish phrase, but it's the name given to a peaceful tribe of Southeast Florida Indians who lived in the Miami area and the eastern Everglades thousands of years ago. They ate oysters, conchs, small animals, fish, turtles, alligators, berries, fruit, deer, and even an occasional bison. The Tequestas created pottery that is still being unearthed in Florida today. Different designs in the clay, especially along the rims, help archaeologists figure out which band of Tequestas made the pieces. The Tequestas were considered peaceful because they usually let neighboring tribes do what they wanted and didn't fight them over territory. To look their ancient best, Tequesta Indians wore shark vertebrae and shells as ear plugs, beads, and hairpins.

98. Biscayne National Park

Landlubbers can learn about the fragile coral reefs of this national marine park at the Convoy Point Visitor Center, east of Homestead on Biscayne Bay. There's a small museum. Be sure to watch the park videos, which introduce you to the colorful species sheltered in this underwater park. The reefs are threatened by pollution, shipping, and divers.

If your children have long attention spans and sea legs, book a three-hour trip via glass-bottom boat out to the protected reefs. You'll spend two hours of sometimes bouncy travel out and back and one hour exploring the reef. Snorkelers like the fact that the reefs are shallow enough for surface-floaters to enjoy the colorful reef fish. Scuba equipment and underwater skills aren't necessary, although swimming skills are a must. Mangroves and shallow areas are also part of the preserve, and you can explore these in a rented kayak or canoe. If you have access to a private boat, you can visit several islands in the park that have nature trails and primitive campsites. The latter are available via reservation only.

Location: From Homestead, about 25 miles southwest of Miami, head east for about 9 miles on Southwest 328th Street to its end on Biscayne Bay. The park entrance is on the left.

Important information: Open daily, with boat trips at 1:30 P.M. in good weather. The park is free, and boat trips are $27.95, including rental of snorkeling equipment. For more information, call 305-230-1100 or visit <www.nps.gov/bisc/home.htm>.

Everglades National Park Area

As intriguing as other regions of Florida are, with their springs, sinkholes, caverns, historical forts, tropical fish, and high sand dunes, the Everglades is the state at its most exotic. Many people think of the Everglades as a giant swamp, but it's actually a shallow "river of grass" flowing 100 miles from Lake Okeechobee to Florida Bay. It's also the largest remaining subtropical wilderness in the nation, covering close to 5,000 square miles.

Deep within this complex and fragile ecosystem of sawgrass and hammock live 14 endangered species, including the American crocodile, Florida panther, and manatee. The vast Everglades encompasses five national preserves—Biscayne Bay National Park (Miami Area), Everglades National Park, Big Cypress National Preserve (Southwest Region), the Arthur R. Marshall Loxahatchee National Wildlife Refuge (Palm Beach Area), and the Florida

Panther National Wildlife Refuge (Southwest Region). The Everglades has been designated an International Biosphere Reserve and a World Heritage Site.

A little less than half of the Everglades is contained within Everglades National Park. Still, the park is larger than some states, covering almost 1.5 million acres. So it's best to plot your visit in advance. The main park entrance is on the eastern boundary at the Ernest F. Coe Visitor Center, about 45 miles southwest of Miami. From this entrance you can continue on to two national park campgrounds along the Main Park Road. This is the only auto route by which you can reach the restaurant, motel, and cottages at Flamingo, an outpost on Florida Bay about 40 miles south of the Coe Visitor Center where the road ends at the tip of the peninsula. If you only have a few hours or less, resist the temptation to rush to Flamingo and back. Talk with staff at the Coe Visitor Center and then spend your time wisely at one or two sites nearby, such as the wildlife-rich Royal Palm Visitor Center, where the Anhinga Trail provides an easy way to view park wildlife. If you have more time and your older children are seasoned hikers, sign up for a free, ranger-led "Slough Slog." This is a mucky, sweaty, buggy slosh through the glades, with the chance to visit an alligator hole.

The national park has three other entrances: Chekika, about 15 miles north of Homestead, where there is a campground but no other access; the Shark Valley Visitor Center and wildlife-watching site, on the northern border of the park on the Tamiami Trail (U.S. Highway 41); and the Gulf Coast Visitor Center at Everglades City, southeast of Naples. From the Gulf Coast Visitor Center, access is possible only by boat. You can bring your own or take a boat tour offered by the park concessionaire or a local guide.

A visit to Everglades National Park is best made in the winter, from November through March, to avoid intense heat, high humidity, swarms of biting bugs, lightning storms, and low-area flooding. Biting bugs are always present in the park, so you should come prepared; wear long sleeves and long pants and bring repellent. Be sure to bring one or two pairs of binoculars, too, and a birding or nature guide. Or rent binoculars at the Coe Visitor Center and get a nature guide at its bookstore.

Properly prepared, you can see a lot of the park in a dawn-to-dusk day trip from Miami. But you'll have a better chance of seeing wildlife and you'll have the opportunity to enjoy a wider range of activities if you stay in a park campground or at the Flamingo resort, which has a campground, motel rooms, and cottages. The park's low topographic profile requires you to get out of the car and walk a footpath or boardwalk, climb an observation tower, or boat around to really see into it.

You'll find more destinations in Everglades National Park described in the Southwest Region, Everglades City Area, of this book.

99. Ernest F. Coe Visitor Center

Stop here to educate yourself about this 1.5-million-acre park, where you may glimpse manatees, dolphins, and flocks of big birds such as herons, wood storks, and roseate spoonbills. You can watch some fast-paced park videos, pick up a schedule of free ranger-led talks and walks, ask rangers about special events, select some free brochures, get a free park map, sign up to take tram rides, schedule bicycle or canoe trips, ask rangers about recent animal sightings, or learn about fishing conditions. Everglades National Park pulses with life, so any new information you glean about its critters or history here can enhance your visit. There are some 500 species of fish, 900 kinds of marine invertebrates, 350 kinds of birds, 100 different butterflies, 40 mammals, 65 reptiles and amphibians, 100 trees, and 1,000 plants to learn about.

This visitor center is a world crossroads, so your children may get to hear people speaking in foreign languages. If your student is studying a language, he or she may want to pick up a park brochure written in one of five different languages.

Location: This park entrance is about 45 miles southwest of Miami and 11 miles west of Homestead via State Road 9336. The Coe Visitor Center is just inside the main park entrance, on the right, at 40001 SR 9336.

Important information: The park is open 24 hours a day. Ask for a return receipt when you pay the $10-a-car national park admission. It's good for a week and can be used at the other park entrances. The Coe Visitor Center is open daily from 8 A.M. to 5 P.M., with extended hours in winter. Call 305-242-7700 for more information or visit <www.nps.gov/ever>. Try to arrive in daylight, because the state road to the park entrance is a winding route through unlighted agricultural fields. It can be confusing, and there is no place to stop for directions.

100. Royal Palm Visitor Center/Anhinga Trail/ Gumbo Limbo Trail

If you're on the eastern side of the park and have time to visit only one site beyond the Coe Visitor Center, stop here. This center's name comes from the stately royal palm trees here, a large variety that grows only in the southern part of the state. This is really a two-for-one site, because Royal Palm offers two very different short walks. The Gumbo Limbo Trail supplies an immediate jungle experience. It leads for a half-mile through a dark, dense hardwood hammock amid strangler figs, hanging vines, and orchids. The gumbo limbo tree has smooth, peeling red bark reminiscent of sunburns, so it's nicknamed the tourist tree.

The second walk, the Anhinga Trail, is a half-mile amble along an airy boardwalk over a marsh thick with alligators, fish, and birds. The anhinga is a black diving bird that emerges from its underwater fishing trips to perch on tree branches and stretch its wings to dry. Rangers lead free walks on the Anhinga Trail daily; check for current schedules. Take as much time as you can at Royal Palm, to absorb the sights and sounds on each walk and to see exhibits at the small visitor center. This site offers some of the easiest, closest access in the park for wildlife watching and plant study.

Location: About 2 miles south of the Coe Visitor Center on Main Park Road, turn left onto Royal Palm Road.

Important information: If you didn't buy a nature guide at the Coe Visitor Center, you can buy one in the bookstore here. You can also rent binoculars and buy insect repellent. For more information, call the main park office at 305-242-7700, or 305-242-7759.

101. Long Pine Key Campground

The only pine that grows in the Everglades, the slash pine, is abundant here. If a radio-collared Florida panther is hunting in the park, this is the neighborhood in which it's most likely to be found. The rare creature is almost extinct; there are only about 35 left in the wild. The campground is on some of the highest and driest land in the park, which is why the pines grow here and not elsewhere. Good features of this campground include 3-mile and 5-mile trails past lakes and an amphitheater where rangers conduct fascinating talks almost nightly. There's also a 7-mile back route via woodland footpath and road to the Royal Palm Visitor Center. Ask a ranger for detailed directions and current route conditions, such as possible water covering the trail.

Location: From Main Park Road, turn south about 2 miles west of the Royal Palm Visitor Center entrance; a sign indicates the Long Pine Key Campground.

Important information: Campsites are rented on a first-come, first-served basis. There are cold showers, so if you've been wanting to try out that black-plastic solar water heater, bring it along. For more information, call 305-242-7700, or 305-242-7599.

102. Pa-hay-okee Overlook

A 100-yard boardwalk leads through the sawgrass to an observation tower, where you can get a bird's-eye view of a portion of this vast marsh. *Pa-hay-okee* is a Seminole word meaning grassy water. It was one of the earliest names for the Everglades region. The sawgrass is so dense and open water patches so scarce at this stop, that you're more likely to see birds than alligators here. Look for great white herons, red-shouldered hawks, red-winged blackbirds, and vultures.

Location: On Main Park Road, about 12 miles southwest of the Coe Visitor Center, on the right (north) side of the road.

Important information: For more information, call 305-242-7700 or visit <www.nps.gov/ever>.

103. Mahogany Hammock

Take a walk to look at the largest mahogany tree in the United States; it's 12 feet around and about 90 feet tall. Most of the mahogany trees in South Florida were harvested by the Spanish to provide lumber for shipbuilding, but a few giants remain. A hammock is a slightly drier area in the midst of a wetland—an island of trees. Park rangers call these areas animal bedrooms, because many creatures that can't live in the sawgrass sleep, hunt, and avoid the blazing sun on these cooler, jungly islands.

Location: About 19 miles southwest of the Coe Visitor Center, off Main Park Road on the right.

Important information: For more information, call 305-242-7700 or visit <www.nps.gov/ever>.

104. West Lake Trail

At this point in the Everglades, you have entered the mangrove coast. A half-mile boardwalk trail—plagued by exceptional numbers of biting bugs in warm weather—will take you past the four species of mangrove: red, black, white, and buttonwood. This is the only lake in the park that you can see from Main Park Road. There's a small visitor pavilion here. West Lake is saltier than other water in the area, so it's crocodile habitat. Use your binoculars to scan the water for a sight of these toothy alligator cousins. And if you see a ranger, ask about the crocodile that made its nest right at the pavilion. Summer visitors were treated to the sight of a crocodile nesting next to the West Lake sign. Mother hatched 13 baby crocs. You may see one of them, all grown up.

Location: On Main Park Road, about 30.5 miles southwest of the Coe Visitor Center.

In a while, crocodile

• •

The lineage of **alligators** and **crocodiles** stretches back to the dinosaurs. These fierce, toothy, armored reptiles are among the most enduring images of Florida, and the Everglades is the one place in the United States where the two species are known to naturally coexist. The crocodile is extremely rare, although surveys show that this species is slowly increasing in numbers, from about 100 just a few years ago to possibly 550 today. At this rate, the species could begin moving into other southern areas of the state to feed and breed.

The crocodile differs from the alligator in a few other ways. It likes its water saltier than the alligator does. It has a prominent tooth that protrudes from each side of its lower jaw when it shuts its mouth. Its snout is pointier and narrower than that of the alligator. Its body is generally thinner. It's often lighter in color—gray compared to an alligator's black. The crocodile's name is from a Greek term meaning "worm of the pebbles." It probably refers to the animal's habit of sunning itself on rocks.

Alligators are considered the salvation of the Everglades. They dig dens and create "wallows" that collect rainwater. These alligator holes are often the only source of fresh water for all wild animals during the winter dry season and during long droughts. Enough fish, turtles, snails, and other creatures live in the water to survive the drought and repopulate the area when the rains return. The alligator's name probably comes from an Old Spanish word, *alagarto*, which means "the lizard."

Don't approach either a crocodile or an alligator, no matter how still and lifeless one appears. You are more likely to come within striking distance of an alligator than a crocodile. At Shark Valley in Everglades National Park, alligators frequently walk out of the water to sun themselves beside footpaths or walk across footpaths to other watering holes. When this happens, you should walk the other way or, at the very least, give them a very wide berth. Report any feeding of alligators or crocodiles to park rangers. Not only is it illegal, but it is extremely dangerous. Alligators taught to associate people with food may lunge at people with their jaws. In recent years, an alligator grabbed a child next to a popular Shark Valley footpath. The child was released but survived but required stitches.

Important information: Unlike other stops, this one has restrooms. The boardwalk over the water and through the mangroves will be plagued with biting bugs in warm weather. For more information, call 305-242-7700 or visit <www.nps.gov/ever>.

105. Flamingo Visitor Center

Make sure to stop here for the exhibits, brochures on Flamingo-area trails, and a schedule of ranger-led events. Don't pass up the opportunity to ask a ranger about events suited for children, canoeing and boating options, how the fish are biting, recent cuckoo and manatee sightings, and tales of park adventure. Plan to attend the afternoon Naturalist Knapsack talk, where you can expect to see a variety of objects ranging from an alligator skull to an ancient shell. The 45-minute chat is fun.

Location: At the end of Main Park Road, 38 miles southwest of the main park entrance on Florida Bay.

Important information: Open from November through April, from 7:30 A.M. to 5 P.M. daily. For more information, call 305-242-7700.

106. Flamingo Campground

This bayside campground is quite large, with 300 campsites. There is no tree cover, which is a drawback during the day, but at night the view of the stars is unobstructed. Hope for windy weather to chase the biting bugs away.

Location: In Flamingo, southwest of the visitor center and Flamingo Resort. Follow the signs.

Important information: There are cold showers and no electrical hookups. Despite its size, this popular campground fills up, especially on winter weekends. Please don't speed the 38 miles to Flamingo from the park entrance to get to the campground. Plan ahead to arrive early in the day so you can get on the waiting list. For more information, call 305-242-7700 or 800-600-3813.

107. Flamingo Lodge

Renting a cottage at this resort is the best bet for families who want to stay a couple of nights in the park. You can more easily make your own meals and

The little town
at the end of the road

The last community on the mainland at the extreme southeastern corner of the United States is named **Flamingo.** For decades it was an isolated outpost of fishing families and charcoal-makers, accessible only by boat. It also attracted rugged market hunters who shot birds for their plumes, trapped otters and bobcats for their pelts, and took alligators for their hides. The ambush of a game warden on an offshore island led to the creation of the National Audubon Society.

Although snowy egrets and many other beautiful birds clouded the skies here in the early 1800s, flamingos were probably never Florida natives. They were seasonal visitors from Caribbean islands, easily scared away by hunters. None are seen in the wild today, except perhaps for a lone bird blown off course by a storm or a zoo escapee. If you see pink birds, they're most likely roseate spoonbills.

The community of Flamingo was hit many times by hurricanes, especially one in 1935. When Everglades National Park was established in 1947, it absorbed what was left of the community. From November through March, it is now a busy resort where you can rent a houseboat, camp, stay in motel rooms or cottages, dine in a restaurant overlooking Florida Bay, rent canoes and motorboats, and explore nearby park sites.

There are plenty of fascinating things to do in the Flamingo area. Especially good for children are the tram ride from Flamingo to the Snake Bight Trail (a bight is a small body of water) and the daily ranger talk, Naturalist Knapsack, offered each afternoon at the Flamingo Visitor Center (see above).

clean up in warm water after a day slogging through the Everglades. Except at Chekika, park campgrounds have cold showers and no electricity. The resort also offers motel rooms and suites overlooking expansive Florida Bay. The Flamingo Lodge restaurant offers an excellent breakfast buffet, as well as lunch and dinner. If you catch a fish, you can arrange for the restaurant chef to cook it. Check restaurant hours ahead of time, so when you arrive for a meal you won't find it closed. The restaurant is on the second floor, overlooking mangroves and Florida Bay. The seafood is generally excellent and desserts are tropical; try the key lime pie or mango cheesecake. There is also a small café.

Another lodging option, but only if you are handy with a boat, is to rent a houseboat. You can make a reservation at the lodge. The resort conducts Everglades boat tours and tram rides, operates a marina, rents canoes and other boats, and runs a small grocery store/gas station at the marina. All the services are available whether you are a resort guest or not.

Although you can stay outside the park and drive in every day to take walks, attend ranger programs, and go on boat rides, staying overnight at Flamingo is one of the best ways for landlubbers to experience the mangrove coast. This is an exceptionally popular resort. If you can get a reservation for a winter-season weekend, consider yourself lucky. Weekdays are also often booked way in advance.

Location: At the end of Main Park Road in Flamingo at 1 Flamingo Lodge Highway.

Important information: Reservations are almost always necessary in the winter season, especially after December 15 and especially on weekends. To make a boat-tour reservation, call 941-695-2591. To make a lodging reservation or get other information, call 800-600-3813 or 941-695-3101 or visit <www.amfac.com>.

108. Eco Pond

No one should come all the way to Flamingo and then leave without a visit to Eco Pond. Take the half-mile boardwalk around the pond, or just watch the feathery sights from the observation platform. The pond supports mangroves that are a bird rookery, or nesting grounds. The place is noisy with birdsong and bird chatter. Visit near dusk and you're likely to see white ibises and several kinds of herons gently winging home for the night. You'll see alligators cruising in the waters, too.

Location: Park near Flamingo Lodge (see above) and walk about a half-mile to Eco Pond. There is very limited parking at the pond.

Important information: In the winter, you're bound to see wildlife anytime, but dawn and dusk are the best times to see lots of it.

109. Guy Bradley Trail

Make this path from the Flamingo Visitor Center to the Flamingo Campground a daily jaunt and bring a picnic. It's a 2-mile round trip along the scenic shore of Florida Bay. You'll see lots of what Robert Frost called "fluttering flowers," or butterflies. Scan the mud flats for roseate spoonbills. They have long, spoon-shaped bills with which they filter the water for food. Guy Bradley, for whom the trail was named, was a game warden who was killed on an offshore island while trying to protect birds like these.

Location: The trailhead starts at the Flamingo Visitor Center (see above) and leads for 1 mile to the campground.

Important information: Try to time your hike with low tide, so you'll be able to see more horseshoe crabs, feeding birds, and other creatures along Florida Bay.

110. Chekika Park

• •

At this park, you can pitch your tent near a lake created from the overflow from an artesian well. As at other Everglades campsites, come prepared for mosquitoes and no-see-ums, tiny biting midges. If it's windy, you're in luck, because many of the insects will be blown away. But if the biting bugs become really bad, there's nothing wrong with packing up and leaving. Rugged world explorers have been driven off by excessive bugs during campouts in the Everglades. Families can hardly be expected to stick out such ordeals. There are nature paths here, and you'll get up-close experiences with sawgrass and isolated, subtropical hardwood hammocks. This 640-acre section of the national park isn't connected by road to any other park units. You drive straight in and straight back out. It's mainly used by campers. But if you have extra time, it's a fine picnic site with restrooms, and it offers a chance to see alligators. There's a small interpretive center. The site is named after a Seminole Indian leader. The area was a Seminole stronghold during the mid-1800s Seminole Wars.

Location: About 15 miles north of the main park entrance. From State Road 997 (Krome Avenue) just north of Homestead, drive west for about 6 miles on SW 168th Street to the park.

The bandit of the Everglades

• •

While many people worry needlessly about snakes, the adorable **raccoon** is a truly pesky Everglades inhabitant. This abundant animal appears cute and cuddly, but it isn't. It bites. It can carry disease. Don't feed raccoons. If you are camping, you should know that these clever bandits can unzip a tent zipper. If you don't want them messing with your food and water, you must keep provisions inside your car, with windows rolled up. This is true for daytime picnickers, too. Tell the raccoons to go fish. It's so much better for them to collect oysters, crabs, and fish, than to eat taco chips.

Important information: This site was closed because of damage caused by Hurricane Irene in October 1999. Call 305-242-7700 or 305-242-7599 to find out whether it's been reopened.

111. Tamiami Trail

● ●

This is a legendary route that was dynamited through the Everglades in the 1920s to open the area to development. Instead, it led to widespread hunting of bobcats, deer, turkeys, and panthers, as well as trapping of otters. Few people wanted to build homes in a wetland besieged by hordes of biting bugs. But hunters who now had a route through all the water were eager to set up camps in the wilderness.

The Tamiami Trail is a two-lane road that is part of U.S. Highway 41. It is an important economic corridor between the two Florida coasts. It connected Tampa and Miami for the first time, hence the name Tamiami. Several stretches of the road are elevated causeways across the famed river of sawgrass. A canal runs parallel to the highway. As it was dug, the fill helped create the roadbed. You'll see people fishing with cane poles in roadside canals, but resist the urge to join. The fish have been found to contain high levels of mercury.

The highway has several marked pullouts at sites where giant gates control the flow of Everglades water. Take care when pulling on and off the road. Shoulders are narrow and often soft. Pull over only in designated areas. Several small commercial sites, such as gas stations, operate along the narrow route, but many sites are the private homes of Seminole or Miccosukee Indians. Some are traditional, palm-thatched, open-air platforms called *chickees*. These aren't tourist villages. They are private homes and aren't open to the pubic, so observe all "No Trespassing" signs. There is a replica Miccosukee village on the Tamiami Trail just west of the Shark Valley Unit of Everglades National Park.

Location: The Tamiami Trail stretches from State Road 997 west of Miami, to Tampa on the Florida Gulf Coast.

112. Shark Valley

● ●

This is a popular winter site. One reason is that it's directly on U.S. Highway 41 (the Tamiami Trail), so it's so easy to reach. It's famous as a dry-weather watering hole for wildlife. Wading birds such as great blue herons, songbirds such as warblers, and field birds such as red-winged blackbirds congregate here. So do otters, fish, turtles, and alligators. Sightings of the latter are practically guaranteed.

Your options here are several. You can stay near the entrance and visitor center and walk along two loop trails from which it's easy to see birds and alligators. Bobcat Hammock Boardwalk is a 500-yard venture into the sawgrass. Otter Cave Trail is a 200-yard loop through a subtropical hardwood hammock.

If you have time, consider taking the 15-mile loop trail for a richer Everglades experience. It's closed to auto traffic. I recommend the narrated, two-hour tram tour. It stops halfway out so you can get a bird's-eye view from the 50-foot-tall observation tower. If you have more time, like a full day, and if your children are quite experienced bike riders, you can attempt to pedal the loop. It's a long haul, so be prepared with water and snacks.

This site was named after the Shark River, which flows out of this area and into the mangrove sawgrass deltas at Florida Bay. It's thought that sharks once inhabited the river. There are lots of alligators here. Expect them to emerge from the water and walk along the same paths that you and your family are traveling. Give them a wide berth! You will see some visitors feeding them. Don't do this! It's illegal. Report any alligator feedings to rangers. Feeding wildlife, especially alligators, is a selfish act. The next child who comes along might well be snatched by an alligator that has been trained to associate people with food. It has happened here.

Location: On the south side of U.S. Highway 41, about 30 miles west of the intersection of US 41 and State Road 997, on the northern border of the park. US 41 is also called the Tamiami Trail.

Important information: Open daily from 9 A.M. to 4 P.M. Sometimes this site gets full and is closed to new visitors, because parking space is very limited, especially on winter weekends. Arrive early in the day. Reservations are required for the tram tours. Occasionally, sunset and nighttime tram tours are offered and are especially worth booking. For more information on the tours, call 305-221-8455. For more information on the Shark Valley park unit, call 305-242-7700.

113. Miccosukee Restaurant/ Miccosukee Cultural Center

No visit to Shark Valley is complete without spending time at two nearby Miccosukee Indian sites. The restaurant is your place to sample catfish, frog legs, and Seminole pumpkin fry bread. The cultural center is a replica of a Miccosukee Indian village of the 1940s. If you have time, take the guided tour to better understand the exhibits in the village. These sites are part of the Miccosukee Indian Reservation. Nearby are the tribal headquarters and a tribal school; they are not generally open for unscheduled visits.

Location: The Miccosukee Restaurant is on the northern side of U.S. Highway 41, opposite the Shark Valley entrance (see above). The Miccosukee Cultural Center is on the southern side of US 41, about a quarter-mile west of the restaurant.

Important information: The cultural center is open from 8:30 A.M. to 5 P.M. daily. The restaurant is closed during important tribal events and sometimes in the summer. For more information, call 305-223-8380.

Key Largo

This is the most visited island in the Florida Keys (not counting Key Biscayne, which some people consider to be the first of the Keys). Key Largo *feels* different. It encompasses a watery part of Everglades National Park and is the land base of a famous coral-reef sanctuary. If you decide to visit Key Largo, realize that getting into and under the water is what makes the visit worthwhile.

There are five island communities: Key Largo, Newport, Rock Harbor, Thompson, and Tavernier/Settlers Park. Plan to spend a whole day—or better yet, two or three days—here. There are two routes onto Key Largo; the road splits at Florida City and rejoins on the key. Each route has its advantages. You might drive down one way and then return the other, so you don't miss anything. If you travel U.S. Highway 1, you'll pass through very urban areas after reaching the key and get a lesson in how easy it is to lose the special character of a place. You'll see annoying spot zoning, such as an adult video store in the middle of a tourist area, and you'll see pavement where limes, pineapples, and melons once grew. Too many fast-food franchises overpower what once was paradise. But US 1 also has "crocodile crossing" signs, warning drivers of these resident reptiles that cross from one saltwater area to another. Kids in cars like to look out for them. Watch out for traffic jams as tourists stop to snap a quick picture. Mile markers on US 1 are often used to identify locations on Key Largo. For example, John Pennekamp Coral Reef State Park is at mile marker 102.5.

The other route, via the toll Card Sound Bridge and County Road 905, offers a bird's-eye view of Key Largo and gets you onto the 30-mile-long island a few miles farther north of US 1 traffic. Heavy traffic is a problem in Key Largo. Be patient and come prepared with cold water and juice, snacks, and back-seat diversions for the little ones.

The island's two public campgrounds, both in John Pennekamp Coral Reef State Park, are so popular that they're almost impossible to get into. Private campground options include Key Largo Kampground and Calusa Camp Resort. Other family lodging includes Westin Beach Resort, Howard Johnson Resort, Mariott's Key Largo Bay Beach Resort, Holiday Inn Sunspree, Bay Harbor, Coconut Bay, Kona Kai, Sunset Cove, and Popp's Motel.

The Jules Undersea Lodge/Key Largo Undersea Park is worth visiting at mile marker 102.5. It's the world's only underwater lodge. If you can scuba dive, you enter the lodge by swimming down through Emerald Lagoon.

About 30 feet below the surface, there's a mini-submarine-type cottage with all the amenities, including hot showers and telephone. NASA has used this site for research. You can find out more about it at <www.jul.com>. Only in Florida!

114. Key Largo Hammocks State Botanical Site

This is one of the best sheltered bike-riding places on Key Largo. Local roads have been closed to auto traffic in this lush preserve, the largest remaining tropical hardwood hammock in the nation. There's also a 2-mile nature trail. Wild cotton and mahogany mistletoe are among the unusual plants growing in this 2,000-acre park. This is crocodile habitat, so ask rangers for tips on spotting this rare reptile. Expect also to see mangrove cuckoos in May and June and white-crowned pigeons year-round. Both are native to extreme South Florida. You'll see rare tree snails and giant land crabs, roseate spoonbills, wood storks, and white pelicans, which are less common than brown pelicans. Raccoons make pests of themselves, begging handouts in the daytime. This is an exceptionally wonderful wildlife-watching site in the winter, as well as a great place for a picnic.

Location: The entrance is a large masonry arch on the east side of County Road 905, about a half-mile north of its intersection with U.S. Highway 1.

Important information: For more information, call John Pennekamp Coral Reef State Park, which supervises this site, at 305-451-1202 or visit <www.dep.state.fl.us/parks>.

115. John Pennekamp Coral Reef State Park

This is the most famous Key Largo stop. It's all about fish and life on coral reefs, so figure out the best way for your family to get onto the water. You have several options for guided reef trips. You can take a glass-bottom boat out over part of the reef. The waves can really get rolling, so plan ahead if any of your group are at all prone to seasickness. Make sure you understand how long the trip will take when you buy tickets. If you don't go out on the glass-bottom boat, consider a snorkeling tour via motorboat. This is really the best way, if your children are swimmers. The ticket includes good and patient lessons on using mask, flippers, and snorkel, and the snorkel is yours to keep. Most important, life vests are provided.

You can take a longer snorkeling tour via sailing catamaran, or take a scuba diving tour, for certified divers only. Another good family option, if your kids swim, is to rent canoes or see-through rafts and drift on your own on sheltered waters. If you prefer to stay on land, be sure to ask rangers which of the park's nature paths are best for wildlife viewing. You'll be able to see some of the subtropical fish that way. It's worth the effort. The awesome sight of some of the 650 kinds of fish and 50 kinds of coral underwater here has set many a child on a path to study marine biology.

At the park's Cannon Beach site, there's an informative visitor center with nature videos, a 30,000-gallon saltwater aquarium, ranger talks, and a campground. There's also a popular campground and an underwater replica of a 17th-century shipwreck. Beaches on Key Largo are of the limerock variety, offering little in the way of sand, but they are excellent places to push off for swimming and snorkeling. Try the park's Far Beach, too.

Location: On the eastern side of U.S. Highway 1 at mile marker 102.5, near the community of Key Largo.

Important information: Open daily from 8 A.M. to sunset. This park gets very crowded. Try to visit on a weekday, early in the day, and avoid student holidays if you can. For more park information, call 305-451-1202 or visit <www.dep.state.fl.us/parks>. For boat-tour information, call the concessionaire at 305-451-1621. Be sure to apply sunscreen frequently. Wear white T-shirts or long-sleeved white shirts when you're in the water or near it, to avoid painful sunburn.

116. Florida Keys Wild Bird Center

Take the boardwalk alongside the natural habitats enclosed in large cages to visit with injured birds that have been hooked in fishing accidents, hit by boats or cars, or shot. The center attempts to heal sick and injured sea birds and other species and return them to the wild. Some residents are permanent, including a roseate spoonbill with an amputated leg.

Location: On the west side of U.S. Highway 1 at mile marker 93.6 in Tavernier.

Important information: Donation requested. Open daily from 8:30 A.M. to 6:30 P.M. For more information, call 305-852-4486 or visit <http://flkeys.fl.us/flkeyswildbird.htm>.

The kings and queens of seashells

Florida is a shell-lover's paradise, and among the many kinds of shells you can find here, the **conch** (konk) family represents the royalty. The horse conch is the largest; it grows from a bright orange infant the size of a fingernail to a 20-inch, orange-brown beauty the size of a football. It's aggressive; it inserts a tubelike snout into smaller, hapless creatures and eats them alive. The horse conch is the official state shell. If you see one, leave it alone so it can reproduce.

Then there's the queen conch, a soccer-ball-sized beauty that only likes the warmest Florida water. It was once found by the hundreds, but overharvesting has drastically reduced its population.

The Florida fighting conch is the size of a juice glass. It is tawny in color and is more common today than the queen conch. Still, it's not as common now as it was in years past. Like other shells, its population has been reduced due to overcollecting.

The most thoughtful way to appreciate shells is to take the empty shell skeletons that are found along the coast and leave the live ones behind to reproduce. Shells purchased at shops were almost always killed only for the shell, without regard for conservation and reproduction of the species. Many shells sold in shops are not even Florida shells but are plundered from far-off shores. I don't buy them.

Few people new to shell collecting know this, but the vivid colors of shells in life often fade after death, just as with tropical fish. Like any living thing, conchs are most attractive when free and alive.

117. Windley Key Fossil Reef State Geological Site

Kids absolutely dig this ancient reef formation, where men quarried coral rock. The small and excellent museum tells the 125,000-year history of this fossil and quarry site. The visitor center is new.

Location: On Windley Key, just south of Key Largo, on the east side of State Road A1A at mile marker 88.5.

Important information: Open from 8 A.M. to 5 P.M. Thursdays through Mondays, but call 305-664-2540 for up-to-date hours and other information, such as tours. Or visit <www.dep.state.fl.us/parks>.

118. Dolphin Research Center

Stop for an educational visit to this bayside nonprofit cove and its captive dolphins. The center is the former home of Mitzi, the mammal that inspired the Flipper TV show, and is dedicated to learning. Children and adults with disabilities can participate in special dolphins encounters. Dolphin Lab is a week-long teen camp. Or you can reserve a spot in a group encounter, Dolphin Splash. Even if you prefer to stay dry, a fact-filled tour will strengthen your resolve to protect these wild mammals and their waters.

Location: Directions are provided when you make reservations.

Important information: Open 9 A.M. to 4 P.M. daily. The splash event is booked a month in advance. Swims are reserved at least two months in advance. Tours occur daily. For fees and more information, call 305-289-1121 or visit <www.dolphins.org>. For splash or swim reservations, call 305-289-0002.

Message in a bottle

As children hunt for treasure along a Florida beach, they may spy that artifact of a hundred shipwreck stories, the message in a bottle. This is just cause for a dramatic pause. The uncorking of the bottle and the reading of the message is a vacation moment meant to last in memory. You'll want to imagine what the seas were like as the bottle made its treacherous way to this very point. You might also try to conjure up the moment when it was set adrift, most likely with a proper sendoff. Maritime etiquette requires that you respond to the sender as soon as possible. You'll want to share the date, time, and place of discovery. It's also helpful to include what the weather was like at the moment the bottle was retrieved and perhaps something about the terrain, the lay of the land where the bottle chanced to wash up.

While I abhor littering, sending a message in a large bottle is a romantic beach tradition that I think few authorities with a sense of history would hold against you. (If they trouble you over this, I'd like to know.) Make sure your container is floatable. Make sure that it's too large to be swallowed by sea turtles, fish, pelicans, or people. Don't use plastic, one of the most damaging, suffocating, lethal materials known to all kinds of sea life. A large, thick glass bottle works well, such as a wine bottle or large sparkling cider bottle. The container ought not to be metal, which may cause a shark or barracuda to become interested in it.

Put your message inside a sealable plastic bag and then into the vessel. Make sure the cork is sealed well, perhaps with candle wax. And don't forget to include a return address for a response. What with modern-day smugglers and brigands sometimes operating along a sea coast, you might want to avoid including a home telephone number, and you might also be wise to share a work or school address rather than revealing private information. But let your message plumb the tradition of seagoing literature. While it's tempting to start off with, "Help! I'm being held captive on a deserted island ...," it's probably better to share something like, "Help! My Florida vacation will soon end and my hopes for extending this paradisiacal mood depend on the kindness of you, stranger. Please respond via mail; post at your earliest moment of leisure to ..." etc., etc.

The launching of a message in a bottle is almost as momentous an event as its retrieval, so be sure to conduct a joyful ceremony. A prayer for its safe voyage is entirely appropriate. Sail on!

SOUTHWEST REGION

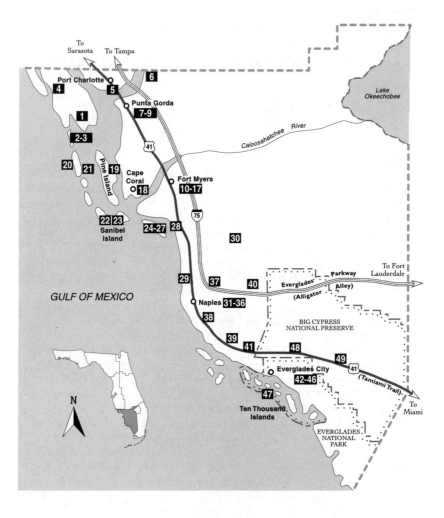

To Sarasota
To Tampa

Port Charlotte

4

5

6

Lake Okeechobee

Punta Gorda

1

7-9

2-3

Caloosahatchee River

41

20

21

19

Cape Coral

Fort Myers

10-17

Pine Island

18

75

22 23

Sanibel Island

24-27

28

30

29

37

40

Everglades'

Parkway

To Fort Lauderdale

GULF OF MEXICO

Naples

31-36

(Alligator

Alley)

38

BIG CYPRESS NATIONAL PRESERVE

39

41

48

49

41

Everglades City

42-46

(Tamiami Trail)

To Miami

47

Ten Thousand Islands

EVERGLADES NATIONAL PARK

N

Southwest
Region

At first glimpse, this region about three hours' drive south of Tampa and west of Miami appears to be a sea of inland shopping centers and other roadside distractions. But stick with your itinerary to reach the mangrove-fringed coast. The great allure of this region is a shore dotted with small back-bay and gulfshore islands, many of which are accessible only by boat. Several resorts, as well as public campsites at Cayo Costa State Park, are for boaters only. Many families plan to hire a boat guide or sign up for a floating tour to see more of the sights.

For the land-bound, there are also delights. Shell skeletons glisten on area sands. At a shell museum on Sanibel Island, you get on a first-name basis with these treasures: lion's paw, alphabet cone, turkey wing. From both boat and shore here, I've seen sea turtles surface, dolphins leap, tarpon jump, giant horse conchs crawl, sharks swim, ospreys nest, roseate spoonbills feed, wood storks pose, manatees drift, and river otters play. When families say they want a beach vacation that's heavy on nature, I send them here. They visit Southwest Florida's aquatic and wetlands preserves, where nature centers interpret the wildlife dramas. Lee County has an exceptional park system. Kayak and canoe adventures are popular bay and harbor trips, allowing your family to drift quietly near gentle creatures as they eat a natural lunch in nature's kitchen.

You will idle along in lengthy traffic lines here, so keep back-seat snacks, books, games, and music handy. Traffic bottlenecks occur most often on the Sanibel Causeway, the only access route to Sanibel and Captiva Islands. Get ahead of the horde by taking day trips early. Early morning and early evening are often good times to catch creatures astir. Or leave the driving to someone else and take advantage of guided nature trips departing from your resort.

There are two roadside state-park campgrounds in the area, but Southwest Florida is better known for family resorts with nature programs than it is for camping. Expect lodging to be casual in appearance but high-priced and booked well in advance. Resort cottages with kitchens are popular with families. Try these homes away from home: Palm Island via boat from Cape Haze; Gasparilla Inn and Cottages in Boca Grande; Sanibel Harbour Resort in Punta Rassa (upscale); Casa Ybel Resort, Sanibel Island Beach Resort, Sanibel Inn, Seaside Inn, Song of the Sea, Sundial Beach Resort (with an Environmental Coastal Observatory), and Gulf Breeze Cottages, all on Sanibel Island; 'Tween Waters Inn and South Seas Resort, both on Captiva Island; Pink Shell Resort at Fort Myers Beach, an excellent alternative to staying at

Sanibel Island; The Registry (with a backyard mangrove preserve) and The Tides Inn in Naples; and Port of the Islands, southeast of Naples near Collier-Seminole State Park.

For more information, contact:

- Charlotte Harbor and the Gulf Islands Tourist Development Bureau
  888-478-7352 or 941-743-1900
- Everglades Area Chamber of Commerce
  941-695-3941
- Fort Myers Beach Chamber of Commerce
  800-782-9283
  <www.fortmyersbeach.org> or <www.coconet.com/fmbeach>
- Lee Island Coast Visitor and Convention Bureau
  800-237-6444
  <www.LeeIslandCoast.com>
- Sanibel and Captiva Island Chamber of Commerce
  941-472-1080
  <www.sanibel-captiva.org>
- Visit Naples
  800-605-7878
  <www.visitnaples.com>

Punta Gorda Area

. . . .

This retirement area of sprawling single-family developments and condominiums stretches from the winding Peace River westward to offshore islands in the Gulf of Mexico that are accessible only by boat. It encompasses the wealthy, low-key retirement village known as Boca Grande, a fishing port at the southern tip of Gasparilla Island that is known for tarpon catches. It also includes the northern reaches of the Gasparilla Sound/Charlotte Harbor Aquatic Preserve, the sprawling retirement development of Port Charlotte, and the charming riverfront community of Punta Gorda.

1. Grande Tours

. . . .

This outfitter can introduce your family to a marine wonderland, the 79,000-acre Gasparilla Sound/Charlotte Harbor Aquatic Preserve, where you might glimpse sea turtles and much more. Guided tours or do-it-yourself kayak rentals take you into a shallow world of aquatic plants, fish, mammals, amphibians, reptiles, and mollusks.

Location: On Cape Haze at 12575 Placida Road.

Important information: Call ahead for times and reservations at 941-697-8825.

2. Gasparilla Island Lighthouse and State Recreation Area

This end-of-the-road spot for picnicking, shelling, and fishing isn't on everyone's list of places to visit. But if you're planning to go to Gasparilla Island anyway, you'll want to see it for the scenic view into one of the great tarpon grounds of the world: Boca Grande Pass. The big draw is the 1890 lighthouse, a squat wooden building shaped like a house. It's open Saturdays and at some other times for tours. Be forewarned that the skyline is marred by the sight of industrial storage tanks at the commercial port next door.

The lighthouse is situated on Boca Grande Pass, a swift waterway that is the entrance to Charlotte Harbor. Do not swim here or leave children unattended near the channel's dangerous water. Children have drowned in the exceptionally strong currents of the pass. This state recreation area has several small swimming beaches farther north along Gulf Boulevard. They are marked with beach access signs.

Location: South of Placida and Cape Haze, at the very southern tip of Gasparilla Island via Gulf Boulevard.

Important information: The park is open daily from sunrise to sunset. Lighthouse tours are Saturdays from 10 A.M. to 4 P.M. and other selected days. Although you shouldn't swim by the lighthouse, there are several labeled swimming-beach accesses on the way to the lighthouse along Gulf Boulevard. For more information, call 941-964-0375 or visit <www.dep.state.fl.us/parks>.

3. Little Gasparilla Island Group

Do your children like fishing, crabbing, swimming, shelling, bird watching, or stargazing? Can they entertain themselves on a castaway island without stores or fast-food restaurants? This group of islands—which includes Knight, Don Pedro, and Palm Islands, and Don Pedro Island State Recreation Area—is accessible only by boat. Palm Island Resort offers lodging in modern rental homes with full kitchens. There is one restaurant. You'll want to load up on groceries, books, art supplies, music, videos, sunscreen, sun hats, playing cards, and other essentials in Englewood, before you ride the ferry over for your long weekend or week here. This outpost gets by fine without car traffic, although you can bring a car over via barge and then leave it parked. There are four swimming pools, 11 tennis courts, a children's activity program, bike rentals, and a gift shop. Maybe your castaway crew won't want to come back!

Location: From Englewood on the mainland in Sarasota County, follow the directions you'll be given when you make your reservations.

Important information: Reservations are required. Make sure you understand what you need to bring with you. For more resort information, call 800-824-5412 or 941-697-4800 or visit <www.palmisland.com>. For information on Don Pedro State Recreation Area, call Barrier Islands Geopark 941-964-0375, or visit <www.dep.state.fl.us/parks>.

4. Cedar Point Park

Cedar Point has 4 miles of trails on 88 acres, where you're likely to see Florida's unique burrowing gopher tortoise. A building with nature exihibits and plenty of picnic tables make this a good roadside stop.

Location: In Englewood at 5800 Placida Road.

Important information: For more information, call 941-475-0769 or visit <www.charlotte-florida.com/chec>.

5. Port Charlotte Beach and Pier

Take a peaceful moment's rest at this popular picnic spot on a bay beach near the wide mouth of the otherwise narrow and winding Peace River. This respite offers a fishing pier on Alligator Harbor, a public pool, a snack bar, a playground, tennis courts, and even a bocci court.

Location: From U.S. Highway 41 (Tamiami Trail) in Port Charlotte, take Harbor Boulevard south about 1.5 miles to the pier.

Important information: Call the Charlotte County Parks and Recreation Department for more information at 941-743-1313.

6. Peace River Cruise

Older children will be delighted by close-up glimpses of alligators, river turtles, and more on this two-hour trip up the lush Peace River. It may prove long for toddlers, so bring toys and coloring books. The ride on a small River Cat pontoon launch follows a fun lunch in an Old Florida setting at the marina restaurant. There is a small museum and a canoe-rental outlet.

Location: From U.S. Highway 41 in Port Charlotte, take County Road 769 (Kings Highway) north toward the rodeo town of Arcadia. On CR 769, follow the signs to the river and the Nav-A-Gator/River Cat. You can also arrive by your own boat from Charlotte Harbor.

Important information: For detailed directions and more information, call 800-308-7506.

7. Florida Adventure Museum

This small, regional museum with hands-on exhibits is a lively rainy-day place to learn about Florida ecosystems.

Location: In Punta Gorda at 260 West Retta Esplanade, off U.S. Highway 41 southbound.

Important information: For more information, call 941-639-3777 or visit <www.charlotte-florida.com/museum>.

8. Babcock Wilderness Adventures

Head inland south of Punta Gorda in Charlotte County for a 90-minute ride through cattle country in a swamp buggy, a large-wheeled sports vehicle that's like an open-air, camouflaged bus. This popular ride, by reservation only, leads through the stunning wet prairie and woodland of the historical Crescent B Ranch and through lush Telegraph Cypress Swamp. You'll see bison; believe it or not, they once were native to North Florida. Learn about Florida's little-known cattle heritage that dates to the Spanish explorers of the 1500s and has strong ties to Cuba. Alligators bask everywhere here. You might also see deer and the red-capped, migratory sandhill crane. Meet a captive panther. There's a small museum with an intriguing emphasis on Florida fossils, a country store, and—from November through April—a camp cook house that serves alligator nuggets and sandwiches.

Location: About 15 miles east of Punta Gorda at 8000 State Road 31. Get directions when you make your reservation.

Important information: Prebooked rides are given in the mornings only from May through October. They are offered between 9 A.M. and 3 P.M. from November through April. All rides must be reserved. Fees are $10 for children 3 to 12 and $18 for all others. For more information, call 800-500-5583 or 941-338-6367 or visit <www.babcockwilderness.com>.

9. Charlotte Harbor Environmental Center

A touch tank, fossils, and an unusual collection of carved animal figures help jump-start an ecology lesson at this center. In mild weather, try a walk on the trails: a 1-mile path through flatwood and mangrove swamp or a 1.75-mile jaunt through old cabbage palms and an oak hammock. The 3,000-acre preserve abounds with birds and other wildlife in the winter, and bald eagles nest here from December through April. Alligators and woodpeckers are seen year-round, and secretive bobcats are active year-round in the morning, although it's unlikely you'll see them.

Location: In Punta Gorda, turn south onto Burnt Store Road (State Road 765) from U.S. Highway 41. After 1 mile, turn right at the marked entrance.

Important information: Summer hours are from 8 A.M. to 3 P.M. Mondays through Saturdays. During the school year, the center is open on school days only. For more information, call 941-575-4800.

Fort Myers Area

It's a challenge for me to limit my site recommendations in this community nestled under some of Florida's most statuesque royal palms on the banks of the Caloosahatchee River. Like Sarasota, to the north, this once was my home. Undeveloped Charlotte Harbor and neighboring subtropical islands accessible only by boat were my playground. North Fort Myers is the gateway to Pine Island, a low-key fishing community of great historical significance. Pine Island has tropical nurseries that are fun to visit, the dock for Tropic Star Nature Cruises heading to Cabbage Key and other nearby islands, and the ferry to Cayo Costa State Park. Fort Myers began life as a military stockade during the Seminole Wars; there is a replica of the fort at a creative museum housed in the city's former railroad depot.

From Fort Myers, you can drive west to Cape Coral and its children's museum, or you can head east through Tice to a popular wintertime manatee viewing area. Many visitors arriving at the Southwest Florida International Airport southeast of downtown Fort Myers travel directly to gulf-island resorts. But few who enter the Fort Myers downtown marina district leave without ambling along one of the most famous streets in Florida, McGregor Boulevard. It's lined with an estimated 1,800 royal palms and is known as the Avenue of Palms. It's hard to resist stopping in exotic garden settings along the boulevard or visiting riverfront museum/homes where Thomas Edison, Henry Ford, and Harvey Firestone once dreamed up some of their brilliant ideas.

The beaches in the vicinity of Fort Myers Beach and Captiva and Sanibel Islands are considered some of the best family seaside destinations in the state. The gulf waters are clear, shallow, and often placid. The sand is soft and snow white, and many beaches are edged with lush palms. You can do your bit to preserve this heavenly habitat by leaving live shells alone (it's the law!), letting birds and resident dolphins fend for themselves, limiting your use of fresh water (that means not asking for clean sheets and towels daily), minimizing littering, and forgoing the use of noisy personal watercraft that disrupt wildlife.

The shell-strewn beaches in this area are world-famous—almost too popular for their own good. My advice if you want to enjoy nature to its fullest is to book at least one experienced guide who can lead you beyond the popular roadside beaches, parks, and preserves, where parking is often at a premium, for kayaking, shelling, birding, fishing, sailing, or a combination thereof.

10. Imaginarium Hands-on Museum and Aquarium

Kids have a tough time accepting rain when they've planned to sculpt sand castles on the beach. So let your rained-out beachcombers broadcast their own more upbeat weather forecast from the miniature TV studio at this science center. Bring a camera to capture them "on air." They can also stand inside a simulated thunderstorm or feel the force of a simulated hurricane. They'll touch live shells, pet a crab, visit a coral reef, "crash" a car, and try dozens of other interactive exhibits. This appealing kids' center teaches visitors about habitats, anatomy, physics, and weather—and it's creatively situated in a recycled city water plant!

Location: In downtown Fort Myers at 2000 Cranford Avenue. Take exit 23 from Interstate 75.

Important information: Open from 10 A.M. to 5 P.M. Wednesdays through Saturdays and from noon to 5 P.M. Sundays. Children under age 3 are admitted free; fees are $3 for ages 3 to 12, $5 for seniors, and $6 for all others. For more information, call 941-337-3332.

11. Fort Myers Historical Museum

Kids delight in strolling through this museum, which once was a bustling train stop, the Peck Street Depot. Meet Seminole and pioneer figures from Fort Myers's past. Learn about the southernmost Civil War battle, fought here when Fort Myers served as the headquarters of the 2nd U.S. Union Federalist Color Troops. See what it was like for early settlers to swat mosquitoes in the 1800s. Find out why cattle and Cuba are such a big part of the region's history. Visit a private railroad car. This is one of three excellent history attractions for families operated by the city in downtown Fort Myers. With a great public library next door, it is an educational break from too much sun or an intriguing rainy-day diversion.

Location: In Fort Myers at 2300 Peck Street.

Important information: Open from 9 A.M. to 4 P.M. Tuesdays through Saturdays. Fees are $1 for children under 12 and $2.50 for all others. For more information, call 941-332-5955.

12. Calusa Nature Center and Planetarium

If limited vacation time keeps you from delving into nearby Corkscrew Swamp Sanctuary in Naples or the Big Cypress National Preserve, this nature center offers a good glimpse of what those wetlands are like. Interpretive exhibits tell the story of the Calusa Indians, who ruled the area beginning about A.D. 800. The planetarium is a cool retreat. The center's boardwalk allows you to move easily through a cypress swamp. It's very hot and buggy in the summer. Expect to see alligators in the wild and in a freshwater aquarium. Many of the captive animals here were injured in the wild and can't return.

Location: In Fort Myers at 3450 Ortiz Avenue.

Important information: Open from 9 A.M. to 5 P.M. Mondays through Saturdays and from 11 A.M. to 5 P.M. Sundays. Call 941-275-3183 for fees and the schedule of planetarium shows.

13. Lee County Manatee Park

East of Fort Myers, the tiny, winding Orange River is one of the premier winter haunts of the endangered manatee. At this public riverside park, you can view these gentle giants, which tip the scales at 1,000 pounds each, from November through early March. Manatees are slow-moving mammals with no natural defenses against cold weather, so they tend to congregate in the winter at warm springs and in areas, like this one, where utilities discharge warm water. The nearest place to view a captive manatee is at a Bradenton museum, so this 16-acre park is an ideal place to see these free-swimming creatures. You'll find an excellent visitor center, three viewing areas, volunteer naturalists who patiently answer questions, a fishing cove, footpaths, a butterfly garden, a picnic area, group kayak adventures on the Orange River, and a nature gift shop.

Location: From the intersection of Interstate 75 and State Road 80 in Fort Myers, travel east 1.5 miles to the park at 10901 SR 80.

Important information: Open daily from 8 A.M. to 5 P.M. in the winter and from 8 A.M. to 8 P.M. other times. Entrance fees are $3 per vehicle or 75 cents per hour. For park information, call 941-432-2004. For up-to-date manatee information, call 941-694-3537.

14. ECHO

This Christian-sponsored plant nursery and agricultural experiment site is an unusual and important stop for families who are interested in helping Third World cultures be self-sufficient with minimal impact on the environment. It features a large collection of tropical food plants, a simulated rain forest, and a farm that you can visit only on a tour.

Location: Call for directions and tour times.

Important information: For more information, call 941-543-3246.

15. Edison-Ford Winter Homes

Take a guided tour through the neighboring riverfront estates of inventor Thomas Edison and car czar Henry Ford. See how these creative men and their families passed time in paradise by enjoying one of the first Florida swimming pools, a long fishing dock, and other diversions. Walk through

Edison's curious laboratory, where he employed a machinist and a glass blower on site to make whatever he needed. Enjoy the garden full of exotic plants, including the 400-foot-wide banyan tree. Find the binoculars he kept in every room for bird watching. If you have time, float on the Caloosahatchee River, on replicas of the electric launch Edison used to entertain guests. Walk through his lush tropical gardens. Enjoy the museum display of invention-artifacts, including dolls that talked, phonographs, and movie cameras, at one of the most appealing historical sites in Florida.

Location: South of downtown Fort Myers at 2350 McGregor Boulevard.

Important information: Guided tours are offered between 9 A.M. and 4 P.M. Mondays through Saturdays and noon to 4 P.M. Sundays. Fees vary. For more information, call 941-334-3614 or visit <www.edison-ford-estate.com>.

16. Six Mile Cypress Slough Preserve

Families can hike across a true cypress swamp via a 1.2-mile elevated board-walk trail. That's at least an hour-long trip through a natural travel corridor for such wildlife as white-tailed deer, river otters, alligators, bobcats, wild turkeys, white ibises, wood storks, bald eagles, and red-shouldered hawks. Highlights of the preserve include miniature hands-on exhibits, an interpretive booklet, seating enclaves, observation decks, restrooms, and guided walks. Like most Florida swamps, this one's full of biting bugs in hot months.

Location: From Interstate 75 south of downtown Fort Myers, take exit 21 and travel west on Daniels Parkway to the intersection with Six Mile Cypress Parkway. Turn north onto Six Mile Cypress Parkway and travel 1.5 miles to the well-marked preserve entrance at 7751 Penzance Crossing.

Important information: Open daily from 8 A.M. to 5 P.M. from October through March and from 8 A.M. to 8 P.M. from April through September. Parking fee is 75 cents per hour, with a $3 maximum per visit. For a schedule of guided walks or other information, call 941-432-2004 or visit <www.lee-county.com/parks&rec>.

17. Lakes Park

Let your kids ride the miniature railroad, sniff the sweet smells of the fragrance garden, and have a fine time splashing around at this 279-acre inland public park. You can rent bicycles, pedal boats or canoes, or enjoy playgrounds or inline-skating paths at this fine picnic spot. The freshwater lakes are open for swimming from Memorial Day to Labor Day.

Location: In south Fort Myers, about 5 miles west of U.S. Highway 41 at 7330 Gladiolus Drive.

Important information: Open daily. Parking fee is 75 cents per hour, with a $3 maximum per visit. For more information, call 941-432-2000 or visit <www.lee-county.com/parks&rec>.

18. Cape Coral Children's Science Center

This small science center and lovely picnic place make a nice local stop if you're traveling in the Cape Coral or Pine Island areas. There are snakes to see, a butterfly garden to explore, and a host of hands-on exhibits to try, including fun with sundials and pendulums. The enthusiastic staff is dedicated to making math and science entertaining.

Location: In Cape Coral, take Del Prado Boulevard north to Pine Island Road (State Road 78). Turn right (east) and continue to 2915 NE Pine Island Road.

Important information: Open from 9:30 A.M. to 4:30 P.M. Mondays through Fridays and from noon to 5 P.M. Saturdays. Children under age 3 are admitted free; fees are $2 for children 3 to 16 and $4 for all others.

19. Museum of the Islands

This small but spellbinding museum documents the elaborate and powerful Calusa Indian civilization. These mound builders and seafood harvesters ruled southwestern Florida 5,000 years ago. They created pottery effigies and dug canal systems for their sturdy cypress canoes.

Location: On the north end of Pine Island in the village of Bokeelia at 572 Sesame Drive.

Important information: Open from 10 A.M. to 4:30 P.M. daily. For more information, call 941-283-1525.

20. Cayo Costa State Park

This 7.5-mile-long shelling beach on the Gulf of Mexico is one of the least-visited parks in Florida's spectacular state park system. If your tribe likes adventure travel, take a day trip or stay overnight here, where clear waters, sand beaches, palm forests, and mangrove swamps are home to flocks of shorebirds, as well as ospreys and brown pelicans. You can spot burrowing gopher tortoises from interior hiking trails. There are no shops or sources of food on the island, so plan your visit as you would a backpacking trip. Thirty primitive campsites and 12 bare-bones cabins are supplied with fresh but cold water; there is no electricity. The island's palm-fringed isolation is so compelling that accommodations are booked a half-year or longer in advance.

Location: There is no bridge to Cayo Costa, so access is via private boat or a concession-run ferry. There are at least seven different embarkation points, including private charters from Boca Grande, Fort Myers, the Burnt Store Road area south of Punta Gorda, Pine Island, Sanibel Island, and Captiva Island. The park-concession ferry operates from the tiny village of Bokeelia, on the northern end of Pine Island.

Important information: The park headquarters is in Boca Grande, within the Barrier Islands Geopark at 941-964-0375. Call for overnight rates and more information or visit <www.dep.state.fl.us/parks>. Day-use admission is $2, and there is a small fee if you decide to ride the park tram from the bayside dock to the gulf shore, which I recommend.

21. Useppa Island

• •

If your kids like glamour, treat them to a lunch on exclusive Useppa Island. There is no public park on this private resort island, but you can indulge in a meal at the century-old Collier Inn, where Teddy Roosevelt once dined. Be sure to stroll to the small museum near the croquet courts to learn about the ancient mound-building civilization that ruled here. Calusa Indian artifacts that may date back as far as 5,000 years are on display.

Location: Accessible only by boat, Useppa Island sits in Pine Island Sound, east of Cayo Costa.

Important information: Hire a private boat in Sanibel or Captiva. For more information, call Captiva Cruises at 941-472-5300 or Captain Mike Fuery's Charter at 941-466-3649 or visit <www.sanibel-online.com/guides/fuery.htm>. The museum is open from 1 to 3 P.M. Tuesdays through Sundays. For more information, call 941-283-9600.

22. J. N. "Ding" Darling National Wildlife Refuge

• •

This 6,354-acre national refuge works hard to protect a beautiful feeding and roosting area for migratory birds. This site on Tarpon Bay attracts roseate spoonbills, mangrove cuckoos, a bevy of statuesque egrets and herons,

A flock of flatware

Pelicans look funny when they swallow fish, and it's a hoot to see a Florida coot "walk" on water as it hops from lily pad to lily pad. But I hope you also have the chance to watch an endangered **roseate spoonbill** in the wild. On shallow mud flats on the southern coasts, look for a bird about 3 feet tall with a pale yellow bill that is flat like a pine board and round at the end, like a miniature Frisbee. The roseate spoonbill bends low and swishes its bill from side to side in the water, searching for a dinner of small fish, fiddler crabs, aquatic insects, snails, and shrimp. It will only feed in shallow water, no deeper than its "knees." When it launches into the air, you can't help but notice the bright swaths of shell pink feathers on its wings and side and the almost-orange tail feathers. Flocks of feeding spoonbills have caused many travelers to stop in their tracks and stare. The birds are colorful winter residents at the J. N. "Ding" Darling National Wildlife Refuge on Sanibel Island.

and a flotilla of wintering ducks. The quiet preserve is thick with alligators, fish, turtles, snakes—in all, about 300 bird, 50 reptile, and 30 mammal species. In cool weather (to avoid mosquitoes!), visit the 0.3-mile walking trail, which leads across shell mounds made 2,000 years ago by the Calusa Indians. An interpretive center orients you to the Calusa civilization and to the world-famous Wildlife Drive, a 5-mile causeway through saltwater and freshwater ponds and wetlands. There is no "people" beach here.

Location: About 15 miles southwest of Fort Myers on Sanibel Island. Take the 3-mile causeway (State Road 867) from the mainland to Sanibel Island and its primary road, Periwinkle Way. The refuge is on Sanibel-Captiva Road 3 miles from the terminus of Periwinkle Way. Because parking is a problem during winter months, I strongly recommend that you take an excellent guided trip through the refuge. Follow the signs to Tarpon Bay Recreation on Tarpon Bay Road. Here, you can also book guided canoe and kayak trips into sheltered refuge waters.

Important information: Open daily from 9 A.M. to 5 P.M. from November through April and from 9 A.M. to 4 P.M. from May through October. Wildlife Drive is open from 7:30 A.M. to a half-hour before sunset. Fee is $4 per car. To give the resident creatures a rest, Wildlife Drive is closed to traffic every Friday. For more information, call 941-472-1100 or visit <http://southeast.fws.gov/dingdarling>. To book a guided trip through the refuge, call Tarpon Bay Recreation at 941-472-8900.

23. Bailey-Matthews Shell Museum

Kids and seashells seem to attract each other, so collect information here to make sense of your family's beach-bucket haul. The museum features two million land and sea shells from around the world, as well as a live-shell tank and kids' play area. It may be the only museum in the nation devoted to shelling. Be aware that the gift shop does not sell shells. Most shells available for sale in Florida souvenir shops were taken live—a practice many preservationists don't endorse. It is illegal in this area.

Location: On Sanibel Island at 3075 Sanibel-Captiva Road, near the Ding Darling National Wildlife Refuge (see above).

Important information: Open from 10 A.M. to 4 P.M. Tuesdays through Sundays. Children ages 8 and younger are admitted free; fees are $3 for kids 8 to 16 and $5 for all others. For more information, call 941-395-2233.

24. Ostego Bay Science Center

Your children will get hands-on experience with inhabitants of area estuaries at this center's touch tanks. Fossils and shells are also on display. You can sign up for guided trips out on the water.

Location: On Estero Island at 718 Fisherman's Wharf, beneath the Fort Myers Beach Bridge.

Important information: Open from 10 A.M. to 4 P.M. Wednesdays through Saturdays. For more information, call 941-765-8101.

25. Lovers Key State Recreation Area

Children and adults alike enjoy riding a park tram from the parking lot through a mangrove tidal lagoon to the gulfshore swimming beach. Along the way, watch for platoons of tiny fiddler crabs massing in the mud flats. Beach shelling is excellent, and a national survey ranked this idyllic spot as the sixth best beach along the Gulf of Mexico.

Location: On Estero Island in Fort Myers Beach at 8700 Estero Boulevard.

Important information: Open from 8 A.M. to 5 P.M. daily. For more information, call 941-432-2000.

26. Matanzas Pass Preserve

Take a boardwalk on the mainland side of Estero Island for a close-up look at a mangrove forest and tropical hardwoods. This is a good bird-watching site for coastal wading birds such as great white herons. You can soak up some of the local history at the Historic Cottage and Nature Center. There's a public library next door.

Location: On Bay Road behind the Fort Myers Beach Public Library on Estero Island.

Important information: For preserve information, call 941-338-3300. The cottage and nature center are open from 10 A.M. to 2 P.M. Wednesdays and Sundays; for more information, call 941-463-0435.

27. Fossil Expeditions

If there's a dedicated young fossil collector in your family, you ought to go adventuring with one of Florida's top fossil finders. Mark Renz is an enthusiastic guide to Florida's natural history, and he leads trips that include the chance to discover fossilized teeth and bones of sea cows, mammoths, mastodons, armadillos, and more. His other jaunts will help you learn about the human history of the region, including the Seminole and Calusa Indian cultures. Renz is president of a regional paleontological society and is author of *Fossiling in Florida*.

When horses were the size of collies

Once upon a time, a horse the size of a collie, *Nannippus,* was probably dinner for a giant Florida bird with razor-sharp teeth that stood between 6 and 10 feet tall, *Titanus walleri.* That is one of many stories you can infer from **Florida's fossil record,** according to Florida fossil expert Mark Renz. Florida was completely underwater in the days of the dinosaurs, so you'll find no fossilized remains of them in the Sunshine State. But once the waters receded, mammals thrived here. Florida was home to wild lions and saber-toothed cats, giant sloths and giant armadillos, pseudo-camels and not-too-woolly mammoths. The alligators that dwell here today are nothing but living fossils, essentially unchanged from the beasts that roamed Florida about ten million years ago.

Location: You'll be told where to meet when you book a tour.

Important information: To book a tour or request a brochure, call 800-304-9432 or visit <www.fossilexpeditions.com>.

28. Koreshan State Historic Site

A turn-of-the-20th-century utopian community is commemorated here in 12 original buildings—Florida's best ghost town—on the lush banks of the Estero River. The Koreshan Unity followed the ideas of a charming religious zealot who brought his followers here from Chicago in 1894. He preached that humans lived inside the globe, that Earth was a hollow sphere with sun, stars, people, water, animals, and everything else encompassed within. The most faithful in this group of 200 professionals also thought that celibacy was important, which is only one reason why the sect eventually died out. The last four members donated the village to the state in 1961.

Exhibits in the 156-acre park interpret the pioneers' daily work and lives. You'll see a sawmill, bakery, sewing shop, concrete-making operation, and more. Community legends, canoe rentals, nature trails, guided ranger walks, and a playground help make this a unique public camping retreat. Every March, the park hosts an archaeology fair to celebrate the Calusa Indians who once inhabited the area.

Location: On U.S. Highway 41 at Corkscrew Road in Estero.

Important information: Contact the park office at 941-992-0311 or visit <www.dep.state.fl.us/parks>.

Naples Area

Naples is a wealthy enclave of condominium towers and sprawling golf developments that cater to upscale grandparents. It dates to the 1890s and is named for the Italian bayside city. Expect to find art galleries, posh shops, and lots of dining options in this community between Naples Bay and the Gulf of Mexico. To the southeast, a state park offers a lovely campground, as does a state historic site at Estero, between Naples and Fort Myers. The famous Audubon Society Corkscrew Swamp Sanctuary is here, as are other excellent nature centers and museums.

29. Delnor-Wiggins Pass State Recreation Area

This beautiful swimming spot set amid sturdy mangroves trees, waving stalks of sea oats, cabbage palm trees, and sea grapes is patrolled by lifeguards. It also has an observation tower, shaded picnic areas, and showers. Summer visitors can register for ranger-guided night walks to see if any sea turtles have clambered ashore to nest. For daytime beach fun, go early on weekdays during the winter tourist season and on weekends year-round, because this is a popular destination. Never swim in the swift pass at the north end of the barrier island; it has a dangerous undertow. Choose a swimming site as far from the pass as possible to avoid both the current and fishing lines.

Location: About 6 miles south of Bonita Springs via U.S. Highway 41 and County Road 901, at 11100 Gulfshore Drive North.

Important information: Open from 8 A.M. to sundown daily. Fee is $4 per car. For more information, call 941-597-6196 or visit <www.dep.state.fl.us/parks>.

30. Corkscrew Swamp Sanctuary

The endangered wood stork, a black-and-white bird with stiltlike legs that is the only stork native to North America, attracts worldwide attention to this Audubon sanctuary. A boardwalk leads 2 miles into the almost primeval swamp. You'll walk through an uncommon bald-cypress forest of 500-year-old trees and dense ferns. Alligators, turtles, river otters, barred owls, and limpkins are year-round residents and may be easily spotted. The visitor center is excellent, and the guided walks are recommended. The walkway is fine for babies in strollers, but toddlers will grow tired and want to be carried. Older children who appreciate nature will enjoy quietly looking for the wood storks that reside here in winter, as well as other creatures.

Location: From U.S. Highway 41 in Naples Park, drive east and then north for 21 miles on State Road 846. Turn left at the sanctuary sign.

Important information: Open daily from 7 A.M. to 5 P.M. from December through April and from 8 A.M. to 5 P.M. from May through November. There is no snack bar, so be sure to bring all your food and drink with you. For more information, call 941-348-9151.

31. Naples Nature Center

This is a place to see how injured wildlife, such as owls and eagles, is cared for. It's also a place to touch a snake, count alligator teeth, peer into saltwater aquariums, take an electric-boat tour through mangroves, or rent canoes and kayaks. It's a fine introduction to area ecology.

Location: In Naples at 14th Avenue North, off Goodlette-Frank Road.

Important information: For more information, call 941-262-0304.

32. Naples Fishing Pier and Beach

Let your family try their luck on this venerable 1,000-foot-long pier just a few blocks from the posh Third and Fifth Avenues shopping district. You'll find restrooms and a concession stand that sells snacks and bait. Anglers catch snook, redfish, and Spanish mackerel, depending on the season. This site is listed on the National Register of Historic Places. About 1 mile to the south is the popular Naples public beach.

Location: From U.S. Highway 41 in Naples, take Fifth Avenue South to Ninth Street and take Ninth Street to Broad Avenue. Follow Broad Avenue to its end at Gulf Shore Boulevard and turn left onto Gulf Shore. The pier is 1 block ahead on the right. The beach is about 1 mile farther south, between 32nd and 33rd Avenues South.

Important information: The pier is open 24 hours a day; concessions are available during the day. For more information, call 941-434-4696.

33. Cambier Park

Here's a nice place to stretch your legs and have a picnic. You'll also find lighted shuffleboard and horseshoe courts, a bandshell in which there are frequent concerts, a community theater, a pavilion, a tot lot, and plenty of play space.

Location: On Park Street near Eighth Street, in the area between Naples Bay and the Gulf of Mexico called Old Naples.

Important information: For more information, call 941-434-4694.

34. Tin City/Olde Naples Seaport

The Old Marine Marketplace at Tin City was once a bustling hub for the area fishing industry. This spot on Naples Bay, including a former oyster house and clam-processing plant, has been cleverly recycled into a vibrant district of tourist attractions, including dolphin-watching and sightseeing cruises at Olde Naples Seaport, the narrated Naples Trolley Tours, rainy-day shopping (check out the Old Naples General Store), and a family food emporium. The Riverwalk Fish and Ale House is family friendly. Grouper is the most popular local fish sandwich in a region also known for fresh gulf shrimp, red snapper, and smoked mullet dip.

Location: Tin City is on the west side of U.S. Highway 41 East, at Goodlette Road in Naples, on the western shore of Naples Bay. Neighboring Olde Naples Seaport is farther south on Naples Bay at Tenth Avenue South. Both are well marked with signs.

Important information: For Tin City information, call 941-262-4200 and for Olde Naples Seaport cruises, call 941-649-2275.

35. Orchids and Egrets Eco-Tours

This outfitter will take children ages 8 and older on unforgettable adventures, such as on a slog through Florida swamps and into bear and panther habitat. The leaders are enthusiastic and full of details about modern-day orchid poaching and old-time panther hunting.

Location: A meeting place is provided when you register for a tour.

Important information: For more information, call 941-352-8586 or visit <www.naturetour.com>.

36. Teddy Bear Museum

If you don't cringe at the sight of an excessive number of toys, this home to more than 3,000 stuffed bears of all ages, descriptions, and places of origin could be a great rainy-day stop. Kids can check out the Three Bears' House. Wallet warning: There's a gift shop, too.

Location: From Interstate 75, take exit 16 and drive about 2 miles west to 2511 Pine Ridge Road in North Naples.

Important information: This is a nonprofit museum; donations of $2 for ages 4 to 12, $4 for seniors, and $5 for all others are requested. For more information, call 941-598-2711 or visit <www.teddymuseum.com>.

37. Golden Gate Community Park/ Aquatic Center

• •

This is one of the best public pools in Florida for families. It has a water slide, toddler activity pool, state-of-the-art swim center, and picnic places.

Location: At 3300 Santa Barbara Boulevard in the Golden Gate neighborhood east of Interstate 75 in Naples.

Important information: For more information, call 941-353-0404.

38. Collier County Historical Museum

• •

A beautiful orchid house is part of this informative, 5-acre historical park. It's well worth a visit to learn about people, places, and events from prehistory through modern times.

Location: About 2 miles south of Naples at 3301 Tamiami Trail East (U.S. Highway 41).

Important information: For more information, call 941-774-8476.

39. Collier-Seminole State Park

• •

A replica of a Seminole War blockhouse, lush nature trails, a canoe trail, and a shady campground are among the allures of this 6,423-acre park southeast of Naples. Black bears roam here, and this is one of the few parks in Florida where the almost-extinct Florida panther has been sighted, so you can imagine that its far reaches protect some very wild places. Every December, rangers lead canoe trips on the scenic Blackwater River, not to be confused with a river of the same name in the Panhandle. When camping, make sure to keep food out of reach of animals. The mosquitoes here are vicious and can be pesky even in winter, so bring repellent.

Location: 17 miles southeast of Naples, just off U.S. Highway 41. The park entrance is on the western side of the highway.

Important information: For more information, call 941-394-3397 or visit <www.dep.state.fl.us/parks>.

40. Florida Panther National Wildlife Refuge

Most of us would like to see a rare Florida panther (*Felis concoryi*), the only wild cougar left in the eastern United States. Only about 30 of these stealthy beasts inhabit this region, and they comprise nearly the whole of the Florida panther population, so your chances are slim. If you do see one, it most likely will be as it crosses a road in front of your speeding car. Traffic deaths, bounty hunting in the early 1900s, habitat loss, inbreeding, and high mercury levels in fish are among the factors that have decimated the panther's population. This new national refuge attempts to provide a haven for these deer hunters. A unique feature of one refuge border road, State Road 29, is a pair of tunnels built on proven wildlife paths and designed so that animals are encouraged to cross under the road and its deadly traffic. Infrared cameras have snapped clear color pictures, some of them published in *Florida Wildlife* magazine, of panthers trotting safely through these tunnels—a small bright spot in the fight to save these tawny creatures. The candid camera has also captured pictures of bears, deer, bobcats, raccoons, armadillos, foxes, and even otters and wading birds using the wildlife crossings.

Location: About 20 miles east of Naples. The refuge is bordered by Interstate 75 (Alligator Alley) on the south and SR 29 on the east. The refuge office is in Naples at 3860 Tollgate Boulevard.

Important information: The refuge is closed to public access and use. You can drive along its southern border via I-75 or along its eastern border via SR 29, which intersects I-75 south of Immokalee. The refuge office in Naples has some exhibits. For more information, call 941-353-8442 or visit <http://southeast.fws.gov/floridapanther>.

Everglades City Area

This part of Florida is bisected by a few straight roads, but just a bit beyond these straight ribbons of asphalt, it's still a wilderness out there. Parts of this area are so wild, so impenetrable, that there are acres of mangrove forests and wetlands through which no human may ever have passed. The area is a vast wetland of cypress swamps, mangrove forests, and tropical hardwood hammocks with wild orchid gardens. The main community is Everglades City. It was dredged from wetlands in the 1920s and connected to the Tamiami Trail, which was also dredged from wetlands.

The western part of Everglades National Park, which has its headquarters in Everglades City, is the least familiar unit of the park to tourists. But this is where President Harry Truman officially opened and dedicated the park in 1947. You can't access this part of the park by road; access is through cruise boats, which weave among some of the mysterious Ten Thousand Islands. Bears and orchids, the almost-extinct panther and potentially extinct manatee are among the endangered and threatened species here. The best way to experience the area is with a wildlife guide. Be prepared to get wet, whether slogging through a swamp on foot or enduring sea spray during a boat trip. Avoid a summer visit, as mosquitoes and other biting bugs are unbearable.

Everglades City, incorporated in 1923, sits on the Barron River and Chokoloskee Bay, just a foot or so above water level on Florida's most remote mangrove coast. Its big draw is the Gulf Coast Visitor Center, where you can arrange boat cruises into Everglades National Park. Families who enjoy fishing and like their nature unmanicured may like this town, where strolling and bike riding beneath stately royal palms suits the pace of life. There are few diversions for kids, other than nature itself. Expect to see wildlife anywhere in town, from wood storks flying overhead to owls sitting in the trees.

41. Fakahatchee Strand State Preserve

This 20-mile-long cypress swamp, the main drainage slough of southwestern Big Cypress Swamp, is one of the state's most unusual natural features. In its deepest reaches, it shelters the largest remaining stand of native royal palm trees, as well as the largest concentration and variety of wild orchids in the continent. It is also prime bear habitat. While the preserve was not intended for public access, there is an easily accessible boardwalk, called Big Cypress Bend, along U.S. Highway 41. This takes you into a green cathedral of ferns, air plants, vines, and more, with interpretive signs along the way to identify the old cypresses and other plants. At the end of the 2,000-foot-long boardwalk, a freshwater pond offers the chance to glimpse basking turtles and alligators. The walk here takes about one hour. Benches along the way make it possible to tote a snack and sit for a bite to eat, but be sure to bring out all your litter, and don't feed the animals.

Location: Just west of Copeland and about 7 miles northwest of the intersection of US 41 and State Road 29.

Important information: The boardwalk is open daily from 8 A.M. to sunset. For more information, call 941-695-4593 or visit <www.dep.state.fl.us/parks>. There are no facilities. Janes Scenic Drive, which runs into the preserve, is a very rough, isolated, dead-end route frequently used by wildlife guides but not recommended for families who don't know the region.

42. Everglades National Park, Gulf Coast Visitor Center

This small center is sometimes overwhelmed with visitors, but it does a good job despite the crowd. The two-story building is a gift shop and ticket office on the first floor. On the second floor, you'll find exhibits and an informative park video. Ask the ranger for recent wildlife sightings and use the opportunity to find out about weather forecasts and water conditions, so you can decide which boat tours to take.

Location: From Everglades City, take State Road 29 about a half-mile south of town to the visitor center, on the right.

Important information: For more park information, call 941-695-3311 or 941-695-2591 or visit <www.nps.gov/ever>. For boat-tour information, call 800-445-7724 in Florida or 800-233-1821 out of state.

43. Museum of the Everglades

Find out how Everglades City starred in a movie and how the residents once woke up, went to work, and ate when a whistle blew. Learn how king snakes fought rattlesnakes on the courthouse steps, and relive the glory days of the Everglades Rod and Gun Club at this museum.

Location: In Everglades City at 105 West Broadway.

Important information: For more information, call 941-695-0008.

44. On the Banks of the Everglades

Spend the night in a former bank and eat breakfast in the vault at this unusual example of adaptive building usage. The stately 1923 Bank of the Everglades is now a beautifully restored lodge. The Board Room, which has a separate entrance, is a large restaurant with a full kitchen. While older children are welcome, toddlers may be too rambunctious for this sedate inn. Also, some rooms have shared baths, so be sure to state your preference.

Location: In Everglades City at 201 West Broadway, a few blocks west of the traffic circle.

Important information: For more information and to decide if this unique experience is for your family, call 941-695-3335 or visit <www. banksoftheeverglades.com>.

45. Everglades Rod and Gun Club

This local landmark began as a pioneer home in the 1870s. It was altered in the 1920s to serve as a private club for big-name fishing enthusiasts. Ask for a table on the porch and try the key lime pie. The lobby walls are lined with trophy fish and old photographs.

Location: In Everglades City at 200 Riverside Drive.

Important information: For more information, call 941-695-2101.

46. Ivy House

This 1920s building, now a bed-and-breakfast inn, is also the base for a creative recreational guide service. Ivy House offers shelling expeditions, canoe and kayak trips, and bird walks and other hikes. Ask the staff naturalist about trips especially designed for families.

Location: In Everglades City at 107 Camellia Street, behind the post office.

Important information: For more information, call 941-695-3299.

47. Smallwood Store Museum and Old Indian Trading Post

This former trading post on stilts, located on tiny Chokoloskee (Chuck-a-LUS-kee) Island, is an opportunity to learn how native residents once traded crops and otter, deer, bobcat, and panther pelts for sugar, flour, and other supplies. Older children are especially intrigued by a true tale of murder and frontier justice that haunts this place, which is listed on the National Register of Historic Places.

Location: From Everglades City, take State Road 29 south past the Gulf Coast Visitor Center of

Who's counting?

The **Ten Thousand Islands** fan out across the Southwest Florida delta. They are perfect examples of the natural order of things. Most began life as a mangrove seed that sprouted in the muck. The seed grew into a single small tree, whose stringy roots grew down into the muck, trapping silt, driftwood, leaves, and more. This began the island-building process. How do we know there are 10,000 of them? We don't. If you want to count them all, become a ranger and return here to work. You might be able to finish the task by the time you retire.

Everglades National Park to Chokoloskee Island. Follow signs to the store, which is at 360 Mamie Street.

Important information: From May through November, the museum is open from 10 A.M. to 4 P.M. Fridays through Tuesdays; it closes at 5 P.M. from December through May. For more information, call 941-695-2989.

48. Ochopee Post Office

This old wooden shed, once part of a tomato farm, today serves the postal needs of three counties, yet is the nation's smallest post office. Other tiny stamp emporiums, such as one in Delaware, also claim the title. But at 60 square feet, this white shack is officially the most diminutive. Pull over, buy a postcard, and mail yourself a future collectible of roadside Americana. Since there are frequently no lines, this is a good time to load up on stamps for the rest of your vacation.

Location: On the south side of U.S. Highway 41 (Tamiami Trail) about 5 miles east of its intersection with State Road 29 and about 10 miles northeast of Everglades City.

Important information: The post office closes for lunch.

49. Big Cypress National Preserve

This wetland is a key part of the Everglades sawgrass-prairie system. It funnels crucial fresh water into the mangrove delta. The preserve is named for the dwarf cypress. The "big" in the name is said to refer to the multitude of dwarf cypresses that once grew here. (The bald cypress, which does grow to towering proportions, can be found in the Fakahatchee Strand State Preserve and at Corkscrew Swamp Sanctuary.) Ranger-led walks and talks are excellent introductions to this preserve, which is mainly wilderness. There are few developed recreational areas. The preserve anchors one end of the Florida National Scenic Trail. The Oasis Visitor Center is the most convenient stop for families. A fast-paced video here includes alligator and panther lore and information about the dramatic cycle of flood, drought, and lightning-caused fires. It also offers a glimpse of the rare ghost orchid, which grows on the preserve. Ask rangers about recent wildlife sightings, especially of otters, bobcats, and alligators. Two campgrounds with very limited facilities—Dona Drive and Monument Lake—are located in flat, open areas along U.S. Highway 41.

Location: The Oasis Visitor Center is on the north side of US 41 about 15 miles east of the Ochopee Post Office (see above). Dona Drive Campground, on the south side of US 41, is about 30 miles west of the Oasis Visitor Center. Monument Lake Campground is about 3 miles west of the Oasis Visitor Center, at the US 41 crossroads called Monroe Station.

Important information: For more information, call 941-695-4111 or visit <www.nps.gov/bicy>.

How *do* you say that?

Because of its multifaceted heritage, Florida is awash in unusual names that sometimes are hard to figure out how to pronounce. So how do you say ...

Ais (ice) — Early natives of the eastern coast of Florida.

Allapattah (al-uh-PAT-uh) — A Native American term for alligator.

Apalachicola (app-uh-latch-ee-KOH-la) — Panhandle town and river.

Caloosahatchee (kuh-LOOS-uh-HATCH-ee) — River that flows from Lake Okeechobee to the Gulf of Mexico, past Fort Myers.

Calusa (kuh-LOOS-uh) — Early natives of the Southwest Florida coast.

Choctawhatchee (choc-tuh-HATCH-ee) — Panhandle river and bay.

Conch (konk) — Several varieties of spiral shells, from 3 to 20 inches long.

Coquina (koh-KEEN-uh) — A pastel-toned, fingernail-sized saltwater clam.

DeFuniak Springs (Deh-FOON-ee-ack) — Panhandle site of a national Chautauqua revival.

Estero (es-TAIR-oh) — Name of the Southwest Florida island on which Fort Myers Beach is located.

Fakahatchee (fak-uh-HATCH-ee) — A swamp preserve southeast of Naples.

Hatchee (HATCH-ee) — This means river in a Seminole language and is part of several Florida names.

Ichetucknee (ish-eh-TUCK-nee) — A spring-fed river northwest of Gainesville.

Loxahatchee (lox-uh-HATCH-ee) — A river and wildlife refuge in Southeast Florida.

Matanzas (muh-TAN-zus) — A national memorial south of St. Augustine and a preserve in Southwest Florida.

Micanopy (mick-uh-NOH-pee) — A Seminole leader of the 1800s and a village south of Gainesville.

Miccosukee (mick-uh-SOO-kee) — A Native American tribe of Florida and the name of a lake and a community east of Tallahassee.

Myakka (my-ACK-uh) — A river, lakes, and a state park near Sarasota.

Ocala (oh-KAL-uh) — An early Native American tribe, a national forest, and a city.

Ochlockonee (oh-CLOCK-nee) — A river in Leon County and a state park in Wakulla County.

Ochopee (oh-CHOP-ee) — A community on U.S. Highway 41 and location of the nation's smallest post office.

Ocklawaha (ock-luh-WAH-ha) — A river on the western border of Ocala National Forest.

Osceola (oss-ee-OH-luh) — A Seminole Indian leader of the 1830s.

Palatka (puh-LAT-kuh) — A town on the St. Johns River and location of a state gardens.

Sabal palm (SAY-bahl) — The state palm tree, also called the cabbage palm.

Sebring (SEE-bring) — A town in the heart of Florida, midway between Sarasota and Fort Pierce, on Lake Jackson.

Slough (slew) — A current of water within a wetland.

Steinhatchee (steen-HATCH-ee) — A river and town on the Gulf Coast.

Suwannee (suh-WAN-ee) — A river flowing from Georgia to the Gulf Coast.

Tamiami (tam-ee-AM-ee) — A highway between Tampa and Miami (U.S. Highway 41).

Tequesta (teh-QUEST-uh) — Early Native Americans of Southeast Florida.

Timucua (teh-ma-CUH-ah) — Early Native Americans of Northeast Florida (there is an ongoing debate over the pronunciation).

Wakulla (wah-KULL-uh) — A spring, river, county, and region south of Tallahassee.

Wekiva (wuh-KEE-vuh) — A spring, river, and state park northeast of Orlando.

Ybor (EE-bohr) — An area of Tampa that reflects its Cuban heritage.

CONTACT INFORMATION

. . . .

Important Phone Numbers

Emergencies: 911
Emergency Tourist Assistance: 800-656-8777
Poison Information Center: 800-282-3171
Florida Manatee Hotline: 800-342-1821
Florida Marine Mammal Stranding Help Network: 800-432-6404
Florida Marine Patrol: 800-DIAL-FMP (342-5367)
Wildlife Emergency Alert:
    Northwest—800-342-1676
    Northeast—800-342-8105
    Central—800-342-9620
    South—800-282-8002
    Everglades—800-432-2046
U.S. Coast Guard Boating Safety: 800-368-5647
National Oil and Response Center (to report chemical spills): 800-424-8802
Florida Bar Association (legal information): 800-342-8011
Florida Consumer Information: 800-435-7352
Florida Lemon Law (auto complaints): 800-321-5366

Tourism Information

VISIT Florida

661 East Jefferson Street, Suite 300
Tallahassee, FL 32301
888-735-2872, 850-488-5607
<www.flausa.com>

This is the official Florida tourism organization. The VISIT Florida website has weather updates, park information, a calendar of events, and more. VISIT Florida produces a free 216-page travel guide; a free 40-page ecotourism/heritage travel guide; free brochures on day trips with such themes as art museums, birding, lighthouses, African-American heritage, Native American heritage, Cuban heritage, and outdoor adventures; and a free booklet of popular canoe and hiking trails, *Florida Trails*. VISIT Florida also offers a free *Planning Guide for Travelers with Disabilities* and a free state map.

Florida Welcome Centers

Florida's five Welcome Centers offer free orange juice, restrooms, state maps, state park guides, advice and information from staffers, and many brochures. You can find a Welcome Center:
- About 1.5 miles south of the Florida/Georgia border and 4 miles north of Jennings, on Interstate 75.
- About 7 miles north of Yulee on Interstate 95.
- About 16 miles west of Pensacola on Interstate 10.
- Just after crossing into Florida from Georgia on U.S. Highway 231, north of Marianna.
- Inside the New Capitol in Tallahassee, at the west-side entrance on Duval Street.

Florida Association of RV Parks and Campgrounds
1340 Vickers Drive
Tallahassee, FL 32303-3041
850-562-7151
<http://floridacamping.com>
The association produces a free guide, *Camp Florida.*

Florida Hotel and Motel Association
P.O. Box 1529
Tallahassee, FL 32302
850-224-2888
<www.flausa.com>

Florida Attractions Association
P.O. Box 10295
Tallahassee, FL 32302
850-222-2885
<www.floridaattractions.org>

Florida Association of Museums
P.O. Box 10951
Tallahassee, FL 32302-3674
850-222-6028

Florida Trail Association
P.O. Box 13708
Gainesville, FL 32301
800-343-1882 (in Florida) or 352-378-8823
<www.florida-trail.org>

Florida Association of Canoe Liveries
P.O. Box 1764
Arcadia, FL 33821
941-494-1215

Florida Disabled Outdoor Association
www.sportsability.org
850-668-7323

All Florida Adventure Tours
305-665-2496 or fax 305-663-9964
<www.all-florida-ecotours.com>

This expert statewide guide service is used by elementary and secondary school groups interested in Florida's natural and cultural history.

State Agencies
Florida Government Information Locator Service
<http://dlis.dos.state.fl.us/gils>

Florida Division of Historical Resources
R. A. Gray Building
500 South Bronough Street
Tallahassee, FL 32399-0250
850-488-1480
<www.dos.state.fl.us>

The division produces a list of historic sites and heritage travel trails, including *Florida Black Heritage Trail* and *Florida Cuban Heritage Trail.* It also produces a free brochure, *State of Florida Heritage and Emblems,* and archaeological information.

Florida Office of Recreation and Parks
Mail Station 535
3900 Commonwealth Boulevard
Tallahassee, FL 32399-3000
850-488-9872
<www.dep.state.fl.us/parks>

The parks division produces the free guide *Florida State Parks.* The information can be faxed to you, or you can write the address above.

Florida Fish and Wildlife Conservation Commission
620 South Meridian Street
Tallahassee, FL 32399-1600
888-347-4356 to order fishing licenses, 800-275-3474 for sportsfishing information, 850-488-4676 for other wildlife information
<www.state.fl.us/fwc>, <www.panther.state.fl.us>

The commission produces brochures on fishing regulations, a guide to popular canoe and hiking trails called *Florida Trails*, *Florida Wildlife* magazine, materials on watchable wildlife programs and endangered species, and other publications.

Florida Division of Forestry
3125 Conner Boulevard
Tallahassee, FL 32399-1650
850-488-6611
<www.fl-dof.com>

This agency administers all state forests and forest facilities and offers brochures on the forests and on forest trails.

State Library Archives Online Catalog
<http://stafla.dlis.state.fl.us>

Florida Wildlife Federation
850-656-7113
<www.fwf.usf.edu>

Florida Wild Mammal Association
850-926-8308

Save the Manatee Club
500 North Maitland Avenue
Maitland, FL 32751
800-432-5046 (out of state)
<www.objectlinks.com/manatee>

Audubon Society
1101 Maitland Way
Maitland, FL 32751
407-644-0190

Florida Native Plant Society
P.O. Box 680008
Orlando, FL 32868

Friends of Florida State Parks
M5535
3900 Commonwealth Boulevard
Tallahassee, FL 32399

National Forests in Florida
325 John Knox Road
Tallahassee, FL 32399-1650
850-942-9300
<www.r8web.com/florida>, <www.fs.fed.us>

National Park Service, Southeastern Region
75 Spring Street
Atlanta, GA 30303
404-562-3100
<www.nps.gov>

National Wildlife Refuges/Florida
U.S. Fish and Wildlife Service, Region 4
75 Spring Street
Atlanta, GA 30303
404-679-7286
<www.fws.gov>

Florida Environmental Citizenship Program
<www.FL-EnviroPage.org>

Florida Anthropological Society
P.O. Box 5142
Gainesville, FL 32602

Florida Historical Society
1320 Highland Avenue
Melbourne, FL 32935
407-690-0099
<www.floridabooks.net>, <www.florida-historical-soc.org>

CAMPGROUND GUIDE

· ·

If your little explorers think a vacation is incomplete without roasted marsh-mallows paired with chocolate squares and graham crackers, then they're campers. Here are sites in this guide that offer bedrooms without walls. Since I've shared tips with you, I hope you'll share with me your family's favorite campgrounds, public or private, if they're not already listed here. Please send your suggestions to me care of Falcon Publishing, P.O. Box 1718, Helena, MT 59624, and tell me why the campground is so super for families.

Panhandle Region
Pensacola and Pensacola Beach Areas

Fort Walton Beach Area

Panama City Area

Apalachicola Area

Panhandle Interior

Southeast Region
Fort Pierce Area

Palm Beach Area

Fort Lauderdale Area

Miami Area

Everglades National Park Area

Key Largo

Southwest Region
Fort Myers Area

Naples Area

Everglades City Area

READ MORE ABOUT IT

. . . .

Books

Fishing Florida, by Kris Thoemke. Falcon Publishing, 1996.

Florida Almanac, by Del Marth and Martha J. Marth. Pelican Publishing, 1999.

The Florida Handbook, compiled by Allen Morris and Joan Perry Morris. Peninsular Books, 1999.

Florida on My Mind, edited by Gayle Shirley, researched by Jan Godown. Falcon Publishing, 1999.

Florida Parks: A Guide to Camping in Nature, by Gerald Grow. Longleaf Publications, 1997.

Florida Wildlife Viewing Guide, by Susan Cerulean and Ann Morrow. Falcon Publishing, 1998.

Hiking Florida, by M. Timothy O'Keefe. Falcon Publishing, 1997.

The Insider's Guide to the Florida Keys & Key West, by Victoria Shearer and Janet Ware. Falcon Publishing, 1998.

Kidding Around: Miami, by Frank Davies. John Muir Publications, 1997.

The Nature of Florida, edited by James Kavanagh. Waterford Press, 1997.

Scenic Driving Florida, by Jan Godown. Falcon Publishing, 1998.

The Young Naturalist's Guide to Florida, by Peggy Sias Lantz and Wendy A. Hale. Pineapple Press, 1998.

Other Publications

Florida Living Magazine
3235 Duff Road
Lakeland, FL 33810
863-858-7244
<www.flaliving.com>

Florida Wildlife Magazine
620 South Meridian Street
Tallahassee, FL 32399-1600
<www.state.fl.us/fwc>

The Seminole Tribune (newspaper of the Seminole tribe of Florida)
6300 Stirling Road
Hollywood, FL 33024
954-967-3416

INDEX

· ·

E

F

ABOUT THE AUTHORS

As a child, Jan Godown moved from rural New Jersey to gulfshore Sarasota, Florida. She has studied Spanish for three months in and published articles from Costa Rica; met a bear on Mount LeConte, Tennessee; climbed Mount Katahdin, Maine; visited much of the West and the eastern seaboard. She graduated from the University of Florida College of Journalism and Communications, and her features on Florida issues have appeared in many state newspapers.

Jan was a 1999 Atlantic Center for the Arts associate artist-in-residence for literary journalism. Her next book will be a children's biography, and her essay on historic travel in the Everglades will be published by Milkweed Editions in 2001. Her first book for Falcon Publishing was *Scenic Driving Florida*.

Jan lives with her husband, Paolo Annino, and their daughter, Anna Annino in Tallahassee, Florida. Anna's artwork and poetry have already received public recognition. The 9-year-old student, a busy Girl Scout, played a major role in researching this book.

"And awaaaay we go!"

Jackie Gleason, Miami Beach

Y'All coming South? Explore rich history, charm, mystique and Southern traditions with The Insiders' Guide® books. More than 30 of our 67 titles cover specific Southeast vacation destinations — Charleston, Atlanta, N.C.'s Outer Banks, N.C.'s Mountains, the Florida Keys & Key West, Williamsburg, Virginia's Blue Ridge and Civil War Sites in the Southern States name a few.

Written by local authors and averaging 400 pages, our guides provide the information you need quickly and easily — whether searching for savory local cuisine, unique regional wares, amusements for the kids, a picturesque hiking spot, off-the-beaten-track attractions, new environs or a room with a view.

Explore America and experience the joy of travel with the Insiders' Guide® books.

Need one now? Call Falcon Publishing at (800) 582-2665 to place an order, inquire about other titles in the Insiders' Guide® series or find a bookstore in your area that carries the guides.

Or visit our website at www.insiders.com.

You can just
Visit,
or you can be an
Insider

FALCON GUIDES® Leading the Way™

FALCON GUIDES® are available for where-to-go hiking, mountain biking, rock climbing, walking, scenic driving, fishing, rockhounding, paddling, birding, wildlife viewing, and camping. We also have FalconGuides® on essential outdoor skills and subjects and field identification. The following titles are currently available, but this list grows every year. For a free catalog with a complete list of titles, call FALCON® toll-free at 1-800-582-2665.

SCENIC DRIVING GUIDES

Scenic Driving Alaska and the Yukon
Scenic Driving Arizona
Scenic Driving the Beartooth Highway
Scenic Driving California
Scenic Driving Colorado
Scenic Driving Florida
Scenic Driving Georgia
Scenic Driving Hawaii
Scenic Driving Idaho
Scenic Driving Indiana
Scenic Driving Kentucky
Scenic Driving Michigan
Scenic Driving Minnesota
Scenic Driving Montana
Scenic Driving New England
Scenic Driving New Mexico
Scenic Driving North Carolina
Scenic Driving Oregon
Scenic Driving the Ozarks
Scenic Driving Pennsylvania
Scenic Driving Texas
Scenic Driving Utah
Scenic Driving Virginia
Scenic Driving Washington
Scenic Driving Wisconsin
Scenic Driving Wyoming
Scenic Driving Yellowstone and
    the Grand Teton National Parks
Scenic Byways East & South
Scenic Byways Far West
Scenic Byways Rocky Mountains
Back Country Byways

WILDLIFE VIEWING GUIDES

Alaska Wildlife Viewing Guide
Arizona Wildlife Viewing Guide
California Wildlife Viewing Guide
Colorado Wildlife Viewing Guide
Florida Wildlife Viewing Guide
Indiana Wildlife Viewing Guide
Iowa Wildlife Viewing Guide
Kentucky Wildlife Viewing Guide
Massachusetts Wildlife Viewing Guide
Montana Wildlife Viewing Guide
Nebraska Wildlife Viewing Guide
Nevada Wildlife Viewing Guide
New Hampshire Wildlife Viewing Guide
New Jersey Wildlife Viewing Guide
New Mexico Wildlife Viewing Guide
New York Wildlife Viewing Guide
North Carolina Wildlife Viewing Guide
North Dakota Wildlife Viewing Guide
Ohio Wildlife Viewing Guide
Oregon Wildlife Viewing Guide
Puerto Rico & the Virgin Islands
    Wildlife Viewing Guide
Tennessee Wildlife Viewing Guide
Texas Wildlife Viewing Guide
Utah Wildlife Viewing Guide
Vermont Wildlife Viewing Guide
Virginia Wildlife Viewing Guide
Washington Wildlife Viewing Guide
West Virginia Wildlife Viewing Guide
Wisconsin Wildlife Viewing Guide

HISTORIC TRAIL GUIDES

Traveling California's Gold Rush Country
Traveling the Lewis & Clark Trail
Traveling the Oregon Trail
Traveler's Guide to the Pony Express Trail

■ *To order any of these books, check with your local bookseller*
*or call FALCON ® at **1-800-582-2665**.*
Visit us on the world wide web at:
www.Falcon.com

FALCON®

FALCONGUIDES ® Leading the Way™

www.Falcon.com

Since 1979, Falcon® has brought you the best in outdoor recreational guidebooks. Now you can access that same reliable and accurate information online.

❏ Browse our online catalog for the latest Falcon releases on hiking, climbing, biking, scenic driving, and wildlife viewing as well as our Insiders' travel and relocation guides. Our online catalog is updated weekly.

❏ A Tip of the Week from one of our guidebooks or how-to guides. Each Monday we post a new tip that covers anything from how to cross a rushing stream to reading contour lines on a topo map.

❏ A chance to Meet our Staff with photos and short biographies of Falcon staff.

❏ Outdoor forums where you can exchange ideas and tips with other outdoor enthusiasts.

❏ Also Falcon screensavers and panoramic photos of spectacular destinations.

And much more!

Plan your next outdoor adventure at our web site. Point your browser to www.Falcon.com and get FalconGuided!

FALCON®